Alley Cat Rescue's Guide to Managing Community Cats

Alley Cat Rescue's Guide to Managing Community Cats

Louise Holton, Author

Maggie M. Funkhouser, *Editor*

Denise Hilton, Joe Zimmermann, and Adam Jablonski, *Assistant Editors*

Alley Cat Rescue, Inc.
Mt. Rainier, Maryland

Acknowledgements

There are many people who helped bring this handbook to life and who helped me in my journey towards helping animals, especially feral cats.

I have mentioned a few in other parts of this book, but I do want to start by thanking the Alley Cat Rescue staff especially, Maggie Funkhouser and Denise Hilton, who helped me not only with the handbook, but with running all of our programs at the office. And of course Joe and Adam, who assisted with the handbook. Plus, Emily and Liz for responding to the hundreds of phone calls and emails from people who need help with cats, and the rest of the ACR staff and volunteers.

My family, Desireé and Robin, Grant and Pauline, and my grandchildren Taylor, Jamie, and Hannah. All of them love cats a lot and have put up with Mom, the crazy cat lady, for many years!

Roger Tabor, Jenny Remfry, Annabell Washburn, and Ellen Perry Berkeley have been great supporters of my work over the years and have always given me lots of encouragement. Thank you to Peggy Carlson, founder of Little Buddies, for standing by me as a wonderful friend and supporter.

Then there are all of the donors and members of Alley Cat Rescue. Without them I would not have the necessary means to continue to help and rescue cats. The feline species is lucky to have this wonderful group of people who are so compassionate and want to make a difference, especially in the lives of alley cats, who are often misunderstood and much maligned. Treated as pests, vermin, and invasive animals, feral cats receive a bad rap, and because of these labels, are shot, poisoned, and killed without second thought, without regrets or compunction, and they need all the support they can get.

Thanks to our board members: Peggy Hilden, Virginia Messina, Dr. Pervaiz Manzoor, Desireé Stapley, and Claudia Delman. They have all supported me and helped Alley Cat Rescue for many years. And there are others who helped me in my journey to help animals: Dr. Neal Barnard, Don Barnes, Kim Bartlett, Batya Bauman, and Tom Regan. Thank you to the numerous cat rescuers who became my good friends, like Judy Zukoski and Barbara Bierly. Judy and I had many late-night excursions in dark alleys and behind dumpsters to trap cats in need. Thank you to Valerie Mullin and Lisa Walker, for donating essential resources over the years, and a huge thank you to Cheryl Noll, our trusted colony caretaker and expert trapper. She has trapped lots of feral cats for ACR and goes out every single day of the year to feed all of our colonies. No matter if it's pouring down rain, there's two feet of snow, or a sheet of ice outside, she knows the cats are waiting patiently for her to feed them; and she will NOT let them down. Thank you Cheryl!

There are of course hundreds of cats I could mention, but because so many have crossed my life let me just mention a few: Mandy, Jupiter, Reggie, Blackie, North Star, Mama Cat, Morris, and of course Adam and Morgan; the first feral kittens I rescued from our Adams Morgan feral cat colony in D.C. in 1990, who spent many happy years living with me. And dogs too! Mickey, the sweetest dog you could ever wish to meet, plus a rescued Chow, Girlie, who first wanted to eat everyone she met, then turned out to be a lovebug! She kept my dear father, who lived with me for the last six years of his life, company when I went to conferences to speak. My Dad used to call Girlie to sit on his bed, and say: "Girlie, she is going off on a vacation again and saying its work!" And two dogs rescued from Mexico, Bandit and Lily, who were going to be killed the night we found them.

I wish also to thank the members of the Cat Writers' Association, who have always been very supportive of humane control for feral cats. They have honored me and Alley Cat Rescue with many awards over the years for our work with feral cats. And a big thank you to the Doris Day Animal Foundation for providing financial assistance for this project, as well as their continued support of Alley Cat Rescue.

And on behalf of the feral cats of the world, thank you Merritt Clifton, Peter Wolf, Verne Smith, Laura Nirenberg, and again Roger Tabor and Jenny Remfry. You have all helped give ferals a better world.

I hope this handbook goes a long way towards helping all the community cats, feral cats, and alley cats of the world live a better and more humane life!

Louise Holton

Founder and President
Alley Cat Rescue, Inc.

Contents

Foreword

Roger Tabor

CBiol, FSB, MPhil, FCFBA, HonFBNA, FLS
Biologist, Feline Behaviorist, Broadcaster, Author

Alley Cat Rescue's Louise Holton has pioneered and promoted, in the United States, the neutering and return of feral cat colonies as the most effective way of controlling and stabilizing numbers. I suggested some time ago to Louise, that a book would be an ideal way to bring the issue before an audience that really wanted to consider the matter. In asking me to write the foreword they have turned the table!

Although cat lovers in America may know me from my TV series on cats and my cat books, Alley Cat Rescue had another reason in mind behind their request. As I was the first person anywhere in the world to scientifically monitor the return of a neutered colony of cats to their site, and the method which has been used so successfully by Alley Cat Rescue in the USA (as well as in many other countries around the world), it seemed appropriate to write as a foreword to this landmark book something of that first study, which was itself a foreword to the work that Alley Cat Rescue undertake so tirelessly.

Mary and I quietly awaited the arrival of the cats back to Fitzroy Square. It had been an anxious time for her while her cats had been taken away and neutered.

"Oh, they look fine," she said with relief as they were released. They settled back into their routine remarkably quickly and soon took some food that she had put out for them.

Mary Wyatt had fed the cats for many years at Fitzroy Square and was typical of the vast army of urban feral cat feeders found around the world who would often spend more of their income on feeding the cats than they could really afford.

There had been cats living feral ("gone wild") in London's Fitzroy Square for many years before Mary had begun to care for them. These were the cats of the Bloomsbury area of London's West One such as had been immortalized years before by T.S. Eliot — these were the black and white "Jellicle Cats." They seemed typically as the dapper puss-about-town in dinner jacket with white gloves and spats, and have become even more familiar around the world in Andrew Lloyd Webber's musical "Cats."

That night at Fitzroy Square, I was also concerned as putting neutered feral cats back on site was a new idea and this was the first colony to be scientifically monitored. I had been studying this group of cats for some time before they were taken away by The Cats' Protection League to be neutered, and at that point I was unsure how well, or even if, the cats would continue to maintain their group ranges.

At that time in the 1970's we did not even know the normal patterns of behavior and size of ranges used by feral or even house cats, and I was one of a tiny handful of researchers throughout the world working on establishing this.

Observing the cats night after night over the following months, I was relieved to find that they continued to hold their ranges despite being neutered.

I continued to monitor the group closely over the following 10 years and they gradually declined in number as the population aged. One of the cats that I named, "Protective Queen" continued to live in her territory for a number of years more, and needless to say I kept a good eye on her and the site. As the cats had all been adult at neutering, this meant that as free-living cats they had comparable life spans to house cats.

I had weighed and measured these cats, and cats from many other colonies, and found that feral cats were not leading starving, undernourished lives, but were virtually the same in weight and size as house cats.

At the time the Fitzroy Square colony were neutered, the normal way of dealing with such groups had been to kill them in the mistaken belief that they would be eradicated. However, I monitored a number of such sites and found that within two years most had nearly recovered in numbers. Such recovering populations had a higher percentage of males than undisturbed groups, as males move in first. As the habitat had been good enough to sustain one group, it was naturally attractive to surrounding cats. I dubbed this the "vacuum effect."

As the Fitzroy Square Group held their territories, it did not fill up in this way with new cats. Hospital administrators with feral cat populations had called in cat killing companies every few years, now instead they had an effective option. The Cat Action Trust was formed which I was asked to launch on television. They implemented the neuter and return method on a large number of sites. In 1984 Dr. Jenny Remfry of the Universities Federation for Animal Welfare followed 17 sites that had begun neutering in 1979, and found that 70% of the cats were still on their original site 5 years on.

The neuter and return method does not just buy time on one site. It was found in London to provide time to neuter adjacent colonies over a period of time and so to gradually reduce the overall population of feral cats in an area. The fast turnover of the previous policy of pointless killings had not allowed that.

The method has since been used effectively in many countries around the world – from America to Australia. One of the first carefully controlled neuter and return schemes to be carried out in the USA was by Karen Heinick at Florida State University. I had the privilege to spend some time there a number of years ago and was impressed by the care with which she had attended to her cats.

I became aware of the tremendous work being carried out in Washington, D.C. by Louise Holton, co-founder of Alley Cat Allies. She had formed a remarkable organization with the aim of making a linked network of responsible cat caretakers throughout the U.S., and were implementing the neuter and return policy as the most effective method for use with feral cats. We communicated frequently 'across the pond,' and she asked me later to become a Scientific Advisor for Alley Cat Allies, as well as her second organization, Alley Cat Rescue. In this capacity Jenny Remfry and myself were flown to Washington, D.C. by the Doris Day Foundation in 1994, as the international speakers at a round-table meeting with the main cat welfare charities in the U.S. The meeting began a much needed dialogue in the USA on neuter and return among the welfare organizations.

The far greater understanding, acceptance and implementation of the neuter and return method for feral cats in the USA has largely been due to the tireless work by Louise Holton. Both organizations have grown, in no small way due to their ability to bring their work to the attention of others, and this book will certainly further that end. In my involvement with Alley Cat Rescue, I have been impressed by their commitment to do their best for cats, people and their environment, and by their appreciation of the need for an understanding of the behavioral geology of the cats as a proper basis on which to act. This book in itself is a testament to that commitment.

When I have accompanied Louise and her colleagues around cat sites in the Washington area, I found myself always aware of more similarities than differences for these cats' way of life and that of my Fitzroy Square group. As I and the cats were alone each evening in the Square, in the hour and a half before Mary arrived gradually more of the cats emerged from the bushes or their basement lairs, and made more anxious anticipatory dashes about until the squeaks from Mary's trolley could be heard approaching. The feeder is the one person who is significant in the lives of

Roger Tabor

these urban feral cats, and they need to be fully involved with any neuter and return program for it to be at all successful.

Roger Tabor

Further details on the Fitzroy Square colony can be found in the following publications by Roger: "The Wild Life of the Domestic Cat" (Pubn. Arrow 1983); "The Changing Life of Feral Cats (*Felis catus L.*) at Home & Abroad" Zool J. Linnean Soc. (1989) 95L 151-161; "Understanding Cats" (Pubn. David & Charles: UK 1995; *Reader's Digest*: USA 1995); "Roger Tabor's Cat Behavior" (Pubn. David & Charles: UK 1997; *Reader's Digest*: USA 1998); "Current Cat Care Options in the UK" in *Best Practice in Pound & Animal Shelter Management* (Animals Australia 1999).

ROGER TABOR, CBiol, FSB, MPhil, FCFBA, HonFBNA, FLS

The cat biologist, behaviorist, and historian Roger Tabor is recognized as one of the world's leading authorities on the subject of cats. He is the author of the David & Charles (UK) book, "Roger Tabor's Cat Behavior," which is published in the USA by *Reader's Digest*. He has researched, written, and presented two BBC television series about these fascinating animals. "Cats" has been shown in Britain, America, and around the world, and subsequently, "Understanding Cats" was shown as pledge programming on PBS in the USA. He is the award-winning, bestselling author of "100 Ways to Understand Your Cat" (David & Charles/F+W), "Understanding Cats" (David & Charles: UK & *Reader's Digest*: USA), "Cats: The Rise of the Cat" (BBC Books), and "The Wild Life of the Domestic Cat" has been recognized by Britain's leading cat charity, the Cats Protection League as the "standard work on the feral cat." Daphne Negus says, it's "the most informative book ever written about how cats have behaved from the time immemorial, and the uncompromising lives they lead in our modern, urban society." Dr. Desmond Morris states, it's "one of the modern classics of feline literature. One of the two best cat books ever written. An original, pioneering study of urban feral cats and their social organization." Roger Tabor has the distinction of having the most books by a single author in Desmond Morris' definitive "100 Best CatBooks" list.

In addition to the videos of his TV series "Understanding Cats," Roger has made a number of cat videos with Bowe-Tennant productions: Understanding Your Cat, Breaking Bad Habits for Cats, The Cat Outdoors, The Cat Indoors, and The Mystery of the Cat. Roger has traveled extensively researching cats, observing them in over 25 countries around the world. He has published research work on other animals, and has also worked on biochemical and electron microscopy studies in strokes and heart attacks in people.

Roger Tabor is the Chairman and Vice President of the British Naturalists' Association, past editor of *Country-side* magazine, and author of a series of books on the Otter, Squirrel, Deer & Fox. He is a keen photographer and has taken most of the pictures in his cat books. In addition to his television and radio broadcasts on cats, he has extensively broadcast for over 40 years in the UK on wildlife and environmental matters, writing, presenting, and producing programs and series' ranging from Animal Magic, Country File, The Traditions of Christmas to The Mill's Life and most recently Going Wild. He has also appeared on many programs in the USA, including hosting his national PBS special, "Wild About Herbs."

Foreword

Dr. Jenny Remfry

PhD, VetMB, MRCVS
Founding Member of the Cat Action Trust

It was in 1991 that Louise Holton introduced me to her free-living alley cats, in the Adams-Morgan district of Washington. They had been trapped and neutered, and I remarked at the time that they looked sleek and contented, and probably had far more interesting lives than solitary cats shut up in apartments all day.

Louise became one of the great pioneers of cat welfare in the United States, in 1990 setting up Alley Cat Allies with Becky Robinson. This was at a time when the established humane societies were convinced that the only solution to the problems caused by unowned street cats was to kill them. Louise and Becky were able to show that the method of Trap, Neuter and Return to supervised sites could be actually a more effective as well as a kinder solution. Alley Cat Allies is now an important campaigning organisation in the USA with half a million supporters.

Louise went on to found Alley Cat Rescue, a hands-on organisation whose vision was to make it unnecessary to kill any healthy cat, whether domestic or feral. This book distills the experience she has gained over 30 years of working with feral, stray and domestic cats and contains much valuable advice and wisdom. If all animal owners and societies involved with cats were to follow her advice, her vision could be achieved.

Jenny Remfry

Preface

Louise Holton

Founder and President, Alley Cat Rescue, Inc.

To this very day, I have vivid memories of my mother feeding all the neighborhood stray cats with scraps from the dinner table. During my early childhood years she always brought in a few of the friendlier cats to live with us, as well as a stray dog or two. So from this perspective, I had a humane background growing up and learned early on that stray domestic animals need our help. No matter how little we had in the home, there was always room for a mutt or two.

Today I care about *all* animals. I also care deeply about the Earth. I am in a fairly constant state of anguish over all the cruelty and suffering in the world, as well as the destruction of our planet. So many humans, who live privileged lives, live in total disregard for the condition of our Earth, and they ignore the sad state of its declining wildlife; of course, many are impervious to the suffering of animals.

Probably my feelings of empathy with the "underdog" throughout most of my life eventually led me to my choice of fighting for a better life for cats, and even more particularly, my fight for better treatment for all feral animals, particularly feral cats. Although I now spend 90% of my life working to defend and protect cats, still as a caring and compassionate human being, I cannot ignore any meanness and cruelty towards *any* animal.

My feelings towards animals have evolved over the years. I have always loved dogs and cats, but I had to learn to extend this compassion to include other animals. As a teenager, I modeled fur coats, never giving a thought to the suffering that went into the making of the coats.

In my opinion, as defenders and protectors of animals, we simply must have empathy for those who have not yet evolved towards accepting that all animals are sentient beings, who experience feelings of joy and happiness, as well as pain and sadness, and they deserve our concern and humane treatment. We must continue to educate these folks and help them to extend their circle of compassion to include all animals.

Learning the hard way

I once spent a couple of weeks on a Karakul sheep farm (Persian fur, as it is known in the U.S.), and really learned the hard way about the suffering of the lambs and the mother sheep used for the fur coats that I used to model when I was a teen-ager. It takes the bodies of around 80 lambs to make one fur coat. And many more are slaughtered and then discarded as "trash" because they are deemed not "good enough" to be made into coats. The sheds on the farm were piled high with the trashed bodies.

The other horrible thing that happened was that every evening the farm workers rode back to the farmhouse on their horses, with dead leopards, jackals, and other predators strapped to their saddles. They were given a small bounty for every dead predator they caught. There were probably African wildcats among the dead too, I don't really remember, as I was so shocked and horrified by this experience.

It was a terribly painful learning experience for me. But it did contribute to my education about how farmed animals are treated. It opened my eyes to this in a most harrowing way. I had nightmares for weeks after we left the farm.

There is so much work to do on behalf of animals, and one's time is very limited, still I do try to spend a small part of my time on the "bigger picture." Actually, to be truthful, I seriously believe that this bigger picture is the solution to any one smaller problem. If we could all accept the interrelatedness of all life, then there would be fewer problems for animals and less suffering for humans.

Frederick Douglass in 1849, made a wonderful statement that I think is applicable to any struggle, whether it is a struggle for besieged people or for the humane treatment of animals, who themselves cannot cry out for help. He said:

> If there is no struggle, there is no progress. Those who profess to favor free-dom and yet deprecate agitation are men who want crops without plowing up the ground. They want the ocean without the awful roar of its many waters. The struggle may be a moral one, or a physical one; or it may be both moral and physical; but it must be a struggle. Power concedes nothing without a demand. It never did and it never will.

Over the years, I have done a fair share of "agitation." This agitation was, in a way, very hard for me. I found myself debating my peers over the feral cat issue and making myself unpopular in some areas. This was difficult for me as I am a "people pleaser" and just hate people to dislike me. I have the "disease to please" — a disease Oprah Winfrey often talks about and tries to cure people from!

When I first found out in 1990, that the humane movement for the most part, advocated killing all feral cats, I was pretty outraged. Well to be honest, shock was my first reaction. I had come to the United States to work in the animal movement and had believed that America was the place to be to make changes for animals. I had believed that the humane groups were pretty progressive and compassionate.

Even after I found out about their negative attitudes towards feral cats, a pretty progressive animal person literally shuddered when she heard I was advocating for feral cats. She called them "fractious animals" and said she hated them. Still, I believed that if I went out and showed them how to Trap-Neuter-Return (TNR), I could persuade them that nonlethal control was the right thing to do. Over time most of the big groups, who had vehemently opposed me, started to embrace TNR!

And as fascinated that I am with domestic cats, the large, exotic cats have also piqued my interest. Loving all the big cats so very much and being concerned by their plight and possible extinction, I cannot in good faith, write a book about domestic cats without talking about the fascinating big cats and the lesser-known, smaller exotic cats who live in Africa. These magnificent creatures are terribly endangered today. The African wildcat, the ancestor of our domestic moggy, is one of my favorite cats. ACR has a program in South Africa, where we help a wonderful local activist sterilize domestic and feral cats to help keep the African wildcat in the Pilanesberg Game Reserve pure; TNR prevents inter-breeding of the two species.

I would like to ask all those who have enjoyed the company of domestic cats to please give a thought to their wild cousins. In the back of this book, we give you a list of organizations that help wildcats, so if you feel so inclined, you can provide them with support. Time is so critical right now. There is not much time left to save wild felids from extinction.

Louise Holton

Alley Cat Rescue's Guide to Managing Community Cats

History and Evolution of the Domestic Cat, *Felis catus*

All cats, large and small, wild and domestic, belong to the cat family Felidae. Within this family are two sub-families: *Pantherinae* — the great cats, including the lion, tiger, leopard, snow leopard, and jaguar, and *Felinae* — the small cats. *Felinae* includes more than 30 different species, such as the lynx, ocelot, serval, margay, leopard cat, bobcat, jungle cat, wildcat, and the domestic cat. These cats are found throughout Africa, Asia, Europe, and the Americas.

Several small wildcats, like the European wildcat, *Felis silvestris*, are similar in appearance to the average house cat. However, it is specifically the African wildcat, *Felis silvestris lybica*, who is considered the ancestor of what is now the most popular companion animal in the world: the domestic cat, *Felis catus* (Driscoll et al., 2007).

The African wildcat is considered the ancestor of domestic cats partly because of its sociability. *Felis lybica* is a little larger and stockier than *catus*, but its coat is similar to that of the modern tabby cat. Even today, African wildcats have been successfully socialized to humans, whereas the European wildcat, *Felis silvestris*, not considered a forebear to modern domestic cats, is almost impossible to tame (Serpell, 2000). Young European wildcats who live in captivity will quickly revert to a wild state as they grow older.

Personal Account from Louise Holton

Many years ago on a trip to the magnificent Kruger National Park in South Africa, I spotted an African wildcat. I did not realize at the time that the cat was *lybica*. The cat looked so much like a tabby cat, I thought a ranger's cat had wandered too far from home. Only later, while reading a book on Kruger, did I discover the cat I had seen was *lybica*! I can still see the wild look on her face as she peered at me from under some bushes. Years later the ACR staff saw several wildcats in a private reserve next to the Kruger National Park and in the neighboring country of Botswana.

Mummified cat remains have also shown the domestic cat's origins to be closer to *lybica* and modern molecular techniques show that the domestic cat is genetically similar to the African wildcat. In 2007, scientists established the origin of the domestic cat by analyzing the DNA of a thousand wild and domestic cats (Driscoll et al., 2007). By sampling genes from several subspecies across three continents, they found that *Felis lybica* living in the Near East were likely domesticated from 10,000 to 12,000 years ago (Handwerk, 2007).

African wildcat (Felis silvestris lybica), considered the ancestor of today's domestic cat.

Domestication of the cat occurred when humans settled the Fertile Crescent, stretching from the Nile in Egypt to the Tigris and Euphrates rivers in the modern-day Middle East. Around this time, human settlements started to grow crops, such as wheat and barley, and with that innovation also came the necessity to store unused grain. The wildcat found easy prey at the grain storage bins, which attracted large numbers of rodents (DK

Publishing, 2014). The two opportunistic species recognized what could be a mutually beneficial relationship; cats benefited from the availability of food sources around humans (as well as shelter from weather and other predators), while humans profited from a feline form of rodent control. Both of them found new companionship and usefulness in each other.

Traditionally, scientists had thought the cat was domesticated around 4,500 years ago in ancient Egypt. In 2004, a group of French archaeologists led by Jean-Denis Vigne discovered the remains of an eight-month-old cat buried with its human companion at a Neolithic site in Cyprus. This cat was dated back to 9,500 years ago. The Mediterranean island was settled by Turkish farmers who brought domestic animals with them. There are no native wildcats on Cypress, so cats were probably imported from Turkey (Vigne et al., 2004).

Most domestic animals were tamed by people, but geneticist Dr. Carlos Driscoll, has written, "The cats were adapting themselves to a new environment, so the push for domestication came from the cat side, not the human side" (Driscoll et al., 2007).

Dr. Stephen O'Brien says: "But this little guy ... chose to be a little bit friendly and also was a very good mouser." The wildcat brought "two very valuable commodities" to these early humans. "One is, he helped dispatch rodents that were living on the grain stores and

3

second he probably provided some amusement to the early families and their children by being friendly," O'Brien says. "So that was the beginning of one of the most successful biological experiments ever undertaken, where a ... deadly predator changed its attitude and became friendly with humans" (Thomet, 2007).

European wildcat (Felis silvestris), similar in appearance to the domestic cat, but much less social toward humans.

Today the descendents of the domestic cat number more than 600 million (Driscoll et al., 2009). Unfortunately, the cat's bigger wild cousins are not faring as well and are in great jeopardy. Habitat loss from the rampant overdevelopment of land has resulted in the loss of prey animals; thus, causing a near-extinction crisis for most of these wildcats.

New studies have discovered genetic markers that distinguish native wildcats from domestic house cats or feral cats (Randi et al., 2001). Since these cats have a similar genetic makeup, they easily interbreed; in some cases, such as the African and Scottish wildcats, interbreeding threatens to "hybridize" their genetically pure wild form out of existence.

In Great Britain and other countries, some true wildcats are protected by law. (Accurate genetic testing is important, so that officials can properly identify protected animals.) David Macdonald of Oxford University has spent ten years trying to preserve the Scottish wildcat, of which only 400 or so remain. "We can use some of the genetic markers to talk to conservation agencies like the Scottish Natural Heritage," he said (Wade, 2007).

The Cats of Ancient Egypt

Because of this new evidence, domesticated cats are now believed to have arrived in Egypt from the Near East, rather than tamed from the resident wildcat species. However, some scientists admit that the African wildcats in Egypt could have been tamed by humans, and I have been told by a few South African friends that they had African wildcats befriend them.

In any case, cats were treated with great respect in Egypt. Many revered the cat goddess Bastet, and celebrated her

4

connection with the moon, fertility, and protection. Another name for Bastet or Bast, was Pasht, from which the word "puss" is thought to have been derived (Zax, 2007). Bubastis, the city of Bastet, became one of the major religious centers of Egypt and in 945 B.C. it was made the capital of Egypt (Mercer, 1919). Bastet was one of the most popular goddesses (Mark, 2012). A temple of red granite surrounded by water was built in her honor (Rosenow, 2008). The Egyptians portrayed Bastet either as a giant cat or as a woman with the head of a cat. The celebration of Bastet at Bubastis continued for two thousand years until it was finally outlawed by the Christian Emperor, Theodosius (Quammen, 2012).

Louise Holton

The ancient Egyptians revered cats and immortalized them in statue form.

Ancient wall paintings show cats and kittens sitting under chairs and on laps in much the same way as our household cats act today. Wall paintings depict the cat as a welcome member of Egyptian households, as well as a prominent figure in myth and legend (Wilkinson and Hill, 1983).

In ancient Egypt the death of a cat was deeply mourned. The entire household shaved their eyebrows to display their grief over the loss (Herodotus, 2008). Millions of cats were mummified and buried in cat cemeteries in Bubastis and other centers (Kurushima et al., 2012). These mummified cats were kept for centuries, but before valuable research could be done to establish the true origins of the domestic cat, the scientific value of these remains was overlooked and most were used as fertilizer (Lorenzi, 2012).

During this period in Egypt, cats were not allowed to be taken out of the country (Mark, 2012). However, the cultural significance of the cat and her ability to control rodent populations so entranced many foreign visitors that slowly many cats were smuggled out of Egypt and began their journey to the four corners of the world (DK Publishing, 2014).

Cats were first taken to the Far East, then, in the 10th Century, to Europe and England. Unknowingly, crusaders also brought rats and mice to Europe from the Middle East and these quickly proliferated in their new environment. The cat's ability to maintain control of the newly burgeoning rodent populations made her welcome in most countries (Serpell, 2000). Her popularity rose quickly in Japan when mice began destroying silk farms. Soon cats were taken on ships to control stowaway rodent populations. When the ships docked in new countries, many cats jumped ship. These seafaring cats are the ancestors of the feral cat colonies found across the world today.

Cats were deliberately introduced to most of the world's islands to control rodent populations (Rodríguez et al., 2006; Courchamp et al., 1999). At least 65 major island groups have populations of introduced cats (Courchamp et al., 2003). This topic will be discussed in more detail in the "Cats and Predation" chapter.

The Persecution of Cats

The early Christian church was aware of the link between so-called pagan religions and cats as deities. As a result, the cat began to fall from favor during the Middle Ages. Western religions started encouraging the cruel torture and burning of cats, condemning them as pagan demons (Lawrence, 2003). During the 13th century the church blamed witchcraft for the social problems of the time, and cats became one scapegoat — along with witches and non-Christian believers (Serpell, 2000).

Many women who practiced ancient healing crafts, using old folk medicines, were accused of being witches. In some cases, women were killed solely because they cared for cats, because the church said they were conversing with the devil (Lawrence, 2003). Cats were accused of being witches' familiars or even witches in disguise. The Festival of St. John was celebrated annually with the burning alive of cats in the town square (Darnton, 1986).

Australian ecologist Frankie Seymour explains in "The Great Feral Cat Con Job: The Ungentle Art of Scapegoating and Scaremongering:"

> By the late Middle Ages, cats in Europe had been hunted, hanged and burned almost to extinction. Then, of course, the Black Death (Bubonic Plague) arrived in Europe and 25 million people ... died in five years because, for several hundred years before, there hadn't been enough cats to keep the rat population healthy. (Seymour, accessed 2014)

The persecution of witches and cats spread to the New World in cities such as Salem, Massachusetts. In 1692, more than 144 were accused of witchcraft, with more than 20 of them executed (Norton, 2007; Doty and Hiltunen, 2002).

This dark age left behind a legacy of superstition, myth, and misinformation about cats, some of which persists to this very day. Although more and more people have cats as companion animals, many others have an unreasonable aversion to cats. Some even suffer from ailurophobia — the irrational and panic-laden fear of cats. In a survey conducted in the 1980s, one out of four people surveyed disliked cats. And Noah Webster, in his dictionary, described the cat as "a deceitful animal and when enraged extremely spiteful" (DeForest, 1874).

Famous Cat Haters

Dwight D. Eisenhower (1890-1969). Eisenhower's loathing for cats was so great, he gave his staff orders to shoot any seen on the grounds of his home.

Johannes Brahms (1833-1897). One of his favorite forms of relaxation was to sit at an open window and attempt to kill neighborhood cats with a bow and arrow.

Napolean Bonaparte (1769-1821). This emperor was once found sweating with fear and lunging wildly with his sword at the tapestry-covered walls. The source of his fear was a small kitten.

Source: "Cat Haters," accessed 2014

Thankfully people do not burn cats at the stake any longer. However, a question resides in the minds of many, and was asked by the Animal Protection Institute (API) in 1994: "Is there a War Against Cats?" And we must agree with API, in that, "The all-out war against cats that Pope Innocent VIII initiated is the stuff of history. But today ... the war against cats goes on" (Lamont, 1994).

Conclusion

It is unfortunate that this "war on cats" is perpetuated to this day, as the negative view of cats is wholly outdated and not based upon facts. We of course no longer believe that cats are conjuring evil spirits, but some are still arguing that cats are violent, dangerous predators who kill for sport and spread disease. Animal control agencies still euthanize untold numbers of feral cats, under the assumption that they are unwanted, uncared for, and have no place in our ecosystem.

Modern science has proven these misconceptions wrong and has brought us a deeper understanding of the feline species. Attitudes are shifting — there are now more pet cats than dogs in the U.S. — and humane policies for cat care and management are spreading. It seems we are finally waking up to our shared responsibility to care for the cats in our communities, and we hope this handbook will be an informative and important tool for those working on behalf of cats.

Introduction to Feral Cats

What Exactly is a Feral Cat?

The word "feral" comes from the Latin *fera*, meaning wild animal. A feral cat is a cat who is born and raised in the wild, or one who has been abandoned or become lost and has reverted back to a "wild," instinctual state in order to survive. A feral cat is commonly referred to as an "alley cat," "street cat," or "community cat." While some feral cats tolerate different degrees of human contact, most are too fearful and wild to be handled. Some feral cats are rarely seen, coming out only at night to look for food. Feral cats often live in groups, or colonies, and reside wherever they can find food. They seek out abandoned buildings, deserted cars, and storm water drains for shelter.

Any domesticated animal, such as a pigeon, pig, horse, or dog, who lives away from human contact can revert to a wild state, becoming feral. In most cases, environmentalists refer to these animals as invasive or exotic species, thereby insinuating that they pose an adverse effect to their habitat. However, Frankie Seymour sees them differently, as "introduced species that have returned to the wild and become naturalized" (Seymour, accessed 2014). This is a much healthier and more accurate view of describing these animals.

Roger Tabor

Feral cats exhibit a wide range of personalities. Some are so fearful of humans that they are seldom seen, while others will patiently pose for a picture!

In the case of feral cats, in our opinion, they should be referred to as "community cats." After all, they belong to the neighborhoods and the communities where they live. The individuals who Trap-Neuter-Return (TNR) them are doing society a huge favor. The cats are now sterilized and vaccinated against disease. And in return, the cats offer our cities and suburbs a service by controlling rodent populations and preventing disease. The term "community cats"also encompasses a broader scope of describing individual cats, including stray, abandoned, free-roaming, and feral.

For the sake of clarity, the term "feral cats" will be used in this handbook. This is the more readily identifiable term in today's world, though we hope "community cats" will one day become the widely accepted term for these cats without having any negative connotation.

Feral cats have lived in the U.S. for around 500 years. Some researchers believe cats came over on the Mayflower, which is probable, since explorers usually took cats with them on their ships to control rodent stowaways (Driscoll et al., 2009). Roger Tabor in his book, "Cats: The Rise of the Cat," says that there were probably cats on the ships of Columbus in 1492, as it is known "from a letter written in 1495 ... that they were taken on his second voyage in 1493-5" (Tabor, 1991). And there are theories that cats came over to the U.S. even before the Mayflower. The Maine Coon cat closely resembles the Norwegian Forest Cat. They both evolved in much the same climate, which has led some to the conclusion that the cats responsible for developing the Maine Coon were brought over by the Vikings (Simmon and Simmon, accessed 2014).

One of the biggest myths promoted by anti-cat folks is that feral cat caretakers are responsible for dumping cats, and that by managing feral colonies, caretakers are encouraging folks to dump cats. The caretakers of these colonies did not put the cats out there. Uneducated and uncaring individuals are responsible for the outdoor cat population.

Cats end up on the streets because (1) they are kicked out; (2) they are let out because of financial constraints and the fear of taking them to a shelter where they will be killed; or (3) they become lost. The majority of the cats who end up on the streets are unsterilized. It's the colony caretakers who are stopping the breeding cycle and humanely managing the cats. When a new cat shows up at a colony, the caretaker ensures she is sterilized and vaccinated. Unfortunately, people are always going to dump animals; that's why organizations like ours work to educate the public about homeless animals to minimize this problem. We also work to provide helpful resources in solving some of the most common behavioral issues facing cats, so that more cats stay in their homes and are not discarded.

Feral kittens are the offspring of a feral mother cat or they can be born to a domestic mother cat who became lost or was abandoned, or one who chooses to have her litter away from humans. In order for kittens to become friendly and completely domesticated, they should be handled from a very early age, ideally from two weeks old. Feral mother cats teach their young to be wary of humans and to run and hide if they feel threatened.

Feral kittens.

Young kittens who have not been handled by humans will spit and hiss. They will be wary of humans and flee when approached. A stray domestic cat who has had to survive on her own for a while will initially be wary of humans. However, she will regain her confidence fairly soon after re-establishing contact. There are varying degrees of wariness and shyness among both feral cats and other cats who have been abandoned to fend for themselves. It requires a certain amount of experience working with stray and feral cats to be able to properly judge just *how* feral a cat may be, or if the cat is even feral at all — maybe she is just a frightened house cat. Sadly, many in animal control refer to these cats as fractious animals. Many domestic cats are killed in shelters merely for acting fearful

and defensive in a frightening situation, because they are assumed to be feral.

Defining and predicting feral cat behavior can be somewhat murky territory. If a domesticated cat becomes lost and has to fend for herself for awhile, she could temporarily revert to some instinctively wild behavior. Some older feral cats can become fairly tame in time, yet other feral cats, even when trapped as young as four months of age, may remain feral forever. Some feral cats bond with their original caretaker, but may never bond with a new person.

During my many years of working with feral cats, I have experienced a wide range of situations with hundreds of fe-

Personal Account from Louise Holton

In Prince George's County, Maryland, a yellow eight-month-old house cat was picked up by animal control officers, along with a few stray cats, at an apartment complex. The cat, Hunter, had been neutered and vaccinated just two weeks earlier, and had apparently escaped from the apartment when someone accidentally left a door ajar. The cat was examined by two experienced veterinary technicians and an animal control officer, and was deemed "feral." He was destroyed that same day. When the family went to claim their cat, they were told that he was destroyed because he "was attacking, spitting and hissing, and trying to bite the officer through his gloves." The agency said they hold most cats for three to five days but often destroy "fractious" stray cats sooner.

ral cats. I've seen them in a wide variety of circumstances — in my home, at the veterinary clinic, in city alleys, and at Alley Cat Rescue headquarters with our own adopted feral office cats. The only conclusion one can reach from these combined experiences is that no two feral cats are alike and one can never predict how *any* feral cat will react to human contact.

The domestic cat is one of the most adaptable mammals on Earth and, as I have said, can become wild easily. When a house cat is lost or abandoned, she will try to find a food source and shelter. She may find a home with humans — 30 percent of Americans obtain their cat as a stray who arrived on their doorsteps — or she may find some old boxes behind a convenience store where other cats have formed a colony, and join this group. Thirty to 60 percent of lost cats, or cats who wander away from home, will eventually come to live in a feral colony (Berkeley, 2001). If she is not sterilized, she will soon become pregnant. Usually around half of her kittens will become ill with treatable illnesses, such as upper respiratory infections; however, most will die. She will teach her remaining kittens to be wild, teaching them survival behaviors inherited from her wild ancestors.

Most house cats do suffer and often cannot survive when they find themselves on their own. However, some survive quite well, which is why there is such a large population of feral cats all around the world. There is generally an enormous amount of discarded food waste in cities and suburbs, where colonies usually form. Feral cats are opportunistic feeders, scavenging on whatever food is available. They will eat from garbage cans or beg for handouts. Cats are also hunters, preying on rodents, reptiles, insects, and birds. Cats, like other predators, prey on young, old, and ill animals. Cats learn very quickly the locations of potential food sources and which households, restaurants, and hotels throw food in dumpsters.

British biologist Peter Neville has studied cats and feral cat colonies for decades. He explains them this way:

> There is perhaps no such thing as a feral cat, a domestic cat reverted to the wild. Instead all cats — feral, stray, and pet — can be viewed as being the same species as their African wildcat ancestor, and the pet cat is simply exploiting an attractive opportunity. The 'normal' lifestyle is living around and with man, but not necessarily to the height of luxury that we offer him as a pet. Then the success of the cat 'living rough' and away from the direct care of man is that much easier to comprehend. (Neville, 1992)

Despite cats being able to survive in the wild, many of those who work in humane organizations are not willing to admit this. It seems to many that, in order to discourage individuals from abandoning house cats to the streets to fend for themselves, they refuse to admit that any cat, even a feral cat, can survive on her own. This is where the myths and misinformation begin and where theories about what constitutes the proper way to protect feral cats becomes muddied. Yet, in defense of those who feel that all cats are helpless on their own, these people have usually witnessed a tremendous amount of suffering and neglect among the animals they have dedicated themselves to protecting. Many cats have been abused, relinquished to shelters for euthanasia when they become inconvenient, and some are treated appallingly by humans. But for every person who treats an animal badly, there are many more who care properly for animals, treating their companion animals as part of the family. And there are many who care for and feed feral cats, to whom they have no obligation, except that their compassion dictates that they must.

Those who advocate that no cat can survive on her own are met with contradiction when colonies of feral cats are seen surviving quite well. When cats have been trapped and sterilized, provided with shelter, food, and water, cats actually thrive. It may seem contradictory to advise people that it is cruel to abandon cats to fend for themselves while saying that many cats can survive quite well on their own. However, we have a moral and ethical responsibility to care for the animals that we have domesticated, whether it be by taking them into our homes or by making their life in our alleyways a little easier. *We do not condone abandoning cats to survive on their own.* However, for those who already live on the streets, we believe it is in the best interest of the cats (and of humans) to sterilize and vaccinate them. These animals deserve the basic medical treatment that our companion pet cats receive.

Where are Feral Cats Mainly Found?

College Campuses

Some students bring unsterilized cats to school and abandon them at the end of the year. Cafeteria dumpsters ensure that a constant supply of leftover food is available. Attracted by this food source, lost or abandoned cats enter from the surrounding residential areas and join the colonies.

Many colleges have students and staff who implement TNR programs on campus. Some of these are: Operation Catnip at the University of Florida, U.C. Davis' Feline Medicine Club, Feline Friends Network at Stanford University, and UT Campus Cat Coalition at the University of Texas, as well as programs at California Polytechnic State University and George Mason University in Virginia.

Military Bases

Transient military personnel abandon domestic cats when transferred to other bases. Many of the cats are not sterilized and, with their offspring, begin forming colonies. Military personnel often assist with TNR programs on bases and try to find homes for adoptable cats; however, many military installations insist feral cats must be removed.

Fast-Food Places, Restaurants, Convenience Stores, Rest Stops

Eating establishments produce a constant source of leftover food in dumpsters that attracts rodents and feral cats. Colonies soon form around this reliable food source.

Densely Populated Urban Areas

Some negligent caretakers allow domestic, unaltered cats to wander. Garbage left in alleys provides an available food source for cats, and they also prey on rodents who are attracted to the leftover scraps; this encourages the formation of colonies. Feral cats find shelter in abandoned houses and buildings. Porch cats are common in cities and surrounding suburbs, as stray and feral cats find shelter under porches and food sources in yards and dumpsters.

Hospitals

In the United Kingdom, hospital grounds represent areas where successful colonies of managed, sterilized cats live. Hospital personnel have found that caring for feral cats is therapeutic for long-term patients, providing a great deal of enjoyment. Such programs have been particularly successful for patients in mental institutions (Remfry, 1996).

One such study considered the feral cat colony at the Gillis W. Long Hansen's Disease Center in Carville, Louisiana. Veterinarians from the Louisiana State

Feral porch cat, Joey.

Louise Holton

University School of Veterinary Medicine first initiated a nonlethal control-scheme, trap-and-remove. They found this method created a vacuum, where new cats entered the colony, introduced new diseases, and exacerbated behavioral problems (Zaunbrecher and Smith, 1993).

A TNR program was then implemented at the Center. The authors found that here, as in England, feeding feral cats can have long-term positive benefits for cats and patients. The overall health of the cats at the Center was found to be improved after TNR, and the size of the colony had stabilized. The authors also found there were fewer behavior-related complaints about the colony; that staff and patients at the Center were eager to participate, as evidenced by their volunteering to perform the TNR; and that the caretakers formed a lasting bond with the cats, eventually treating them as companion animals (Zaunbrecher and Smith, 1993).

Farms

Many farmers allow feral cats to live in barns to control rodent populations. Sometimes these cats may be underfed in the mistaken belief that this will make them better "mousers." This is a false belief, as hungry cats will move away to areas where better food sources exist. Poorly fed cats are also susceptible to disease. All too often, farmers do not sterilize the animals, causing further overpopulation problems. However, farms can offer an excellent opportunity for relocating sterilized feral cats from cities and urban areas. The new caretakers must agree to confine the cats for a three week period to allow acclamation to their area and food should be provided on a daily basis, with basic medical care given when necessary. For detailed relocation instructions, please refer to "Guidelines for Safely Relocating Feral Cats."

Judy Zukoski

Relocated barn cat.

The Evolution of a No-Kill Approach to Animal Welfare

> "Whose interests does shelter euthanasia serve? The traditional answer asserts that animals are the beneficiaries — it alleviates suffering and protects helpless creatures against fates worse than death. Based on this belief between 20,000 and 30,000 mostly healthy companion animals daily are ushered out of this life. In the face of those numbers still alarming even if improved over recent years, the question of whose interests it serves and the validity of euthanasia's guiding assumptions deserve reexamination."
>
> - Craig Bestrup, Ph.D., author and former Executive Director of the Progressive Animal Welfare Society (1997)

The reexamination of animal welfare in the United States began in 1989, when Ed Duvin, a long-time animal and political activist and historian of social change, wrote an article titled, "In The Name of Mercy." He wrote this after his own realization that many animal activists had essentially walked away from helping companion animals. Commenting on his article, Duvin said:

I was thoroughly immersed in articulating a larger vision for other beings, and there was no time or inclination for the dog-and-cat set. After all, the 'new movement' was charting an exciting course for the future, and there were ample humane societies and SPCAs to cope with unfinished business from the past. It will be to my everlasting shame that so many years passed before I heard the screams of those animals closest to me. (Duvin, 2013)

Duvin continued by saying:

When I finally wrote 'In the Name of Mercy,' it did not take long to recognize that I had struck a nerve. This was the intention, as 'Mercy' was crafted to produce discomfort with the status quo — so much that never again would millions of companion animals be 'euthanized' as a matter of routine. (Duvin 2013)

In 1990, I co-founded Alley Cat Allies and later established Alley Cat Rescue (ACR), as a means of changing the way feral cats have traditionally been managed and viewed by our society. Wrongly considered by some to be pests, these cats are labeled "dangerous and a nuisance" by some animal agencies and environmental groups and, as a result, are trapped and killed. ACR is committed to the development of viable no-kill policies. We agree with Ed Duvin that when shelters kill companion animals, they turn a blind eye towards the "damaging long-term effects of devoting most of their energy to collection, processing, and killing,

[while] leaving sparse resources for bold preventive measures" (Duvin, 2013).

In 1993, the San Francisco SPCA, under the direction of Richard Avanzino, re-evaluated its programs and created the "Feral Fix Program" (Maddie's Fund, 2006). Free vaccinations and sterilizations were made available for all feral cats in San Francisco at no cost, five days per week. On April 1, 1994, the SF SPCA and the city's Department of Animal Care and Control signed an Adoption Pact (Maddie's Fund, 2000). This historic agreement guarantees a home to every adoptable dog and cat in San Francisco. In the agreement, the SF SPCA takes sick, traumatized and under-socialized animals from Animal Control, and rehabilitates them, finding new homes for these animals who otherwise would have been killed.

In 1994, Lynda Foro established the nonprofit organization, Doing Things for Animals (DTFA). DTFA published an annual directory of over 1,100 humane organizations whose mission was to provide humane education to help end the tragedy of killing healthy, adoptable animals. The groups listed provided shelter for animals, adoptions, spay/ neuter programs, and Trap-Neuter-Return (TNR) programs for outdoor cats. Foro, quite progressive and ahead of the times, served only vegetarian

Personal Account from Louise Holton

In 1990, I had come full circle. Having been involved in the animal movement for many years and with wildlife and conservation groups, I was under the impression that companion animals and even community outdoor cats, were being taken care of by the thousands of animal shelters in the country. Unfortunately, that all changed when I became involved with my first feral cat colony in Washington, D.C. I got quite a shock to find out that the feral cat issue had been almost totally ignored, or viewed in a very negative light. The local animal control, and even rescue groups, called these cats "fractious" animals, with catch-and-kill considered the only solution.

Having worked with the Johannesburg SPCA in South Africa on TNR in the mid-1970's, and knowing of all the fine work being done in Britain for outdoor cats, I decided to focus on stray outdoor cats and co-founded the first national network for outdoor and feral cats, Alley Cat Allies. Several years later, I founded my second organization, Alley Cat Rescue, to focus on helping all cats — domestic, stray, and feral.

food at her conferences, saying: "How is it that we can kill an animal to eat while advocating for no-kill?" (Foro, 2001).

The first no-kill organizations pledged never to euthanize healthy animals — only those who could not be treated, had terminal diseases, and were suffering. Many of these no-kill organizations cultivated relationships with their local animal control agencies to take shelter animals slated for euthanasia.

Contributing much success to the No Kill Movement is former lawyer Nathan Winograd, who helped run programs at the San Francisco SPCA and the Tompkins County (NY) SPCA. In 2004, Nathan founded the No Kill Advocacy Center and in 2005, he organized the current annual No Kill Conference.The No Kill Advocacy Center promotes saving lives by implementing the No Kill Equation. The equation emphasizes progressive programs, such as TNR, high-volume, low-cost spay/neuter, and community partnerships around adoption, foster care, and transfers to rescue groups, all with the goal of keeping animals out of shelters that do kill.

All those who work in the humane and animal welfare movement would like a no-kill country. No one who works in animal shelters condones the killing of healthy animals. We should therefore all be working together towards the goal of no-kill. Let those of us who are able to take in a small number of animals and who do not euthanize healthy animals

work with those agencies who are overwhelmed by the numbers of animals brought to them. If all the groups and concerned individuals worked together, if all those who place animals in homes spayed or neutered them before adoption, if all the feral cat caregivers could be given the resources to sterilize their colonies, it would go a long way towards this ideal of a no-kill society.

> "Killing 'surplus' animals does nothing to solve the homeless problem. In fact, it perpetuates the problem by continuously 'making room' for more and more outcasts. 'Excess' animals are not the problem; the problem is in people's heads and hearts, in the way they think and feel — or fail to."
>
> - Amy Blount Achor, author of "Animal Rights: A Beginner's Guide" (1996)

Unfortunately, two other problems exist in the U.S. that are not easy to solve — the dumping of companion animals and individuals not spaying or neutering their animals, which creates litters of unwanted kittens that overwhelm shelters each spring. The two most common reasons people relinquish companion animals are due to a move or a "no pet policy" at their new residence (Salman et al., 1998). Other common reasons include behavioral issues, no time to care for the animal, death or illness in the family, and divorce or having a new baby.

The economy also plays a large part in why individuals abandon companion animals. The loss of a job, foreclosure on their house, and the inability to pay bills forces many families to give up their animals. And upon learning their local shelter is full and fearing their cat will be euthanized, they often release the cat outdoors hoping she will have some chance at survival.

As a compassionate society, it is our responsibility to use all available resources to address each of these problems mentioned above in order to progress toward being a no-kill nation.

Will Community Cats Suffer if We Don't Take Them to Shelters?

Dr. Kate Hurley, head of the shelter medicine program at U.C. Davis, initially believed outdoor cats should be

Working with outdoor cats where they are, out in nature, is more humane than bringing them to a shelter, where they will likely be killed.

rounded up and taken to a shelter where they would of course be killed. But today she travels to conferences to give a very powerful presentation on why this practice should end (Hurley and Levy, 2013).

She and Dr. Julie Levy make a really good case for leaving outdoor cats where they are living, regardless of whether they are spayed or neutered. Taking them into shelters (where most will be killed) will add to shelter overcrowding, which leads to the spreading of viruses and diseases, resulting in the deaths of even more healthy animals who would otherwise have a chance at adoption.

In a discussion through the no-kill Maddie's Fund foundation, Hurley and Levy argue against long-standing assumptions that claim nothing but suffering and untimely deaths await outdoor cats not admitted to shelters. The veterinary experts cite growing evidence that these cats not only survive on their own, but that feral cats brought to TNR clinics are generally healthy; less than one percent require euthanasia for disease, trauma, or other incurable conditions (Scott et al., 2002, print; Wallace and Levy, 2006).

They also note veterinarians find less than 10 percent of cats have a medical condition on intake at shelters (Wenstrup and Dowidchuk, 1999). Though community cats have a higher risk of infection by parasites than owned cats, they have an equal risk of contracting feline leukemia virus (FeLV) and feline immunodeficiency virus (FIV), and a lower risk of feline infectious peritonitis (FIP) (Lee et al., 2002; Luria et al., 2004). (Refer to "Health Care for Feral Cats: Guidelines for Colony Caretakers" for more information on viral diseases.)

Additionally, in what Hurley and Levy call "the most complete long-term study of community cats in a TNR program" (Hurley and Levy, 2013), researchers found the cats in a TNR'd colony lived an average of three to five years. Yet after the 11-year follow-up period, the cats still living on the property had been there for an average of seven years, meaning they live even longer than expected (Wenstrup and Dowidchuk, 1999).

Hurley and Levy argue to shelter directors that taking in and killing cats, regardless of whether they are friendly or feral, does not resolve complaints. They say it does not help reunite lost cats with their families. These cats usually do not find new homes while in a shelter; although there is a very good chance that community cats will be taken in and given a permanent home by local residents if left where they are living (Hurley and Levy, 2013).

Most community cats are being cared for in some capacity, with feeding being the most common activity. Studies have found that up to a quarter of American households are feeding one or more cats they do not own (Levy and Crawford, 2004; Lord, 2008). Hurley and Levy note that the 14-month survival rate "was 90 percent for 'semi-owned cats'

(free-roaming cats fed by a community member who did not consider themselves the cat's owner)," according to one study (Schmidt et al, 2007).

Community cat in Mount Rainier, Md.

Free-roaming cats are sometimes so well cared for that it is not unusual for cat lovers to adopt them into their homes from the streets. Surveys show that more cats are directly taken in as strays, Hurley and Levy say, than are adopted from shelters or rescue groups (Hurley and Levy, 2013).

However, as Hurley and Levy point out, though adult cats are able to thrive in the community, kittens are often not as lucky. In a rate similar to that of other small carnivores, a study found 75 percent of feral kittens died within six months of birth (Nutter et al., 2004), a terrible statistic that TNR could lower by decreasing reproduction.

"The bottom line," says Dr. Hurley, "[is that] traditional sheltering is not an effective tool to eliminate or protect community cat populations" (Winograd, 2013).

Alley Cat Rescue's Own Backyard in Maryland

Change comes slowly sometimes, but after many years of community advocacy, work with government officials, and even law suits, our county animal control agency is now required to work with community cat caretakers and those performing TNR. Whereas feral cats brought to the shelter in the past were promptly deemed unadoptable and euthanized, there now exist regulations that require a three-day holding period and notification of rescue groups, like Alley Cat Rescue, when an ear-tipped cat is brought to the shelter. The agency still does not practice or approve of TNR, and "stray" animals with no readily discernible vaccination or ownership history have little chance of survival once at the shelter. But, it is at least recognizing ear-tipped cats as cared-for members of the community.

Alley Cat Rescue is working towards a goal of having everyone on the same page regarding overpopulation of companion animals: 1) We sterilize every cat, and work hard to place every friendly cat in a home, while leaving outdoor cats in their outdoor homes and providing

them with proper medical care; 2) We educate the public on the importance of spaying and neutering their companion animals and providing committed, lifetime care. Nowadays, most animal shelters work with other rescue groups, and together we can do even better.

However, we have much hard work still ahead. The current shelter system continues to kill 3 to 4 million companion animals every year, and that is far too many for a country like the United States (The HSUS, May 2013). Of those, 1.4 million are cats, and 41 percent of all cats taken to shelters are euthanized (ASPCA, accessed 2014). Still, it is a vast improvement compared to the 12 to 20 million animals euthanized each year in the 1970s. Previously, about 25 percent of American dogs and cats were euthanized every year, now only about three percent meet this fate (Pacelle, 2007).

Though euthanasia rates may be decreasing, the overpopulation of domestic animals remains a concern, and several factors are at the root of this problem. Despite growing campaigns promoting the spaying and neutering of companion animals, many guardians — as many as 35 percent in the U.S. — still fail to have their companion animals fixed (Scheer and Moss, 2011). This results in many unintended litters and many more cats and dogs who need homes. Unfortunately, guardians often find that they cannot take care of their animals.

The majority of companion animals relinquished to shelters are turned in by their caretakers, perhaps as many as six to eight million animals every year (Scheer and Moss, 2011). Alley Cat Rescue receives calls every day from individuals looking to give up their cat(s) for a number of reasons: the person is moving, the person brought in another companion animal who does not get along with the cat, the arrival of a baby, behavioral issues, medical issues, financial constraints, or the person simply no longer wants the cat.

Along with this abundance of animals being born and abandoned, there are simply not enough animals being adopted from shelters. Every year, 17 million Americans get a new companion animal, with only 20 percent being rescued from shelters (Scheer and Moss, 2011). Because of this, rescue groups and shelters often deal with a huge number of animals and a shortage of homes to adopt them into.

Whatever the reason fueling overpopulation, Alley Cat Rescue and other

Backyard cat.

Alley Cat Rescue

organizations are working hard to form partnerships with local county-run shelters to continuously improve the situation for community cats. Merritt Clifton of *Animal People* states that the introduction of TNR into the U.S. has contributed greatly to the reduction of killing of cats in shelters (Clifton, 2003). We strive for a day when no healthy cats — domestic, stray, or feral — are killed in U.S. shelters.

TNR in a Nutshell

"I have now been studying cats and the people who try to help them for many years, and I am continually struck by the mutual attraction between cats and people, the lengths which people are prepared to go to in caring for their pet cats and in protecting ferals, and the amount of pleasure which those people derive from the grace, comforting presence and displays of affection of their cats."

- Dr. Jenny Remfry, author of "Ruth Plant: A Pioneer in Animal Welfare" (2001)

Trap-Neuter-Return (TNR) is the most effective and humane way to treat feral cats and manage their colonies. Cats are trapped and taken to a veterinarian to be sterilized and given any necessary medical attention. At this point friendly cats are moved to an adoption program — immediately (and most importantly) reducing colony size — while those not suitable for indoor life are returned to the place of trapping. All cats are scanned for a microchip and returned to their guardian. Anyone (including you, dear reader!) can learn to safely practice TNR, and those who do can witness first-hand the benefits of a humane approach to outdoor cats.

Spaying and neutering colonies of cats:

- stabilizes populations at manageable levels;

- eliminates annoying behaviors associated with mating (fighting, yowling, and spraying);

- improves the overall health of outdoor cats;

- is more effective and less costly than repeated attempts at eradication;

- is humane to the animals and fosters compassion in the community.

Key stakeholders (cat caretakers, citizens of the local community, volunteers, and any property owners where the cats reside) should work together to implement a management plan. Financial support may be available from an already -established organization; if not, then money may have to be raised by voluntary contributions. Local governments should be approached and asked to contribute to the fund, as TNR will save them money over time. The initial investment may seem high, but in the long-term a proper TNR program will cost much less than repeated eradication attempts. The major expenses are for equipment, veterinary services, and food.

Before you Begin

So, you've made the decision to help your local feral cat community and want to use TNR to do it: Congratulations! The work you do in your area will go a long way towards ending cat homelessness. The following is an outline of the steps you can take to put your ideas into action, and how to work with others in your community to achieve the greatest impact.

Assessment

It is important when implementing a new TNR program to get a broad view of how (or if) your community is currently managing feral cats in some way and who is involved. Identify all individuals who feed community cats and all locations of feeding sites. Create a spreadsheet tracking pertinent information regarding the cats (i.e., number of cats, sex of each cat if possible, state of health, whether females are pregnant, if there are kittens). Also, identify the cats who are only occasional visitors or who are very friendly, as these may be companion animals and could have an indoor home.

While TNR programs are increasing in number and gaining wider acceptance,

there are still few laws or regulations that specifically govern it. When addressed in the law, it is usually at the local municipality level. Refer to Addendum 2 in the back of the handbook for more information.

Mama "Squirrel" and kittens, Bronx, New York City, NY.

Main Steps for Implementation

Once the assessment is done, you're ready to start work in the field.

The location should be evaluated as to whether it is an appropriate environment in which to keep the colony. Spots near vacant buildings and other uninhabited areas can be good locations for colonies, but be careful, as buildings scheduled for demolition or areas too close to major highways may not be suitable.

For the most part, the area where the cats are currently living is the best place to keep them. If relocation is necessary, after careful consideration start searching for a suitable new location (i.e., farms, neighbors with land). (Refer to "Guidelines for Safely Relocating Feral Cats" for more information.) Euthanasia, the final option, is recommended only for very sick cats, who cannot be treated and released.

Notify your neighbors of your plan before trapping begins to prevent them from thinking that you will harm the cats, and also to allow them to keep their cats indoors so they are not trapped.

Planning

Make arrangements for kittens and cats who may be socialized after veterinary treatment so they can be placed into an adoption program. Foster homes should be arranged prior to trapping. All cats and kittens should be sterilized prior to adoption, and caretakers can charge an adoption fee to help recover part of the cost. Obtain humane traps and transfer cages and learn how to properly use them. Make arrangements for transport, overnight stay prior to being released, and delivery to and from the veterinary clinic.

Don't leave a cat in an unprotected trap and never leave the cat where she might be threatened by other animals, people, or weather. Immediately cover the trap with a towel or blanket when the cat is caught in order to calm her down. When one cat has been trapped, move her to the transfer cage so you can use the trap for a second cat.

Do not trap in inclement weather, especially during heat waves; traumatized cats are very susceptible to heat stroke. The use of rabies poles and tranquilizers are discouraged. Tranquilized cats may leave the area before the tranquilizer takes effect and can get into situations that could endanger their lives, such as wandering onto busy streets. Do not trap lactating mothers, if possible. If, however, a lactating mother is trapped you need to make a decision on whether to have her spayed — she could be hard to retrap. If you decide to have her spayed, find her kittens as soon as possible.

Refer to "Steps for Successful and Safe Trapping" for information on equipment.

Veterinary Care

If you're not working with a cat rescue organization, then you will need to reach out to local veterinary clinics to find one that is willing to help. Discuss your plan with the veterinarian and confirm beforehand that the doctor(s) and technicians are prepared to treat feral cats. Some veterinary clinics are not equipped to treat and house feral cats. Once you find a veterinarian who works with feral cats and is willing to help with your colony, you may want to inquire about a possible fee reduction, since you will be bringing the doctor several cats to be sterilized. Many veterinarians who treat feral cats are willing to negotiate cost.

All cats to be returned must be identified by clipping one quarter inch off the top of the left ear. Ear-tipping is the universal marking to identify a cat who is part of a managed TNR program. Ear-tipping can be a life saver for feral cats — if trapped by animal control, they can be returned to their colony. This procedure is performed while the cat is under anesthesia, and the ear is properly cauterized to stop bleeding. All cats should be treated for internal and external parasites, inoculated for rabies and distemper, and given a long-term antibiotic injection. Microchipping is also recommended, in case the cat is ever trapped and taken to animal control. She could then be identified and returned to the colony.

After surgery, male cats should be fostered overnight and females should be kept for two nights prior to being released. No cat should be released immediately after surgery. Most veterinary clinics do not hold feral cats after surgery, so you will have to make arrangements to hold the cats for a few days.

You may leave the cat in a trap or you may carefully transition the cat from a trap to a larger cage if fostering for more than two days. Place newspaper under the trap to absorb urine and provide food and water. Keep the trap or transition cage in a basement, shed, covered porch, or other area that is out of extreme weather conditions. Keep the trap covered with a towel or blanket to keep the cat calm.

Refer to the chapters "Health Care for Feral Cats: Guidelines for Colony Caretakers" and "Guidelines for Veterinarians" for more information.

Domestication

Although some older cats can be domesticated or socialized, the best time to tame feral cats is when they are kittens; ideally before they are eight weeks old. While it is possible to domesticate older kittens (12 weeks old), if no homes are available and your local shelter is killing unwanted domestic kittens, a more humane and practical solution for all is to sterilize the kittens, vaccinate, and return to the colony.

Refer to "Feral Kittens and Pregnant Cats" for more information.

Relocation

When returning a cat to the original site is not possible, relocate the cat to a different site, such as a farm, a riding stable, or even a backyard, as long as new caretakers are willing to take responsibility for consistent care. Relocation may take several weeks or months and must be undertaken with the utmost care. "Dumping" feral cats in rural areas, forests, or farmland is strongly discouraged. If the cat is unable to find a reliable food source, she may starve to death.

When relocating a feral cat, you must confine the cat for three to four weeks, to allow her to get familiar with the new sights, sounds, and smells. This period allows a new bond of trust to be established. If this confined transition period is not adhered to, the cat may not remain on the property, which can lead to a traumatic situation for the cat.

Refer to "Guidelines for Safely Relocating Feral Cats" for more information.

25

Long-Term Maintenance

The long-term management of a colony should include arrangements for daily feeding, fresh water, provision of insulated shelters, and providing and cleaning litter boxes. (Refer to "Winterizing Feral Cat Colonies" for more information.) Dust the shelter bedding with flea powder to prevent infestations, and keep feeding areas clean and tidy. It may take several months to bring a large colony under control and achieve stable groups of content and healthy cats. Any new cats attaching themselves permanently to the colony should be trapped and sterilized. Many of these new cats may be tame, domestic strays, able to be resocialized and placed into homes.

Feral cats can be retrapped a few years later for booster rabies vaccinations, health check-ups, teeth cleaning, etc. At this time, they will be more trusting of their caretaker and can be tricked into cages and traps. A plan should be worked out with the veterinarian where mild illnesses can be treated with antibiotics placed in moist food.

Cat shelter, Adams Morgan, Washington, D.C.

Louise Holton

The Community Benefits of Feral Cats

Animals are good for us. Many people who have contact with animals, whether from an indoor companion animal or a colony of outdoor cats, would agree. Having a managed feral cat colony in your neighborhood can benefit the entire community. The colony can demonstrate to all that compassion for cats teaches nonviolence and tolerance towards others.

- Feral cats can minimize rodent problems. While cats do not hunt rats and mice into extinction, they do keep their populations in check and discourage new rodents from moving into the area. Feral cats fill in a gap in the current ecosystem. For example, bobcats (*Lynx rufus*) used to live up and down the East Coast, but were hunted ruthlessly and driven away by development. Feral cats exhibit similar behaviors to these native feline predators, and they help to control the same species of small prey animals.

- An established, stable, sterilized, and vaccinated colony of feral cats will deter other stray and feral cats from moving into the area. This actually decreases the risk that residents will encounter an unvaccinated cat, and will virtually eliminate problem behaviors like fighting and spraying.

- Many people enjoy watching feral cats, and observing animals has been shown to lower blood pressure in medical studies (Sakagami and Ohta, 2010).

- People who help to care for feral cats by feeding them and taking them to the vet enjoy many benefits. Often cat caretakers are elderly and live alone, a population at risk for depression, loneliness, and isolation. Cats relieve these conditions and often bring a sense of happiness and purpose to people who help them. Just as companion animals have been shown to extend life expectancies, lower blood pressure, and relieve stress (Qureshi et al., 2009; Levine et al., 2013), caring for feral cats can improve the health and happiness of the caretaker.

The author, feeding a colony in Adams Morgan, Washington, D.C.

Alley Cat Rescue

- Individuals who cannot take on the full-time commitment of adopting a companion animal can particpate in programs to help feral cats. This provides a viable alternative to irresponsibly purchasing an animal one is not prepared to care for.

Talk to Your Neighbors

Depending on the size of the colony, you may need to address some concerns from one or more of your neighbors. By addressing any specific concerns and showing that you want what is best for the cats and your neighbors, you may be able to defuse many common conflicts.

The most common complaints about cats include the soiling of lawns or gar-dens, the late-night yowling, the leftover food scraps attracting wildlife, the sight of sickly animals, the unpleasantness of dirty feeding areas, and sometimes just the fact that free-roaming cats are around. A feral cat caretaker can alleviate many of these problems and concerns.

- First and foremost, it is critical that you open a friendly dialogue with your neighbors. Rather than being emotional and angry, appear reasonable and professional, even if your neighbors are not. This will give them confidence that you know what you are doing and that you care about their concerns.

- Let them know that you did not create this situation. Explain that the feral cats are there because someone else failed to sterilize their pet cat, abandoned the cat, or the cat became lost.

- Explain the benefits of TNR and the ineffectiveness of eradication. Tell them that withholding food is not only cruel but also pointless, as the cats will continue to breed. Explain how many fewer cats there will be due to your efforts. Make them realize that you are doing them a favor by caring for the cats and preventing the birth of more.

- You may also want to call a community meeting or gathering of concerned neighbors to discuss the situation and possible solutions. They may be more comfortable when they learn that groups across the country and around the world are implementing TNR programs for feral cats.

Steps for Preventing Problems with Neighbors

- All cats should be spayed or neutered to prevent the noisy and objectionable breeding behavior that neighbors dislike: yowling, spraying, fighting, and excessive roaming.

- Make sure cats are vaccinated against rabies to alleviate health concerns. Immediately retrap and vet any cats who become ill or injured. Maintain good vet records, including a rabies tag number for each vaccinated cat, to provide evidence that the feral cats are healthy. Be sure your cats are ear-tipped so neighbors can easily identify cats who are sterilized, vaccinated, and cared for.

- Clean areas where urine has been sprayed. White vinegar or Nature's Miracle can eliminate any odors or staining. Cats will continue to spray in an area that smells of urine, so reclean the site if needed. Avoid using ammonia products; they smell so similar to cat urine that they may encourage more spraying.

- To prevent cats from soiling neighbors' yards and gardens, dump sand in an out-of-the-way area, or in covered wooden litter boxes that can be built outdoors at the colony site. Cats much prefer to use the clean sand and will do most of their eliminations there. (Continue reading for more information on cats and gardens.) Scoop daily to keep sand boxes clean and to prevent odor. Scoop more often in hot weather. Pouring a layer of baking soda beneath the clean sand or litter can be helpful in preventing odors. Cats will stop using the litter or sand if the odor becomes too strong. Odor is another reason neighbors might complain.

- Keep food areas clean. Pick up any and all trash regularly, even if it's not your trash. Remove empty food bowls, old dried-up food, dirty bedding materials, etc. Make the area as attractive and clean-looking as possible. Never leave cans lying around. They are not only an eyesore, but they also attract flies and other animals to the area.

If the area where the cats are fed is a particularly objectionable one for neighbors, gradually move the feeding station to a less objectionable area a few yards away. This can be done in increments and completed in one to two weeks. The cats will follow their food. Create a small, partially enclosed feeding site to make food and water bowls, as well as cats, less visible. Hide it behind or under some bushes.

To keep from attracting wildlife, feed only in the morning or daylight hours when raccoons and other wild animals are not active. Cats will quickly adjust to the new schedule. Again, be sure to remove leftover food after feeding.

Try to make the shelters you have erected look clean and unobtrusive. Many caretakers have built creative shelters and feeding stations. These structures can be painted in natural colors, like dark green and brown, to blend in with surrounding foliage.

If fleas are a concern, treat feral cats with a flea product, like Advantage, when you trap the cats. Only a few drops need to be applied to the back of the cat's neck; your veterinarian can do this for you. Be sure to change the bedding material or hay in shelters regularly. Some herbal products will deter fleas. Try sprinkling mint, dried pyrethrum flowers, or a non-toxic herbal flea powder, like Diatomaceous Earth, beneath the bedding.

There are also some oral flea treatments available. But use caution and make sure that a cat eats only one dose and does not go around eating the food of other cats if the medicine is in all the cat food.

Advantage Multi for Cats is a broad-spectrum parasite preventive in a monthly topical application. It prevents heartworm disease, kills adult fleas, and will treat flea infestations. In addition, Advantage Multi treats roundworm infections caused by Toxocara cati, hookworm infections caused by Ancylostoma tubaeforme, and ear mite infestations caused by Otodectes cynotis. This medication is for use on cats and kittens at least nine weeks of age and weighing at least two pounds.

Desireé Stapley

Feral colony in Key Largo, FL. Feeding stations are tucked out of sight amongst lush vegetation.

Capstar (nitenpyram) is an oral medication designed to kill adult fleas. The pills can be crushed into wet food and used daily. Capstar is intended for cats who are at least four weeks of age and weigh more than two pounds. It begins to kill adult fleas within 30 minutes of ingestion.

Cats and Gardens

Here are some helpful and humane suggestions for neighbors who wish to keep community cats out of their yards and gardens. For more information on the products mentioned in this section and where to purchase them, please see the Helpful Resources section in the back of the handbook.

- Push wooden chopsticks or 10-inch plant stakes into flowerbeds every eight inches to discourage digging and scratching.

- Push Cat Scat Mats into flowerbeds and gardens to prevent digging. These plastic mats can be cut to fit any size area and consist of flexible plastic spikes that are unpleasant for cats to walk on.

- Cover exposed ground in flower beds with large attractive river rocks, to prevent cats from digging. Rocks have the added benefit of deterring weeds and beautifying the landscape.

- Cats dislike citrus smells. Scatter orange and lemon peels or spray a citrus-scented solution on areas you don't want cats. You can also scatter citrus-scented pet bedding such as Citrafresh. Cayenne pepper, coffee grounds, and pipe tobacco work to repel cats as well. Some suggest lavender oil, lemongrass oil, citronella oil, eucalyptus oil, and mustard oil.

- Cat Repellent Clips are biodegradable clips filled with a blend of natural, organic garlic, citronella, lemongrass, and cinnamon oils. These clips can be placed anywhere you don't want cats, like in gardens or flower beds. Clip onto plants and shrubs that cats tend to nibble the leaves of. These clips safely and effectively repel cats for six to eight months.

- Spray a cat repellent (available at pet supply stores) around the edges of the yard, the top of fences, and on any favorite digging areas or plants.

- Plant the herb rue to repel cats or sprinkle the dried herb over the garden.

- Try an ultrasonic animal repellent, which emits high frequency noise inaudible to humans. Cats find the noise to be an extremely loud and annoying alarm, repelling them from the area. These devices are available at lawn and garden stores.

- Use a motion-activated sprinkler, such as the Scarecrow sprinkler. Any cat coming into the yard will be sprayed but unharmed, and it is good for the lawn. These are also available at lawn and garden stores.

- Reppers Outdoor Sticks contain methyl nonyl ketone, which is a cat (and dog) training aid and repellent, that can be used both inside and outside. These repellent sticks are nontoxic to plants, mammals, and humans and can safely keep animals out of your garden, flowerbed or potted plants for up to 60 days. These repellent sticks have been tested and proven to work by Alley Cat Rescue staff and neighbors!

You may want to offer to help your neighbors with any of the above, whether purchasing supplies for them or setting up the deterrents. They will appreciate the offer and your willingness to help even if they don't accept it.

Addressing Other Problems

If neighbors express concern about the effects of feral cats on local wildlife, provide them with copies of ACR materials on feral cats and predation. Explain that cats are rodent specialists and keep rodent populations in check, and if rodents are left unchecked, they could potentially spread deadly diseases.

Also, some neighbors may fear feral cats will pose a threat to their children. Explain to them that feral cats are naturally wary of people and will not approach humans they do not know. A feral cat will not attack a person unless the cat is cornered or feels threatened. Advise neighbors to teach their children not to approach or touch unknown animals. Children should ask an adult for help if they think an animal may be trapped, sick, or injured, or if they find a baby animal.

Feral cats do not pose a health or disease risk to humans, but some neighbors may need to be reassured. Give them copies of ACR's factsheet on "Zoonotic Diseases." Also advise them that they can avoid any risk by not touching community cats and by washing their hands after gardening. Sometimes, even after having expended your best efforts, neighbors may continue to complain, or even be hostile towards you and the cats. This can be very frustrating. In these difficult situations, it may be beneficial to bring in a professional mediator to help solve the problem in a way that is satisfactory to all concerned.

Remember: It is vital that you maintain detailed, up-to-date health records on all feral cats under your care. Ear-tipping is key to identifying which cats have been sterilized, vaccinated, and are being cared for. It is recommended to microchip all feral cats, in the case that someone takes a cat to the shelter. If the shelter does check for a microchip after seeing the ear-tip, the shelter should contact you to come pick up the cat. Again, you may need to prove the cat has been vaccinated, so keep up-to-date records; it can save a cat's life if animal control becomes involved.

If any complaints are made to you or to animal control, it is important to act quickly and demonstrate that you are willing to cooperate with neighbors. Even if there have been no complaints, you may want to avoid any conflicts by minimizing the impact of the outdoor cat colony on the neighborhood.

Conclusion

If any of the above seems overly complicated or time-consuming at first glance, remember that you are fighting for the lives of feral cats and building good public relations for the future. In addition, you might be strengthening your community by getting more people involved! All feral cat problems that are solved positively and amicably help leave a better overall impression regarding feral cats and caretakers, and will serve to make it easier for all of us to continue to care for our outdoor cats.

31

The Effectiveness of TNR Programs:
Why Eradication Does Not Work

Every day more and more sterilization programs for feral cats are being implemented across the United States and around the world. Compassionate communities are embracing this humane, nonlethal method of managing community cats, not only because it preserves the sanctity of innocent life, but also simply because it is effective. Unlike its traditional counterpart catch-and-kill, which has been practiced for decades, Trap-Neuter-Return (TNR) programs stabilize populations, improve the overall health of outdoor cats, and reduce both shelter costs and euthanasia rates. In addition, such programs drive community involvement and encourage compassionate actions.

TNR is Effective, Reduces Costs, and is Humane

Proven Effective to Reduce Feral Cat Populations and Reduce Shelter Euthanasia Rates

Along with sterilizing community cats, all kittens are removed from the colony and placed into an adoption program, which immediately reduces the size of the colony. Friendly, stray cats are scanned for microchips and returned to their guardian or rehomed. Any cats who can be socialized are also placed into an adoption program, further reducing the number of cats in a colony.

A University of Florida study found that spaying/neutering community cats in an area of high animal-control impoundments led to a dramatic decline in the number of cats who were admitted to and euthanized by the local shelter (Levy et al., 2014). During the two-year study, the shelter staff TNR'd 2,366 community cats (an estimated 54 percent of the feral cat population in the targeted area), with most of the cats being returned to the site and some being adopted (Levy et al., 2014). After implementing TNR, the animal control intake for cats in that targeted area decreased by 66 percent and the shelter euthanasia rate for cats dropped by 95 percent (Levy et al., 2014). In addition, this TNR project reduced cat intake by animal control for the entire county by 13 percent and shelter euthanasia rate by 30 percent (Levy et al., 2014).

Another study analyzed data from a TNR program for feral cats living in Orange County, Fla. When the authors compared data from six years before the implementation of the TNR program to data collected during the program, they found both the number of calls to animal control about cats and the number of cats killed by animal control greatly decreased after the TNR program was initiated,

Colony cats, Key Largo, FL.

Desireé Stapley

even while the human population grew significantly. The number of sterilization surgeries and the number of cats adopted out of the shelter also increased (Hughes et al., 2002). Another study that focused on a North Carolina community found that the number of cats euthanized at the local shelter decreased significantly after a spay/neuter clinic was established nearby. The number of service and complaint calls to animal control also declined or leveled off annually (Scarlett and Johnston, 2012).

In Italy, where the national law for managing feral cats is a no-kill policy, TNR programs have been in place for more than a decade. One study examined TNR programs for feral cats living in the city of Rome and found the number of registered feral cat colonies greatly increased (Natoli et al., 2006). This allows for more detailed documentation of the program's effectiveness, while helping to drive community involvement. Colony caretakers, who once worked under a shadow of fear

and persecution for their actions, now have the freedom to carry out the necessary steps in implementing a proper TNR program. The study revealed that, with TNR, the average number of cats per colony decreased between 16 percent and 32 percent over a few years, but the researchers also concluded that further education of the larger community would be necessary to make TNR fully effective (Natoli et al., 2006).

One well-known cat sanctuary in Rome, Torre Argentina, believes this to be precisely the situation. The sanctuary, even today, must push back against the uninformed who fundamentally misunderstand TNR, and believe that all community cats will simply disappear shortly after a TNR program begins. These detractors do not consider that TNR cannot stop irresponsible people from abandoning cats, nor does it keep a cat from getting lost away from her home. Torre Argentina stresses sterilization in its outreach to the public as

33

the key factor to reducing the feral cat population. It has sterilized more than 30,000 cats in the last decade, but has in fact seen a decline from the peak number in 2008. They believe that greater public education and awareness has led to more Romans sterilizing their own companion animals, which in turn has led to the decline in sterilizations at the sanctuary since 2008 (Torre Argentina, accessed 2015).

After researchers established a TNR program at Texas A&M University, they conducted a study where they compared the feral cat colony from the year of implementation of TNR to the year after. In the first year, they caught 123 cats, compared to 35 the second year (Hughes and Slater, 2002). Additionally, while they found 20 kittens the first year, they found only three kittens the second year, and all of them in unusual places and alone (not in litters), leading them to conclude these kittens were likely born elsewhere and abandoned. They found no litters or nursing mothers after one year of TNR. Though most cats were returned to campus, 32 were adopted. The study found that, while such programs required substantial money and time to start, they would cost less money over time as the size of the cat colonies decreased and fewer new cats migrated into the colonies. Returning the cats to their outdoor environment after trapping was deemed to be an effective method of colony management that stabilizes the population of feral cats over time (Hughes and Slater, 2002).

Less Costly and Less Time-Intensive

Unlike eradication programs, which are paid for using tax dollars, most TNR programs operate using private money and use volunteers to carry out the workload. A study commissioned by Best Friends Animal Society and funded by Petsmart Charities found that TNR programs for free-roaming cats can cut costs in half. The study says that with an estimated 87 million free-roaming, community cats in the United States, it would cost governmental entities about $16 billion to trap and kill these cats as opposed to about $9 billion to support TNR programs run by rescue organizations and individual volunteers (Best Friends, 2010).

As part of a population modeling project for the Alliance for Contraception in Cats and Dogs, a team of researchers conducted a more recent economic analysis of both TNR and catch-and-kill. Their results also support TNR as the more cost-effective solution to managing community cats. According to the study, the cost of catch-and-kill methods are 4.5 to 9 times *greater* than TNR, as projected over a seven-year period (Zawistowski, 2013).

The Orange County, Fla., study mentioned prior also supports the cost-effectiveness of TNR. Researchers calculated the estimated cost associated with neutering feral cats and compared the data to the cost of impounding and euthanizing feral cats. They found that "neutering would be less costly as well as less labor intensive" than impounding the cats (Hughes et al., 2002).

Addresses Public Health Concerns

TNR programs provide community cats with vaccinations that prevent the transmission of diseases to humans and to other cats. A rabies vaccine is administered, which creates a buffer zone between wildlife and humans. "By keeping a critical mass (usually 80 percent) of feral cats vaccinated against rabies in managed colonies, a herd immunity effect may be produced, potentially providing a barrier between wildlife and humans and preventing one of the major public health threats caused by feral cats" (Slater, 2002). The distemper and feline leukemia (FeLV) vaccines also prevent the transmission of disease to other cats.

Providing community cats with vaccines decreases the chance of the public coming in contact with an unvaccinated cat and instills good public health policy. Ron Cash, the former business administrator of Atlantic City, who oversaw the Department of Health and Human Services, has said, "TNR is good public health policy." Prior to implementing TNR for the cats living on the Atlantic City boardwalk, Cash said he received numerous calls from the public about the cats. However, after observing the results of TNR he said, "The [cat] population that's here is much healthier. They're coexisting with people very well now. Most people don't even know the cats are there" (City of Atlantic City, accessed 2013).

Returning feral cats to their outdoor homes after sterilization also ensures rodent populations are kept in check; maintaining low rodent populations helps prevent the spread of disease. Fitzgerald and Karl, among others, studied cats and their prey for over 20 years in a mostly uninhabited forest in New Zealand, and their research clearly shows how cats keep rodent populations in check. In the beginning of the study, cats were common and the rat population was "low and stable." However, as the study continued and cats were trapped, leaving only a few individuals in the area, rats began to increase slowly. After several years with only a few cats present, the rat population "peaked at about five times their original numbers" (Fitzgerald and Turner, 2000).

During the 14th century, the Black Plague claimed the lives of over 25 million people, because years earlier, Europe's witch hunts had brought the country's cat population almost to extinction. The low cat population meant a high rodent population and that made for the spread of disease. It wasn't until the Age of Exploration, when cats began accompanying sailors on their voyages to new lands (to eat the rat stowaways) that the cat became popular again.

TNR Improves Cats' Health, While Helping Them Become Better Neighbors

Along with reducing and stabilizing feral cat populations, TNR programs also improve the overall health of outdoor cats; cats are relieved from the constant stress of mating and pregnancy. In one study, veterinarians examined the effects of sterilization on feral cat health by measuring the body condition of 14 feral cats upon trapping, and then taking measurements one year following sterilization. When trapped initially, the cats were lean but not emaciated. One year after being sterilized, the cats showed significant increases in weight and improvements in body condition. In addition, caregivers reported that the cats had a decreased tendency to roam after being neutered (Scott et al., 2002, web).

Park, London to determine whether sterilization had any negative effects either on the social structure of the colony or on the individual cats. No negative health effects were observed, and the colony's social structure seemed to strengthen after the cats were neutered. Cats were seen spending more time in groups, they showed fewer aggressive behaviors toward each other, and they fought less (Neville and Remfry, 1984).

On average, spayed females live 39 percent longer than unspayed females, and neutered males live a full 62 percent longer than those unneutered (Banfield Pet Hospital, 2013). Sterilization greatly decreases the risk of certain cancers (uterine, mammary, testicular, prostate), while providing vaccines will prevent the spread of disease. Neutering male cats also decreases fighting (for mates and territory), which leads to the reduced risk of disease transmission, FIV in particular (Banfield Pet Hospital, 2013).

In addition, sterilizing both female and male cats decreases their need to roam in search of mates, which decreases the risk of injury. Unneutered cats are at four times the risk of being hit by a car than neutered cats, and three times more likely to need treatment for an animal bite (Banfield Pet Hospital, 2013). And most

Linda Tanner

Feral family at Crescent City Harbor wharf, Crescent City, CA.

In another study, researchers followed two colonies of feral cats in Regent's

TNR programs treat cats for internal and external parasites to address disease and potential malnutrition. Lastly, caretakers provide daily food and fresh water; a proper diet leads to improved health and reduces the need to roam in search of food. Any cats showing signs of illness or injury are promptly trapped and treated accordingly.

Once reproduction stops, so do the mating behaviors, which helps improve their relationship with local residents. Sterilization greatly reduces yowling, fighting, and spraying, so complaint calls to animal agencies are decreased. Helping feral cats become better neighbors improves community morale (Hughes et al., 2002).

Drives Community Involvement and Promotes Compassion

Implementing local TNR programs helps drive community involvement and encourages compassionate action. TNR also creates opportunities for outreach, education, and cooperation. Today, three times as many individuals in this country are sharing their homes with companion animals as compared to 40 years ago (The HSUS, 2014). Cats and dogs play a large role in the lives of most Americans and these animals are treated like family members. Today's society also has a heightened awareness of the staggering euthanasia rates occurring in animal shelters, and there is more determination than ever to reduce the killing of healthy animals. Rather than a simple problem of too many animals, many view the situation "as a people problem — the result of the human-animal bond failure," which makes "the killing of animals an unacceptable response" (Hughes et al., 2002).

This shift in attitude has brought a change in the role humans play when managing these animals. The traditional catch-and-kill method is no longer viewed as morally acceptable; many individuals would rather see a cat sterilized and returned to the site over having the cat trapped and killed. A case study conducted by The Humane Society of the United States found that 85 percent of cat owners who were surveyed would rather have a cat TNR'd than trapped and killed (Gibson, 2012). And in the Orange County, Fla., study, it was noted that prior to implementing a TNR program, citizens "had requested help from the county to keep their colonies rather than having them euthanized" (Hughes et al., 2002).

Surveys have shown that most individuals acquire cats by rescuing strays in their neighborhoods. Compassionate people feed and care for homeless cats. They use their own time and money to provide the basic needs for these animals. When they are given the proper tools (access to low-cost TNR services) and they are permitted to conduct TNR without penalty (fines, jail time), they are able to help more cats. This is illustrated by the study of Rome's no-kill policy that showed an increase in the number of registered feral cat colonies (Natoli et al., 2006). TNR programs *encourage* individuals to get involved and make a difference in their communities. TNR also establishes a point of contact for concerns about the cats and for resolving any community concerns.

Eradication is Ineffective, Costly, and Cruel

Once an eradication program has started, it must continue until all targeted individuals have been killed in order to be successful. A primary weakness of eradication programs is that it is close to impossible to determine if all targeted subjects have been killed, let alone identified, and when they are not, the breeding cycle will repopulate the area. Since individuals become trap-shy or immune to introduced disease, it becomes more difficult to kill the last few individuals. However, the killing cannot continue indefinitely and the program must cease at some point.

But an eradication program cannot just stop at *any* given time. A mistaken assumption that eradication is complete when it really isn't can have disastrous consequences: "the species can bounce back and even expand its range, causing environmental and economic damage, and rendering the initial eradication campaign redundant" (Rout et al., 2013). And although scientists try to predict the appropriate time to stop eradication programs, "imperfect detection methods make it difficult to tell whether an invasive species has been successfully eradicated" (Rout et al., 2013).

The "Vacuum Effect"

History has shown that the catch-and-kill method does not effectively reduce feral cat populations. Killing is a temporary, "quick fix" that may appeal to authorities but it does not stop the breeding cycle. When cats are trapped and removed from an area, new cats quickly move in to fill the vacated territory and start the breeding process all over again. This phenomenon was discovered by British biologist Roger Tabor and is referred to as the "vacuum effect" (Tabor, 1983). However, if a colony of cats is "neutered and returned to its area it will continue to hold the location and keep other cats out by its presence" (Tabor, 1995). If new unsterilized cats are permitted to join the colony, they will be sterilized and returned.

A perfect example of the vacuum effect is illustrated by a recent study conducted by Lazenby et al. (2015) in the forests of Tasmania, Australia, where "low-level culling of feral cats" actually caused an *increase* in the number of cats in the area, despite the initial *illusion* that there was a decrease in population. Over the course of 13 months, researchers attempted to "simulate the resource-effort that typically might be available to and expended by natural resource managers," which entailed trapping cats and shooting them in the head (Lazenby et al., 2015). At the end of the study, researchers noted a significant *increase* in feral cat numbers with an average of 75 percent at one site and 211 percent at the other site. It was also noted that "cat numbers fell, and were comparable with those in the pre-culling period, when culling ceased" (Lazenby et al., 2015). More importantly, the researchers acknowledge their efforts "did not constitute a sustained, multi-faceted, long-term downward pressure on [their] study populations, which may be required if culling is to be used in programs of feral-cat control" (Lazenby et al., 2015). Subsequently, the catch-and-kill method of managing feral cats continues to prove ineffective and also counterproductive.

Counterproductive

Eradication programs for feral cats can be highly counterproductive with potentially catastrophic consequences on local ecosystems. After cats were eradicated from Macquarie Island, near Antarctica, the rat population exploded, decimating the ground-nesting bird populations (rats feed on eggs and baby birds)(Strickland, 2009). Rabbits, too, increased in population, which destroyed the island's vegetation; this resulted in decreased materials for birds to build nests and left the native penguin population more susceptible to predators. Scientists spent seven years eradicating the rats, mice, and rabbits to combat their increased predation on birds (Strickland, 2009; Australian Department of the Environment, 2009). And on Wake Atoll, part of the Pacific Islands, a U.S. military base eradicated the cat population (though a few cats have since been sighted), which allowed for the rat population to dramatically increase. The base continues to implement rat control measures (Rauzon et al., 2008).

"Other counterproductive eradication attempts include: the explosion of the local rat population in Albany, Ore., after "aggressive city efforts in recent years to control the feral cat population" (Harlan, 2013), and an increase in the local skunk population in Cape May, N.J., following the removal of a colony of feral cats (Cox, 2008)." An eradication effort on Little Barrier Island near New Zealand resulted in a proliferation of rats, who then preyed on the petrels meant to be protected from cats (Rayner et al., 2007).

In a letter to *Nature*, biologists Kevin R. Crooks and Michael E. Soulé explain that when large mammalian carnivores disappear (or in the case of eradication programs, they are lethally removed), this causes small carnivores, or meso-predators, to increase (Crooks and Soulé, 1999). In other words, when a top predator, such as the cat, is removed from the food chain, smaller predators like rats — along with prey animals like rabbits — increase in abundance, which is often bad news for an ecosystem. As seen on Macquarie Island, removal of the top predator (cat) left prey populations (rats and rabbits) unchecked and vegetation was decimated, causing the entire ecosystem to collapse.

Costly and Very Time-Intensive

Eradicating feral cats is a futile endeavor that comes with a hefty price tag — at the expense of the taxpayer — and requires decades of continual killing. It took over 15 years and cost AU$3.5 million (about

39

$2.5 million USD) to eradicate the 2,500 cats on Macquarie Island (which is only 21 miles long and 3 miles wide), with another AU$24.7 million (about $20.2 million USD) allocated to eradicating the rats and rabbits over seven years (Veitch et al., 2011). Marion Island near South Africa is only 15 miles long and 10 miles wide, yet it took 19 years to kill 3,400 cats (Bester et al., 2002). Additionally, it cost $1.3 million to eradicate the cats living on Ascension Island (located in the South Atlantic Ocean), which is only 34 square miles (Veitch et al., 2011). These eradication programs that are deemed "successful" within the scientific community have been carried out on small, isolated islands with little to no human habitation. Attempting to eradicate an entire population of feral cats on a continent, with far more variables and unpredictable outcomes, would be futile.

Cruel and Inhumane

Along with being ineffective and costly, eradication programs are also cruel and inhumane to the animals being culled. In most cases, the animals die slow, painful deaths due to asphyxiation, starvation, dehydration, dismemberment, or over-exposure to weather elements. Killing methods used for feral cats include poisoned bait, cage traps, leg-hold traps, shooting, gassing, drowning, hunting dogs, and deadly viruses. Some countries have even invented new ways of killing feral cats.

In Australia, cats are lured into tunnels where they are sprayed with a toxic sub-stance (Murphy et al., 2011). The country's government is currently working to create a deadly virus to be released nationwide to control the feral cat population, along with producing a toxic bait known as "Curiosity" (Owens, 2014; Arup and Phillips, 2014).

In the above island examples, every eradication program required more than one method of killing to eliminate most or all of the feral cats. On Marion Island, nearly 100 cats were intentionally infected with the feline panleukopenia virus (feline distemper), which ultimately killed around 2,800 cats. Some cats, however, built up an immunity to the disease, so the remaining individuals were shot at night (Bester et al., 2002). On Ascension Island, the cats were killed by live trapping and shooting, poisoned bait, and leghold traps (Ratcliffe et al., 2010). And one study of 87 island eradication programs, including Macquarie Island, revealed that "on average, each campaign employed 2.7 eradication methods including leg-hold traps (68%), hunting (59%), primary poisoning (31%), cage traps (29%), and dogs (24%)" (Ratcliffe et al., 2010).

Collateral Damage

Eradication programs rarely kill only the one intended species; more often, many non-target animals are killed as well. Poisoned bait does not discriminate between a cat and another meat-eating animal, and intentionally unleashed viruses like, feline distemper, infect feral cats and domestic cats alike. In these programs, when live-trapped cats show

Perpetual Killing

Australian Environmentalist Frankie Seymour explains that: "Reducing a population of mislocated animals is a complete waste of time (and money) unless you are prepared to keep on reducing it — killing and killing and killing, generation after generation. The moment you turn your back for a year or a season, the population will return to full occupation of all available niches."

Seymour also points out that, "when you kill animals to control their numbers, you are constantly culling for individuals who are clever or fast or strong enough to thwart your attempts to kill them — and they pass those faster, smarter, stronger genes (as well as their experiential knowledge) on to their offspring. This is basic Darwinianism — survival of the fittest — yet the thought of it does not seem to have entered the heads of those who advocate lethal control of 'feral' animals" (Seymour, accessed 2014).

no sign of ownership (i.e., a collar or microchip) they will be killed even if they are someone's pet.

Non-target animals and species sometimes pay quite a high price when people try to eradicate cats. On Ascension Island, 38 percent of domestic house cats were killed, causing "public consternation" (Ratcliffe et al., 2010). Over 6,000 land crabs were also killed by ingesting poisoned bait, and "a moratorium on crab claw consumption" was implemented to prevent secondary poisoning of humans (Ratcliffe et al., 2010). In some cases, eradication of feral cats is done through secondary poisoning, meaning prey animals are intentionally poisoned in order to kill cats who eat the tainted prey. On the New Zealand island of Tuhua, cats were removed through secondary poisoning by attempting to eradicate two types of rats living on the island (Ratcliffe et al., 2010).

Even on Marion Island, where "acceptable" numbers of non-target animals were killed, hundreds of birds died in traps set for cats, including some of the petrels that the eradication of cats was meant to protect (Bester et al., 2000). After most or all of the cats had already been killed, researchers set out across the island 30 thousand slaughtered chicken carcasses that had been laced with poison. There is no record of how many cats or other animals died from consuming these tainted birds (Bester et al., 2000).

Perpetuates Animal Abuse

Implementing catch-and-kill to manage *any* animal population, not just cats, perpetuates the idea that animal cruelty is tolerable. When policy supports lethal methods of control, it sends a message to the public that it is morally acceptable to kill sentient beings. Humans created the situation that feral cats are currently in: we domesticated them, we relocated them to every corner of the Earth, and we allowed them to reproduce. There-fore, it is our responsibility to manage them humanely. Killing is the highest form of abuse; it is certainly not humane.

Feeding Bans

Some authorities blame caregivers for perpetuating and even starting the prob-lem by feeding stray and feral cats. They think the cats can be "starved out," so they implement feeding bans and threaten anyone caught feeding outside cats with fines and jail time. These plans never work because cats are territorial animals, who won't quickly abandon an area, and they are also very resourceful scav-engers, finding new food sources even when supplies are scarce. In addition, compassionate people continue to feed outdoor cats regardless of potential fines and other repercussions; it seems to be a natural act for humans to feed an animal to keep her from starving. One recent study concluded that as much as 25 percent of U.S. households, approximately 30 million, are feeding at least one community cat (Lord, 2008). Instead of blaming feeders/caretakers and criminalizing their ac-tions, we should encourage their acts of compassion by assisting them with the resources and information to help steril-ize the animals.

Conclusion

As demonstrated by the above studies, TNR programs are highly effective in stabilizing feral cat populations, reducing shelter costs and euthanasia rates, and improving overall health of outdoor cats. All kittens and adoptable adult cats are immediately removed and placed into adoption programs, which decreases a colony's size instantly. All remaining cats are sterilized to stop the breeding cycle. Euthanizing cats who are too sick or injured also decreases the number of cats in a colony, and, over time, natural attrition will further reduce the size of a colony.

When feral cats enter a traditional shelter they are usually euthanized immediately. Most agencies do not have the time nor the resources to house feral cats. However, by working with local rescue organizations to implement TNR programs, fewer cats end up in shelters, fewer cats are killed, and the feral cats who do come in can be returned to their appropriate colony.

The traditional method of controlling feral cats by catching and killing them is not only outdated but it has been prov-en ineffective, counterproductive, and costly. The few examples scientists like to provide of "successful" cat eradication programs took several years, millions of taxpayer dollars, and were carried out on tiny islands, most uninhabited by humans. Removing the cats in these ex-amples also released prey populations of rats and rabbits, so eradication programs were implemented to remove those animals from the ecosystem as well — because rats prey on ground-nesting birds and rabbits destroy vegetation. Even removing one species from an ecosystem can have catastrophic consequences, setting off a chain reaction that could result in the total collapse of that ecosystem. Once you start killing, you have to continue to kill until all targeted animals are removed or the breeding cycle will repopulate the area.

Unlike killing, which has a dramatic effect on the environment with uncertain results, TNR provides a practical solution with a more subtle way of interacting with the environment. TNR stops the breeding cycle without removing the animals from the ecosystem. This does not create any open niches and keeps nature in balance. Professor Andrew Linzey of the University of Oxford, England, once said:

In the name of biodiversity, these 'managers' regularly kill one form of life in order to 'allow' another to survive ... perhaps populations rise and crash as a matter of course ... we seem to have forgotten ... that it is a self-regulating system. In the end, everything depends upon our own moral vision of ourselves in the world of nature. I believe that we should be not the master species, but the servant species. That means as little interference as possible, and only then with genuinely benign intentions. Biodiversity is a classic tale of how an idealized view of the world can result in individual harm. (Linzey, 2001)

With more individuals sharing their homes with companion animals, the bond between humans and animals is strengthening. People are making more compassionate decisions and becoming more vocal regarding animal concerns. And they are awakening to their place within the environment and moving away from the view that humans are separate from the environment. The public no longer finds it morally acceptable to use lethal animal management practices, such as catch-and-kill. Today's society supports programs, like TNR, that preserve and respect life.

In the Name of Mercy

In his 1989 essay entitled, "In the Name of Mercy," Edward Duvin had this to say about traditional animal sheltering operations:

"Shelters cannot continue to be slaughterhouses and friends of animals cannot continue killing healthy beings in the name of mercy. A new and larger vision is needed, a vision in which shelters hold themselves accountable for meeting demanding performance standards that preserve life — not destroy it."

Roger Tabor

Steps for Successful and Safe Trapping

Once you've assessed the situation and devised a plan with all key stakeholders, it's time to proceed with trapping and transporting. Following the below instructions and guidelines will help ensure the safety of the cats and you.

Preparing to Trap

Pre-Exposure Rabies Vaccinations

These are recommended for those working with feral and stray cats, and for veterinary staff and wildlife rehabilitators who handle small mammals. The chance of contracting rabies from an infected cat is extremely slight (the last documented occurrence in the U.S. was in 1975); however, it is always best to take all precautions.

Pre-exposure prophylaxis is given to provide protection for any possible exposure to rabies. It also protects people when post-exposure therapy is delayed.

For those who have been bitten by a rabid animal, if they have already been vaccinated, they need only receive two additional injections as post-exposure treatment.

If you have not had pre-exposure vaccinations, and you are bitten by a suspected rabid animal, an initial dose of rabies immunoglobulin, along with the first rabies vaccination, is given on day zero. After that, THREE vaccinations on these exact days: 3, 7, and 14. (Note: The first day of vaccine administration is referred to as day zero).

Rabies from animals is usually transmitted to humans through actual bites, although the virus can be transmitted by scratching or contact with saliva. In either case, your doctor will most likely administer a series of vaccinations to be safe.

If you are bitten by an animal you suspect may have rabies, see your doctor IMMEDIATELY! And with any injury, immediately wash the wound with hot, soapy water for several minutes, and clean it with peroxide. Apply an antibiotic cream and cover the wound with gauze and tape.

If a wound caused by a cat requires medical treatment, animal control may confiscate the cat. Some animal control agencies still insist on killing a cat to test for rabies rather than quarantining the cat. When you visit a doctor or emergency room for treatment of a cat bite, the medical practitioner may have to report the bite to the authorities, especially if it is discovered that the cat has not been vaccinated against rabies and has no known medical history. Again, some animal control agencies are adamant that a cat with an unknown medical history must be killed if she injures someone.

You can try to convince the authorities to hold the cat in quarantine, but they may insist on a six-month holding period with very strict holding procedures. In any event, a quarantine period of at least 14 days is advisable for a feral cat who has bitten someone.

Refer to "Zoonotic Diseases" for more information.

The Correct Equipment

If you are only trapping a couple of cats, you may borrow a trap from a friend, a feral cat group, or an animal control agency. Remember, though, that some agencies may require that the cat be brought to them in the trap for euthanasia. If your local agency has this policy, you will need to find another group to borrow a trap from or purchase one. Also, please feel free to have this agency contact Alley Cat Rescue; we have a shelter outreach program to assist and inform shelters about the Trap-Neuter-Return (TNR) protocol as a better way to control outdoor cat populations.

If you are trapping a large colony, you should probably buy several traps for your own use. If you use several traps at once, you can catch the cats far quicker and this will make it easier for you, before the remaining cats become trap-shy.

Remember, never try to catch a feral cat or kitten by hand. These animals are usually very afraid of humans and can inflict painful bites.

Supply List:

- One humane trap per cat, properly labelled with your contact information and a short note explaining that you are trapping cats as part of a humane TNR program, and the cats will not be harmed.

- One bed sheet or large towel for each trap. The cloth should be large enough to cover the entire trap on all sides. Covering the trap will calm the cat and lessen the risk of injury.

- One large blanket, bed sheet, or plastic cover to protect your vehicle seats.

- Folded newspaper to line the bottom of each trap.

- An easy-open can of tuna in oil, sardines in oil, mackerel, or other enticing bait.

- A spoon, or use the lid from the can to scoop out bait. (Do not leave the can in the trap.)

- A flashlight or headlamp. If you are trapping early in the morning or late at night, you'll need the flashlight to identify the cats you've caught.

- Masking tape to use to identify and label traps.

- Tracking sheets to identify cats and to record information.

- A pen and a marker.

- Extra cat food and clean water to leave for any cats remaining in the colony and not being TNR'd at that moment.

- A pair of thick gloves.

- A roll of paper towels and hand sanitizer.

- A few twist ties (bread ties).

- Pliers, a pocket knife, a can of WD40. (Optional but comes in handy when you need to make a quick trap repair.)

Always inspect your equipment prior to trapping. Make sure traps are working properly and gloves are free from major holes or tears.

Establishing a Regular Feeding Schedule

Establishing a routine feeding schedule will make trapping easier. Feed the cats at the same time and place each day and for at least one week prior to trapping.

During this period, the colony should be assessed. Determine if some cats are tame (friendly) and can be adopted into homes, and plan ahead for fostering any kittens you trap. Create a spreadsheet to record such information as the name of the cat, description, spayed/neutered, etc. This information will help establish proper health records for your colony.

Trapping

The first step to trapping is to withhold all food for 12 to 24 hours before setting a trap. This will ensure that the cats are hungry enough to enter a trap. Also, surgery will be easier on the cats if they have not eaten for the past 24 hours. While this may be hard, particularly if the cats appear hungry, know that you are doing what is best for them. Continue to provide the cats with clean, fresh drinking water.

Perform the trapping during the late evening or early morning; this usually coincides with a regularly scheduled feeding. Get the trap(s) ready near your vehicle or away from the trapping site before placing them there, as you don't want to scare off any cats if a trap goes off accidentally.

Place the trap on a flat surface. Unlatch the rear door and take it off so you can get your hands inside the trap. If your trap does not have a rear door, then you might want to secure the front door open with a twist tie so that it won't keep falling shut while you work.

Fold several pieces of newspaper lengthwise and place them inside the bottom of the trap. This disguises the wires and trip plate. Do not use newspaper if it is windy, or make sure to use several sheets that will stay down and not scare the cats.

Place approximately one tablespoon of bait in the rear center of the trap. You can place the food directly onto the newspaper or use a lid or small container. Next, drizzle some liquid from the bait the entire length of the newspaper inside the trap. Place about 1/4 teaspoon of bait in the middle of the trap and 1/4 teaspoon inside the front of the trap. This strategy is meant to entice the cat into the trap, making her way to the larger amount of food at the rear of the trap. However, it is important not to put too much bait in the front or middle of the trap, because this may satisfy the cat and she will leave without setting off the trap.

Set up the traps at the trapping site, most likely in the feeding area. Place the trap on the ground and make certain it is stable and will not rock or tip. Cover the entire trap with a sheet or towel, leaving the opening uncovered and ensuring the cover won't interfere with the door shutting.

If using multiple traps, stagger them, so they are facing in different directions. Try to think like a cat and place the traps where they will be tempted by the smell of the bait. Move quietly and slowly, and try to remain relaxed so your behavior won't frighten cats away.

Set the traps. Leave the area quietly. The cats are unlikely to enter the traps if you are standing nearby. You may want to sit in your car or take a short walk. If you are trapping in your yard you can go inside.

Traps should never be left unattended for more than one hour under any circumstances. It is good to check the traps frequently and quietly, from a distance. Never leave a cat in a trap unattended. Also, traps may be stolen, damaged, or set off; a trapped cat also might be released by someone who doesn't understand your intentions.

Trapping feral cats may take some time. Be patient. Once a cat appears, it may take a few minutes for her to go into the trap. Make sure the trap has sprung, and the cat is securely trapped, before you approach.

Desireé Stapley

Trapping cats at Adams Morgan colony, Washington, D.C.

Do not attempt to transfer a trapped cat to another cage or carrier unless you are very experienced in dealing with feral cats and have the proper equipment to do this. A transfer cage is the best item to use for safe transfer. It fits snugly up against the trap and a sliding door on each piece of equipment will allow a safe transfer. You should have another person assist with this task.

Before moving the trapped cat, ensure the trap is covered with a sheet or large towel. Covering the trap will keep the cat calm. Still, it is normal for the cat to thrash around inside the trap. It may be tempting to release her but she will not hurt herself if the trap remains covered. If a cat has already hurt herself, do not release her. Most injuries from traps are very minor, such as a bruised nose or torn claw. The cat will calm down eventually. Use twist ties to ensure the rear door is secure.

Alley Cat Rescue

ACR colony cat, Thomas Cattington, trapped for a vet visit.

Once you have trapped as many cats as you can, transport them in the traps to the veterinary hospital. Remember to inform your veterinarian that you are releasing the cats in 24 hours so that she

uses dissolvable sutures and surgical glue during surgery. If you trap cats at night and need to hold them until their appointment in the morning, keep them in their traps and make sure they are in a dry, warm location. They can stay in a shed, basement, or isolated room if the weather is poor. Do NOT leave trapped cats in extreme cold or heat.

Postoperative Care

After surgery, allow the cat to recover overnight in the same trap, still covered. Usually the veterinarian's staff will replace any soiled newspaper in the bottom of the trap with fresh newspaper. If they do not do this, ask them to. Fresh newspaper will make the cats more comfortable during recovery.

Female cats usually need to be held for 24 to 48 hours after surgery. Male cats can be returned to the trapping site 12 to 24 hours following surgery, as long as they are fully awake and do not require further medical attention. Make sure all cats are fully conscious and alert prior to being released. If the cat needs further care (longer than 48 hours) you will need to transfer her into a holding cage.

Kittens must be kept warm during recovery because they are vulnerable to anesthetic-related hypothermia. A heating pad can be used to keep kittens warm, but be sure it is not too hot. Kittens also must be fed around four to six hours after surgery. Feeding the kittens after they have recovered from the anesthesia is recommended to prevent hypoglycemia.

Adult cats can be given a small amount of canned food, which is easier to digest than dry food, eight hours after receiving surgery. However, the cat may not have an appetite. When you open the carrier or trap to put in food, be careful that the cat does not escape. Keep your hands out of the trap and always re-lock the door.

Normal behaviors during recovery include: deep sleep, head bobbing, wobbly movements, fast breathing, and shivering. Slight spotting and bleeding from the left ear tip is expected but should stop by the time of release. There should be no continued bleeding from the surgery area, and prolonged recovery time (still inactive and lethargic, six-plus hours after surgery) or getting drowsy or weak again after waking up is not normal. If any abnormal behavior is suspected, contact your veterinarian immediately, as the cat may need intravenous fluids.

Once the cat has fully recovered and she appears to be alert, clear-eyed, and not displaying any abnormal behaviors, she may be released. Release the cat in the same place you trapped her. Pull back the cover and open the rear door. Step away from the trap quickly and quietly. Do not be concerned if the cat hesitates a few moments before leaving. She is simply reorienting herself to her surroundings. It is not uncommon for the cat to stay away for a few days after release; she will return eventually. Continue to provide food and water, she may eat when you're not around. Do not release a cat during inclement weather, and always have the phone numbers of your veterinarian or a nearby emergency clinic on hand in case of emergencies.

Additional Trapping Tips

If some cats won't go into the traps, you may want to try feeding them in unset traps for several days before trapping. Feed the cats in the same place and time as always. Tie up the doors to the traps so they stay open, and place the food inside. When the cats see other cats eating inside the traps they will try it themselves. Once they become accustomed to the traps, they will be easier to trap.

If you are still unable to trap a cat, or if the cat has learned how to steal bait without springing the trap, consider using a drop trap instead, which provides the trapper with more control. Refer to the Helpful Resources section in the back of the handbook for more information on drop traps.

Never release the cat into a new area. If the cat needs to be relocated, please refer to "Guidelines for Safely Relocating Feral Cats." Relocating cats without following the proper steps can endanger a cat's life. She will try to return to her old home, and may become lost or attempt to cross major roads. Also, feral cats form strong bonds with other cats in their colonies. Separating a cat from her colony members and leaving her alone in a new environment will cause stress, depression, and loneliness. So do try to relocate several cat buddies at the same time.

Avoid Trapping During Spring

Spring is also known as "kitten season." Try to trap before or after this season so that you allow the mothers to nurse their young properly. Around mid-May is usually when the majority of kittens are old enough to eat on their own.

If you do trap a lactating mother you have several choices:

- Release the cat without sterilizing. You may struggle to retrap her, however.

- Have her sterilized, requesting that your vet uses the flank incision. This will allow the mother to be back with her kittens the next day and she can continue to nurse them.**

- Have her sterilized, if you are able to locate the kittens and they are old enough to be safely fostered without the mother (around eight weeks old).

- Keep her (and you'll have to catch her kittens) in a foster home until the kittens are weaned, and then spay the mother (and sterilize the kittens).

If you trap a pregnant cat, here are your options:

- Release the cat without sterilizing. Again, you may struggle to retrap her.

- Keep the cat and have her spayed. If she is in the early stages of pregnancy, the pregnancy can be terminated.**

- Keep the cat and allow her to birth her kittens in foster care. Once the kittens have been weaned, the mother can be spayed, and the kittens sterilized.

**It is important to discuss these options with your veterinarian prior to trapping, so you can devise a plan. Your vet will determine which is the safer option for the mother cat.

Springtime also means increased activity of other wildlife. If you should accidentally trap a non-target animal such as a raccoon, opossum, or skunk, carefully open the back door and release the animal where it was trapped. Most wildlife are afraid and will run away. Do not release the animal in another area. Taking animals away from their homes is cruel and inhumane. They may have families around and they are usually immune to local diseases. Moving them causes disorientation and they do not know where to find food sources.

Do Not Use Tranquilizers Before or During Trapping

Tranquilizers have the potential for being extremely dangerous for outside cats. The cat will not fall unconscious immediately. It will take some time for the cat to react to the drug. During this time the cat may become disoriented and cross busy roads or get into other dangerous situations. Some cats need smaller doses, others need larger doses. You will not know how much to feed the cat. In any event, tranquilizers are not recommended. Some people get desperate with hard-to-trap cats. Just be patient and realize that your persistence will pay off, and that it may take a long time and require using different tricks before the particular cat is trapped.

If you have a female cat who is constantly giving birth to kittens and you cannot catch her, this may be a time to consider the contraceptive drug, Ovaban. But remember, this is only to be used for a short period. Long-term use can have serious side-effects. (Refer to "Chemical Sterilization" for more information.)

Judy M. Zukoski

It takes a real stroke of luck to catch two feral cats in a single trap!

Feral Kittens and Pregnant Cats:
Guidelines for Fostering and Socializing

Female feral cats usually look for safe, hidden places to give birth. The young offspring of feral female cats, or of abandoned domestic cats, learn from their mothers to be wary and distrustful of humans, and to hide and defend themselves against any perceived threat. The tiny kittens will spit and hiss if approached by humans, and though small, will bite and scratch if not handled properly. When dealing with feral kittens, as with any wild animal, you should have a pre-exposure rabies vaccination and keep your tetanus shot current. Minimize all risks by using the correct equipment.

In most areas of the U.S., except Northern regions with extreme cold, kitten season can extend from February through November, however, most kittens are born during spring. Cats can have three litters each year, although two are more likely, with a gestation period of approximately 65 days. Cats, like many wild animals, overproduce to ensure survival of the species.

Kitten mortality rates are usually very high — often around 75 percent (Nutter et al., 2004). Many become sick from diseases that are treatable, such as upper respiratory infections (URIs), but without medical care and supportive treatment, weak kittens usually perish. Those kittens who survive this initial period often build up immunities to common diseases, and once a colony has been sterilized and stabilized, most of the cats remain healthy and viable for many years under the care and supervision of caretakers.

To Tame or TNR?

If your local shelter is euthanizing domestic kittens for lack of homes, you may want to consider trapping any pregnant feral females and having them spayed. You can also TNR any kittens when they are eight to

Spring brings lots of mama cats and babies.

Alley Cat Rescue

52

twelve weeks old and return them to the colony. Even at the young age of twelve weeks old, many kittens may be difficult to tame and socialize; returning them to the colony will free up available space at shelters for more adoptable cats. It is much easier to place tame kittens than feral ones, who may always retain some of their wild instincts. Peter Neville notes that even under ideal conditions "around 15 percent of kittens seem to resist socialization and demonstrate only limited willingness to becoming generally sociable adults" (Neville, 1992).

The critical socialization period of a feral kitten is from two to seven weeks of age. During this period the kitten should form bonds with humans and other animals. Friendliness is also a gene that passes along to kittens from the mother or the father. Researchers at the Waltham Centre for Pet Nutrition in Leicestershire, Great Britain have found that friendly fathers produce friendly kittens, and unfriendly or fearful toms propagate timid kittens — independent of the fact that the fathers are neither present nor involved in rearing the youngsters (Jablonski, accessed 2014).

The process of taming kittens can take four to eight weeks depending on their age and degree of wildness. First and foremost, any person attempting this process should be patient and totally committed. Do not take on too many kittens at one time. And always be cautious when working with feral kittens. Remember they are wild and will defend themselves if they feel cornered or threatened. Never handle a new or strange feral kitten

until you know how she will react towards you, and always wear protective gear.

Cara Frye

It is critical to begin the socialization process for feral kittens early, between two and seven weeks of age.

There are many feral kittens, even if not socialized during the critical period, who can become affectionate and loving companions. They will need to be placed in adoptive homes as soon as possible because feral kittens tend to bond with one person. Be aware that a young feral cat who may be completely tame and loving with one person can revert to her wild state when placed in another home. It can sometimes take six months, a year, or even longer for that cat to bond with the new caretaker.

Alley Cat Rescue strongly advises that kittens be spayed or neutered before being placed in adoptive homes. The goal is to stop the killing of healthy animals in shelters, and those of us who care about animals should <u>NOT</u> contribute to the problem by allowing unneutered cats to be placed in homes. Currently, compliance rates for sterilization of cats and dogs from public and private shelters is less than 60 percent (Marrion, accessed 2014).

Trapping Feral Kittens

Kittens will make themselves visible when they are about four to six weeks old, once they begin eating solid food. ACR recommends trapping kittens between the ages of five and eight weeks, when they have developed enough to leave their mother but still young enough to be tamed.

Shaida Tala Sabin

ACR recommends trapping feral kittens when they are between five and eight weeks of age; old enough to survive away from the mother, but still young enough to be tamed.

They are usually hard to catch and will hide in any small hole not accessible to humans. ACR recommends using baited traps for safe handling and transporting of feral kittens. They look just like any domestic kitten; however, they have wild instincts and can be aggressive. They have been taught by their mother to defend themselves with teeth and claws. So always wear gloves when handling feral kittens.

How to Safely Foster a Feral Kitten

All feral kittens should receive their first vaccines around six to eight weeks of age. Your veterinarian will administer a series of vaccines at three- or four-week intervals until the kittens reach 16 weeks of age. Kittens can receive their initial distemper vaccine around six to seven weeks of age, and their rabies vaccine as early as 12 weeks of age. If fostering kittens too young to receive vaccines, it is important to use caution when allowing the kittens to interact with other cats.

It is also important to treat for internal and external parasites around six weeks of age. The majority of feral kittens are born with internal parasites, such as roundworms, and they can get fleas and ear mites from their mother. Parasites can cause loss of appetite, diarrhea, anemia, and can be deadly for a kitten. Most internal and external parasites can be treated with a topical medication, such as Advantage Multi.

When kittens reach about eight weeks of age and they weigh around two pounds, they should be sterilized. Take care to ensure their incision site remains clean and heals properly. A long-lasting antibiotic injection, such as Convenia, should be administered.

A feral kitten is usually frightened at first and may hiss and spit. Begin the taming process by confining the kitten to a large cage in a spare room or other location that has limited foot traffic. Adding a cat den or other small box to the cage will help the kitten feel safer and more comfortable. Line the cage with newspaper and provide a litter box, along with food, water, and kitten milk replacer (KMR) if necessary.

For the first day, do not attempt to handle the kitten. She must first learn to feel safe. Set up the cage in a quiet environment and visit her frequently. Talk to her so she gets used to your voice. You can also turn on a radio or TV for her to get used to human voices. Remember to always move slowly and quietly.

If the kitten needs to be medicated, use liquid medicine in moist food, or crush tablets into baby food. Whole tablets should not be administered to a feral kitten or cat because it may cause trauma and can undo the taming process. It also increases the risk of you being bitten.

If the kitten escapes from confinement, do not grab her with your bare hands. Use gloves or a carrier to catch her.

Caring for Orphaned and Newborn Kittens

If kittens are under five weeks of age and unable to eat solid food, bottle-feed them with kitten formula (KMR, Similac, or Just Born) obtained from veterinary clinics or pet supply stores. (Cow's milk does not contain enough fat or protein for kittens.) Make sure you hold the kitten upright and do not force too much milk into her mouth or the fluid will go into her lungs and she could aspirate.

Young kittens should be kept in a box lined with absorbent paper towels; make sure they stay dry. Keep the box warm (around 90 degrees F) during the first two weeks of life, using a heating pad covered with a towel, or you can use an infrared lamp. It's very important to keep kittens warm.

For three-week-old kittens, decrease the temperature to around 80 degrees F. If a kitten is too weak to drink from a bottle, feed her with an eye dropper. Massage the belly to stimulate digestion, and use a cotton ball or paper towel to stimulate elimination of urine and feces after each feeding. Moist cotton balls can be used to clean the area afterwards. Rub Vaseline on the anal area. The mother usually cleans the babies during the first few weeks so you will have to take on this task. Begin weaning from three to four

Using a cat den helps feral kittens and cats feel safe

When a feral cat must stay at Alley Cat Rescue's clinic, we always have a cat den inside the cage. A feral cat finds safety in the small box. When it is time for a technician to clean the cage, the feral cat is either already in her den or will go into the den when the main cage door is opened; this makes cleaning the cage much easier and safer. A cat den also makes transporting a feral cat easier and safer.

weeks old. Mix canned kitten food with kitten milk formula and hand feed until the kittens are accustomed to eating on their own, then gradually change over completely to canned food.

Orphaned feral kitten fostered and bottle-fed by the author.

If you do not have kitten formula on hand, use the following formula for temporary feeding only (12 to 24 hours): Add one egg yolk to eight ounces of cow's or goat's milk. Feed kittens two table-spoons per four ounces of body weight daily. Divide total amount into equal feedings. Small weak kittens should be fed every three to four hours.

The milk that is produced by the mother cat for the first two days after birth is called colostrum. This milk is high in protein and antibodies that protect the newborn kittens. Orphan kittens who do not have this protection should be vaccinated against rhinotracheitis, cali-civirus, and panleukopenia at four weeks of age. Vaccination at an early age should only be considered for orphan kittens. If kittens remain with their mothers, they should receive their first vaccinations at

eight to ten weeks of age when they lose their maternally derived immunity.

Common Infectious Diseases

Kittens are susceptible to respiratory diseases such as feline herpes virus and calicivirus. Panleukopenia (feline dis-temper) and feline leukemia (FeLV) may be contracted in utero. Panleukopenia, if contracted before birth, can result in cerebellar hypoplasia causing balance and walking problems in a kitten, which start at two to three weeks of age. In un-vaccinated populations, feline distemper is a very deadly and contagious disease. In rare cases, feline immunodeficiency virus (FIV) can be transmitted in utero.

Respiratory diseases cause sneezing, coughing, and nasal discharge. The exact cause of the URI is often difficult to diag-nose and treat. The most probable cause is either rhinotracheitis or calicivirus. Often the disease becomes chronic and sometimes cannot be completely cured. The cat may sneeze or have runny eyes for most of her life.

A mild case can be treated by provid-ing a warm environment, cleaning the eyes and nose areas, and using a vapor-izer. Antibiotics will not help treat URIs, which are viral infections, but are some-times used to combat secondary bacte-rial infections. Conjunctivitis of the eyes requires constant cleaning with moist, warm cotton balls and application of Terramycin or Chlorasone a few times per day directly in the eyes. If left untreated, upper respiratory infections can cause severe health problems, pneumonia, eventual blindness, or even death.

Nearly all feral and stray kittens have internal parasites (worms), as well as external (fleas, lice, mites) parasites. Once kittens weigh about two pounds, they can be treated with a monthly flea and tick medication, that also helps prevent worms.

Refer to the chapter on "Health Care for Feral Cats: Guidelines for Colony Caretakers" for more information.

How to Tame Feral Kittens

After you have given the kittens about two days to settle in, select the least aggressive kitten, place a towel firmly around the kitten's body (do not cover her head) and pick her up. Keep her wrapped securely in the towel as you remove her from the cage and set her on your lap. If the kitten stays calm, pet her gently on the head from behind. Never approach from the front. Initially, hands will frighten feral kittens and they may bite when approached from the front. Continue to softly pet her head while you talk to her in a soothing voice. Some kittens may respond quickly to being petted, while others may take more time adjusting. Practice this step several times a day for several days, until each kitten is comfortable with being picked up and petted.

You can also offer the kittens baby food from a spoon to help increase trust and build up their courage. Food can be a great incentive in taming a feral kitten; just make sure if using baby food, you only use plain meat-based foods that do NOT contain onion or garlic ingredients, which are toxic to cats.

As the kittens become more comfortable with being handled, you can try to pet them without the towel. Gently grip the kitten's skin at the nape of her neck, put the towel on your lap, and set the kitten on the towel. Relax your grip and slowly stroke the kitten's body while speaking in soft reassuring tones. Some kittens may get scared and want to jump from your lap, so be prepared to wrap the towel back around her; but be careful not to scare her. Go through this process with each kitten, and give a special treat after they all have been handled; it's important to reward them for their progress. Repeat this handling process as frequently as possible.

Within about a week the kittens should have made considerable progress. Remember that each kitten will develop at a different rate. As the kittens become more comfortable being around you and other humans, they should be allowed access to the entire room and no longer be caged. It is important to limit hiding places and make sure the door to the room remains closed.

Continue to make frequent visits to handle and play with the kittens. Use toys to encourage interaction and build trust.

Toys are a great way to distract a kitten, while discreetly petting her. Provide a variety of scratch posts to train them on appropriate scratching areas. You may also want to leave open carriers in the room to help acclimate them.

Spring kitten rescued by Alley Cat Rescue.

If there is another tame cat in the house who enjoys the company of kittens, this will help the taming process. Kittens are "copycats" and will follow the tame cat's behavior, coming over to be petted if they hear the tamer cat purring while being petted. Remember to always use caution when introducing new cats.

Please note, you should also be prepared to find barn homes or a sanctuary for any kittens who are unable to be socialized. No matter how much time has passed and how much effort you put into taming a feral kitten, some individuals do not warm up to human contact and will remain feral for life. It is in the best interest of the kitten to be placed in an appropriate outdoor home, rather than forcing her to live indoors if this is not the environment suited for her.

As emphasized previously, feral kittens may try to bite and scratch. If you do get bitten or scratched, wash the wound immediately with soap and water. Apply antibiotic ointment and cover with a bandage. If the wound is deep or does not heal after a few days, seek medical treatment. If the kitten has not been vaccinated and the doctor is concerned about rabies, assure him/her that you will quarantine the kitten for 14 days, an adequate time for determining rabies infection.

Placement in Adoptive Homes

Sadly, most people who wish to adopt a cat want a friendly, fully socialized animal. Some people are afraid to tell potential new adopters that kittens were once feral, for fear they will not be placed. Alley Cat Rescue believes this is not in the best interest of the kitten. The cats or kittens may retain some feral instincts and it is important to disclose this information to the adopter. "Unsocialized" or "not completely socialized" can be more appealing words to use when describing the kittens, rather than saying "feral."

People's perceptions about feral cats need to change. Education is important, and people must be made aware of the millions of feral cats living in alleys who need our understanding and our help, not fear and disdain. Most people who have lived with cats before will understand that many are shy and can act wild at times.

Feral kittens do best if there are no small children in the home. All the work you have done can easily be reversed by a child's spontaneous activity and noise. This is vital to remember when placing kittens for adoption. The most suitable home is a calm environment so the kittens feel secure. Ideally, two kittens should be placed together in a home, or with another cat or friendly dog, or where an adult person is at home part of the day.

The taming process is extremely rewarding. Many tamed feral cats will continue to be a bit elusive, while others will demand human contact constantly. People who have tamed formerly feral companion animals have reaped many pleasures from their company.

When a feral kitten is placed into a new home, ACR strongly recommends that the new guardian go through a similar "mini-taming" process with the kitten. The new home may be very confusing and scary at first; reinforcing the basic handling and trust-building exercises will help the kitten feel more relaxed and at home. Most kittens soon settle down happily into their new environment and start enjoying the luxuries offered.

Any kittens who never really seem to outgrow their wild nature and are not good candidates for adoption can be considered for placement in barn homes. Refer to "Guidelines for Establishing an Effective Adoption Program" for more information on rehoming cats and kittens and "Guidelines for Safely Relocating Feral Cats" if a barn home is necessary.

Caring for Pregnant Feral Cats

As discussed previously in the chapter on "Steps for Successful and Safe Trapping," there are several options to consider before trapping a pregnant feral cat. All available options should be discussed with your veterinarian prior to trapping, so an appropriate course of action can be established.

Feral cats may become stressed when they are held in captivity. Stress can cause illness and a mother's inability to properly care for her kittens, especially when giving birth. Providing a safe, quiet place for her, where she won't be disturbed, will minimize any stress and reduce the risk of birthing complications.

To safely foster a feral mother cat (or any feral cat) you will need a large cage and a cat den for her to hide in to feel safe. It is highly recommended that you keep the cage in a spare bedroom or other room that has limited foot traffic. Line the cage with newspaper and provide plenty of fresh, clean blankets or towels. Cover the top of the cage with towels or sheets to give her a safe environment. Limit your access to the room and the cage; only disturb her when changing food/water, the litter box, and blankets.

Leave her alone to give birth in a quiet environment. Some of the kittens could die, either at birth or from viral infections. If the mother does not show any interest in caring for a particular kitten, it is usually because she instinctively knows the kitten is not going to survive. Try to encourage the mother to care for any kittens she is ignoring, but only do this safely — don't stress her. If she clearly is not going to care for a particular kitten(s), you will need to remove the kitten and begin bottle feeding as described above.

The mother cat should allow all kittens to nurse. She should be washing and grooming them regularly. Make sure the mother is also taking care of herself: eating/drinking, going to the bathroom, and cleaning herself.

When the kittens are around two to three weeks old, you can attempt to pet them. You will have to gauge the mother cat and how agreeable she is to letting you handle her kittens. Mothers can be very protective of their young, so take extreme caution. The easiest way to begin the taming process is to sneak pets when you are cleaning the cage. As you're reaching into the cage to change the blankets or food, you can quickly and calmly give each kitten a few pets. The more you work with them and the mother cat, the easier and faster it will be for them to become socialized. (Refer to "Adopting an Adult Feral Cat" for more information.)

Conclusion

Fostering cats and kittens in a home environment can be an enjoyable and rewarding experience, and it also frees up shelter space, so more cats can be assisted. However, it is important to keep in mind that being a foster parent means increased responsibility; most cats and kittens who need to be fostered require a lot of time and energy to prepare them for adoption. Prior to fostering, make sure you are fully aware of and fully equipped for what it means to be a foster parent. For more detailed information on fostering cats and kittens, and guidelines for establishing your own foster program, please refer to Addendum 3. An example foster parent agreement form can also be found in the back of the handbook.

Guidelines for Safely Relocating Feral Cats

Alley Cat Rescue receives numerous calls from people across the country who want to move feral cats. Often the first thought when someone finds a feral colony is to remove the cats, or to "find a home" for the cats. Many people do not realize that the cats are living in their home — their outdoor home. The colony has probably lived there for some time, in some cases for a decade or more. (Refer to "TNR in a Nutshell" for solutions to common complaints about community cats.)

Unless the cats' lives are threatened or the building they live in is to be demolished, the present home of the feral cat colony is the optimal place for them. As we said, they have been living there for some time, and most likely a food source already exists.

Many people would like to find a cat sanctuary for feral cats to live out their lives. However, few cat sanctuaries exist that can accommodate ferals, and most ferals will not be happy living in such an environment. They are wild animals and prefer to live without confinement.

Feral cats are social animals. Many biologists have completely overlooked this and consider lions to be the only social felines. However, colony cats develop strong bonds with one another and become dependent on each other. When you relocate feral cats, you may be separating them from family members and consequently causing them undue stress.

The author, relocating cats to a farm home.

George Smith

Only in certain cases — if a caretaker is unavailable to care for the colony, or if the cats simply cannot remain at their present location for safety reasons — does ACR believe relocation can be a viable option. But this has to be undertaken with great care and used as a last resort. Relocating a colony of feral cats is time-consuming. New homes are difficult to find and certain procedures have to be followed, otherwise the relocated cats may not remain on the new premises. If proper procedures are not followed, the cats can become disoriented and lost. In an attempt to find their way home, they might travel hundreds of miles, putting themselves in danger.

Despite these challenges, if proper procedures are followed, it is possible to successfully relocate feral cats. ACR has relocated hundreds of feral cats to new, safe homes, and you can too, by following the steps below.

Alley Cat Rescue

Packing cats up for relocating to a sanctuary.

Steps for a Successful Relocation

Once you have decided that relocation is the only option left for the colony, several steps should be followed:

Assess the Colony

Determine how many cats are in the colony so you know how many homes you will need. Also, determine if any of the cats need to be sterilized. If some or all cats need to be sterilized, this should be performed in conjunction with the relocation efforts. Keep in mind that all cats should be relocated in pairs. They have usually bonded with one another and the move will be less traumatic if they are not alone. Adjusting to their new home will be easier if they have the security of a familiar companion.

Find a New Outdoor Home

Farm homes or horse stables make the best places for relocating feral cats. Most farmers are willing to take two to four cats to help control rodent populations. Rarely can you relocate eight or more to one site, so you will want to look for several homes if relocating a large colony. And there is no reason to worry about horses getting along with cats; in most cases, cats and horses get along very well. A cat may seem surprised at the size of the horse at first, but after a while both cat and horse seem to enjoy each other's company.

Make sure the new caretaker is interested in providing a good home. When they hear you need a farm home, some people think that all you need is the place and not supervision or food. A country home that is only occupied on weekends while the owners work in the city is not acceptable. The cats need daily food and water. People must agree to provide basic needs, including veterinary care if necessary and sign an adoption contract similar to one used for domestic cat placements.

Be wary of homes on busy country roads. One may presume that these roads are less dangerous because they are usually not as busy as city roads. However, city cats are used to slower city traffic and although there may be fewer cars on country roads, they tend to go much faster. Most city cats are not used to this. ACR has had reports of cats being killed on a rural road soon after the relocation process, so this is also something to keep in mind when looking for outdoor homes.

Be careful of dogs at the new home. Although it may not be a problem, the new caretakers should be willing to introduce the dogs to the new cats slowly and not allow the cats to be chased, or they will leave. The new caretaker should also be mindful of other animals such as raccoons, opossums, and skunks. In most cases, cats and these animals will peacefully coexist with little interaction. However, do take more care if cats and especially kittens have the potential of coming in contact with predator animals, like foxes, coyotes, and owls. Erecting tall fencing or confining the cats to a barn during night-time hours will minimize the risk of confrontation.

In searching for an appropriate location, contact friends and relatives who live in rural areas and see if they have any sug-

gestions, or if they have any neighbors who have land or outbuildings. Ask them to place notices in newspapers and flyers in local tractor and feed supply stores, or run newspaper ads yourself. Besides word of mouth, hanging flyers and placing newspaper ads, the Internet is a good source for finding new homes. Just make absolutely sure that the new home checks out before relocation; thoroughly do your research prior to trapping.

Although the above locations are most ideal, feral cats can also be relocated to a backyard, particularly one in a suburb, to another alleyway, especially if it is close to the original home, or in some instances, feral cats can be relocated to an already established colony. Extra care should be taken when introducing new cats; introduce them slowly and keep new cats confined for a few weeks. You may need to put a cat playpen outdoors to keep the cats confined. Note there will be a transition period where the cats establish a "pecking order;" some mild fighting is normal.

Trapping and Transport

Refer to the chapter on "Steps for Successful and Safe Trapping" for proper trapping techniques. As mentioned previously, any cats who are not already sterilized will need to be vetted prior to relocation. Once the cats are trapped, either transport them to your veterinarian to be sterilized (and then relocated) or transport them to the new location.

Whether transporting one cat in a trap or several, keep the traps covered with a sheet or large towel; this will help calm the cat. Make sure both ends of the trap are secured with twist ties. Use old sheets to protect your vehicle's seats and floors. Check that there is good air circulation in the vehicle, especially on hot days, and travel the most direct route to the new location. You want to minimize the cat's time spent in a trap and in a vehicle. Do not place the cat in the trunk of a car or any unsafe area.

Confinement Period

Judy M. Zukoski

Cats can be relocated to barns or stables. A three-week confinement period is very important for acclimating a cat to her new home.

It is very important that cats be confined in their new home for the first three to four weeks. This is enough time to familiarize the cats to their new environment, so they will remain on the premises. Even though there are instances of cats remaining when they have escaped upon arrival, this is rare and most cats will take off, never to be seen again. Other than being dangerous for the cat, this can be traumatic for the rescuer who has usually put a lot of time, energy, money, and care into the rescue. So prior to relocating any cats, ensure the new caretaker is aware of this vital step in the process.

Some people may see confinement of a wild cat as cruel, but a short confinement period is a very necessary part of any relocation. This will give the cat time to get accustomed to new sights, sounds, and smells. She will learn that the new caretaker provides food, water, and a warm, safe place to sleep. Providing a secure environment for the cat will ensure she considers this her new home. You should warn the new caretaker that during the first couple days the cats may struggle to find a way out. Most cats settle down in the cage after a day or two when they realize that no harm will come to them.

A large cage or playpen should be used for confinement. Be skeptical if you are told that the new barn is completely cat-proof and that the cats will not escape. There are few barns that really are escape-proof. Always take cages/ playpens, litter boxes, and food/water dishes with you, just in case. Make sure the confinement area is located near a place where the cats can hide once they are allowed out of the playpen. They will likely run and hide when first released.

Take care not to confine the cats for longer than a month. Doing so is unnecessary and can be harmful to the cats and to the relocation process. When confined for so long, the cats may run away after release, due to the fear of being confined again. There is definitely a period of time when animals have had enough of close confinement. Even friendly, domestic cats cannot tolerate a lengthy confinement period.

If a cat does escape, set food and water out and sprinkle her used litter (for scent) around the barn. Cats often hide for a period of time but will stay in the area. Leave plenty of food and water to prevent them from leaving in search of food.

During the confinement period, it is also important for the new caretaker to make contact with the cats by talking to them or by playing a radio softly. This will help them get used to human voices. It is noted that people who make the effort to communicate with the cats are also those who have the most successful relocations.

Follow-Up

Make sure to call or visit after the relocation. You will want to stay in touch to make sure the cats are doing well and also to keep a contact for future relocations.

Conclusion

Relocation can be a safe and viable option for feral cats if undertaken properly and if these guidelines are followed. But remember the best option for the cats in a feral colony is for them to remain in their original home. Sometimes this may mean finding caretakers or speaking out for the cats to stay at their present location.

If you do remove a whole colony, make sure that the food sources disappear completely, or other stray cats will move in to repopulate the area. Removing the food sources can be difficult to achieve, especially when garbage is thrown out in backyards and alleyways. Check from time to time to ensure that no new cats have moved into the vacated territory.

Zoonotic Diseases

The World Health Organization (WHO) defines zoonoses as diseases and infections that are transmitted between animals and humans (WHO, "Zoonoses and the Human-Animal-Ecosystems Interface," accessed 2014). A zoonotic agent may be a bacterium, a virus, a fungus, or other communicable disease agent. According to the Centers for Disease Control and Prevention (CDC), at least 61 percent of all human pathogens are zoonotic, and have represented 75 percent of all emerging pathogens during the past decade (CDC, "Emerging and Zoonotic Diseases — At a Glance," accessed 2014).

Newly emerging zoonotic diseases include Severe Acute Respiratory Syndrome (SARS), which sparked an epidemic in 2002 and came from animals sold in Chinese markets (WHO, "Severe Acute Respiratory Syndrome (SARS)," accessed 2014), and the avian influenza H5N1 virus, which came from Asia and can be contracted through handling infected poultry (U.S. Dept. of Health and Human Services, accessed 2014).

Although many anti-cat campaigns use the fear of zoonotic diseases to push for the eradication of feral cats, history has shown us the important role cats have played in preventing the spread of disease. For instance, during the 14th century, the bubonic plague, or the Black Death, took the lives of 25 million people living throughout Europe. For hundreds of years prior to the plague, cats were hunted and killed because they were thought to be associated with witches. While cat populations were virtually eliminated, rat and mice populations exploded, which allowed for the spread of the disease. It wasn't until the Age of Exploration that cats became popular again and were welcome passengers aboard ships as rodent control specialists (Seymour, accessed 2014).

While it is true that cats can transmit a few diseases to humans, the Cornell Feline Health Center reports you are much more likely to contract infectious diseases from other humans than you are from your cat (Cornell, "Zoonotic Disease: What Can I Catch from My Cat?," 2014). For this very slight risk, simple precautions, common sense, and good hygiene, including careful handling of litter boxes and treating cats aggressively for fleas and other parasites, can further reduce any possible risk of zoonotic disease transmission from cats (Cornell, "Zoonotic Disease: What Can I Catch from My Cat?," 2014). Individuals with immature or weakened immune systems, such as infants, individuals with acquired immunodeficiency syndrome (AIDS), the elderly, and people undergoing cancer therapy should take extra precautions.

Below are a few zoonotic diseases that can be transmitted from cats to humans and the precautions that can be taken to prevent transmission.

Nancy North

Zoonotic diseases are a consideration for colony care-takers, but simple precautions can serve to mitigate the risk of transmission for them and the millions of people living with outdoor cats across the world. This colony is in the Buenos Aires Botanical Garden in Argentina.

Rabies

Of all zoonotic diseases, rabies is the most feared and most misunderstood. Rabies is an acute and deadly disease caused by a viral infection of the central nervous system. The rabies virus is most often spread by a bite and saliva from an infected mammal. Although there is an extremely low incidence of contracting rabies in the U.S., the virus still causes great panic.

The primary carriers of rabies are wild animals, although any unvaccinated mammal can be a vector for rabies. The CDC reports that wild animals accounted for 92 percent of reported cases of rabies in the U.S. in 2013 (Dyer et al., 2014). Raccoons accounted for 32.4 percent of the cases, followed by bats (27.2 percent), skunks (24.7 percent), foxes (5.9 percent), and other wild animals (Dyer et al., 2014).

In the last 100 years, the number of human deaths from rabies in the U.S. has fallen from 100 or more per year to an average of one or two (CDC, "Rabies in the U.S.," accessed 2014). In most fatal cases, death occurs largely because the victim failed to recognize the health risks associated with bite wounds and did not seek medical advice or treatment.

Several programs have been responsible for the decline in rabies cases. First, vaccination programs for dogs and cats began in the 1940s, virtually eliminating the chance of contracting the disease from our beloved companion animals. Secondly, an oral rabies vaccination program for wildlife was introduced in the 2000s (Wildlife Services, 2011). Thirdly, effective pre-exposure and post-exposure rabies vaccines have not only reduced the risk of infection for those who receive the pre-exposure vaccine, but they also reduce the effects of the illness and prevent death in those who receive post-exposure treatment.

Some countries in Asia, Africa, and Latin America have a high incidence of rabies infection. These countries have large populations of domestic and feral dogs who live in cities and come in close contact with humans. These countries do not have the resources to provide spay/neuter and TNR programs; therefore, dogs remain the major vector species for rabies in these countries. While there are far fewer cases of rabies infection in the U.S. than in many other countries, the virus is still widespread among wildlife here and it remains a serious public health concern.

The first symptoms of rabies in humans are similar to a flu-like illness, which includes fever, headache, and general discomfort. However, within days, the infected person will experience symptoms such as anxiety, confusion, agitation, abnormal behavior, delirium, and hallucinations. Once the latter symptoms appear, the disease is almost always fatal. Therefore, any person who has been bitten or scratched by a potentially rabid animal should see a physician immediately for post-exposure treatment.

Any unvaccinated cat who bites a human should be quarantined for at least 14 days, examined by a veterinarian, and then vaccinated prior to release. If a cat appears ill at the time of the bite or becomes ill during the quarantine period, a veterinarian should evaluate the cat for signs of rabies and continue to monitor the cat's health closely. Once infected

with the rabies virus, a cat will only survive for about three or four days. Obvious signs of rabies infection in cats include, foaming at the mouth, trouble walking, lethargy, and erratic and extremely aggressive behavior. Unfortunately, if such symptoms are present, the only option is to euthanize the cat to prevent suffering and transmission of the virus.

To prevent the transmission of rabies, never approach or attempt to handle an unfamiliar cat (or wildlife). Always use a humane trap and wear thick gloves when handling or transporting a cat whose vaccination history is unknown. It is highly recommended that anyone handling feral or stray cats (or other animals, especially wildlife) should receive the pre-exposure rabies vaccine.

It is also important to make sure all domestic cats (and dogs) receive the rabies vaccine, and TNR programs are implemented for community cats. In TNR programs, feral cats receive a three-year rabies vaccine, which studies have shown to be effective for longer than three years. Vaccinated cats provide a buffer zone between wildlife and humans, and vaccinating community cats will reduce the risk of an individual coming in contact with an unvaccinated cat.

If a cat bites you, <u>immediately wash the wound</u> with hot soapy water for several minutes and clean with peroxide. Apply an antibiotic cream and cover the wound with gauze and tape. Monitor for infection (redness, swelling, pus) and seek medical attention if the wound doesn't seem to be healing.

If a cat (or other animal) is showing signs of rabies infection, the animal should <u>not</u> be approached and the appropriate authorities should be alerted immediately. For more information on rabies and preventing the transmission of the disease, please refer to Addendum 4 in the back of the handbook.

Bacterial Diseases

Bites are the most common animal-human health concern. Bacteria in the mouths of cats can cause serious infection if a bite wound is left untreated, including swelling, inflammation, and pain. If you are bitten by a cat, immediately wash the wound with hot soapy water for several minutes and clean with peroxide. Apply an antibiotic cream and cover the wound with gauze and tape. Monitor for infection (redness, swelling, pus) and seek medical attention if the wound does not seem to be healing.

Always use caution (wearing thick gloves and using a trap if possible) when handling an unfamiliar cat. This will help prevent being scratched or bitten.

Cat Scratch Disease

Cat scratch disease, or cat scratch fever, most commonly occurs in children following a cat scratch or bite. Typical symptoms include enlarged lymph nodes, fever, fatigue, sore throat, and headaches. Although most patients do not become seriously ill and recover with or without treatment, all cat scratches and bites should be thoroughly cleaned and properly bandaged.

Again, always use caution (wearing thick gloves and using a trap when possible) when handling an unfamiliar cat. This will help prevent being scratched or bitten.

Lyme Disease

Lyme disease is caused by bacteria and is transmitted by ticks. In 70-80 percent of cases, a rash will appear at the site of the bite, often in a bull's eye pattern. Early symptoms can include headache, fever, and fatigue. In most cases, the infection and its symptoms are eliminated by antibiotics, especially if the illness is treated early. Delayed or inadequate treatment can lead to more serious symptoms that affect joints, the heart, and the nervous system (WHO, "Lyme Borreliosis," accessed 2014).

Lyme disease can also affect cats (and dogs). It is highly recommended that domestic cats who spend some part of their day outdoors, and all community cats (when possible), should be treated with a monthly topical (flea and) tick medication. Shelters and bedding should also be treated, using flea and tick powders or sprays. Providing cats with tick preventative treatments, not only protects the cats but it also protects the caretaker and others from contracting Lyme disease.

If you do find a tick biting you or a cat, carefully remove it using a pair of tweezers.

Make sure to completely remove the head and the mouth parts, which can be difficult to remove if the tick has become engorged. Clean the area, apply antibiotic ointment, and monitor for infection (redness, swelling, bull's eye rash). If you see signs of infection, seek medical attention immediately. Dispose of the tick by flushing it down the toilet.

Campylobacter

Campylobacteriosis is usually transmitted through raw or undercooked meat, but humans can also catch the infection from other humans or animals. The main source of contamination in both humans and cats is ingesting undercooked poultry. Although campylobacter is not common in cats, it can sometimes be found in kittens, who usually get it from kennels (PetMD, accessed 2014). The bacteria causes cramping, diarrhea, fever, and abdominal pain (NIH, "Campylobacter Infection," accessed 2014). Symptoms usually last about one week and can be treated with increased hydration or antibiotics, if necessary.

Wearing gloves when handling cat feces can prevent possible contamination. Making sure the living space of cats is clean will also prevent them from becoming infected.

Salmonella

A foodborne pathogen with symptoms similar to campylobacter, salmonella causes diarrhea, fever, and stomach pains within hours or a few days of infection. Again, the main source of contamination is raw or undercooked food, largely poultry or eggs. Infected humans often recover without treatment, though hospitalization is sometimes necessary in severe cases.

Cats and other animals can pass salmonella in their stool. The bacteria is common in cats who are fed raw meat or cats who eat birds and rodents. If a cat has diarrhea, wear gloves when cleaning her litter box and wash your hands thoroughly afterward to avoid contamination (CDC, "Salmonella," accessed 2014).

Fungal Infections

Fungal infections can be common occurrences in cats, with skin lesions typically appearing on the tips of the ears, nose, tail, and also on the feet and hocks; however, the rash can spread to all parts of the body. The skin around these lesions is often flaky and bald; not always red in color; and the rash is usually itchy. In humans, the infection is called Ringworm because the outside of the spots usually appears more red than the inside, resulting in the characteristic ring shape (NIH, "Ringworm," accessed 2014).

Fungal infections are highly contagious and can spread to other animals, as well as to people, through simply touching an infected animal or person. It can also be transmitted through unwashed clothing and showers. It is important to keep the infected cat quarantined and to wear gloves when applying ointment.

Treatment for humans (and cats) depends on severity, but may include antifungal ointments and oral medications. Topical treatment sterilizes the outside of the body, while oral medications kill the infection internally. For small outbreaks, over-the-counter antifungal creams (i.e. athlete's foot cream) can be used to treat cats, dogs, and humans.

Parasites

There are a few diseases common to cats and humans caused by parasites. They include cryptosporidiosis, giardiasis, and toxoplasmosis. Cryptosporidiosis and giardiasis can cause diarrhea in both cats and people, usually through drinking contaminated water. To prevent the spread of infection, everyone should have a veterinarian perform an annual fecal examination on their cats. If a cat should have one of these parasites, use extra caution while cleaning litter boxes by wearing gloves and washing your hands.

Cats and dogs can have these parasites, but a much larger concern is contaminated water. No one should drink water directly from lakes, rivers, streams, or springs (CDC, "Parasites - Cryptosporidium (also known as "Crypto")," accessed 2014). Those who want to take extra precautions may wish to boil water to eliminate parasites such as *Cryptosporidium* or *Giardia*. These precautions are especially important for travel outside the U.S. because water standards elsewhere may be different.

Toxoplasmosis

Toxoplasma gondii is an intestinal parasite that is most often associated with cats. The parasite causes the disease toxoplasmosis, which is a human health concern for pregnant women. Raw meat, especially pork, is the primary mode of transmission of the parasite to humans. Consuming raw or undercooked meat is a danger, as is failing to wash your hands properly after handling meat or utensils used with contaminated meat. *Toxoplasma* cannot pass through the skin, but oocytes left on the skin can unintentionally be ingested if hands are not washed properly, resulting in infection (CDC, "Toxoplasmosis," accessed 2014).

This parasite is estimated to infect as much as one third of the world's human population, but very rarely do those infected get sick (Montoya and Liesenfeld, 2004). Most healthy people have immune systems that can fight off the parasite and will never become sick. However, the parasite can be dangerous in rare cases. Individuals with weakened immune systems, such as AIDS patients, can sometimes become seriously ill as a result of infection, and pregnant women can pass on the parasite to their unborn child. For this reason, doctors are quick to tell pregnant women to get rid of their cats. However, it is important to note that there is less risk of acquiring toxoplasmosis from cats than eating raw vegetables and undercooked meat (Vittecoq et al., 2012). Additionally, owning a cat does not increase the risk of contracting toxoplasmosis (Vittecoq et al., 2012).

Still, pregnant women can take certain precautions when in contact with cats to be safe. If pregnant, one should avoid cleaning litter boxes if possible. Infected cats could pass the oocyst of *Toxoplasma* in feces. If a pregnant woman has no alternative but to clean the litter box herself, she should wear disposable gloves and wash her hands thoroughly afterwards. The same goes for if she is gardening, as it is possible for the parasite to live in soil (CDC, "Toxoplasmosis," accessed 2014).

Pregnant women should also keep their cat indoors, where the cat is not exposed to other animals who may be infected, and all newly adopted cats should be tested for the disease. Pregnant women can also be screened for toxoplasmosis. The only risk occurs when the parasite infects a woman during pregnancy — if she was exposed to toxoplasmosis before pregnancy, there is no risk to her child since she will have developed antibodies to fight the parasite. However, some experts recommend waiting six months after an infection before trying to become pregnant (CDC, "Toxoplasmosis," accessed 2014). If a woman is pregnant when she contracts toxoplasmosis, medication is available.

Web MD reports:

> It is important to understand the mode of transmission from cats to understand how minimal the risk is. Even a cat with an active toxoplasmosis infection is only capable of passing it on for seven to ten days of her entire life, when there's an acute infection. It takes anywhere from one to three days for oocysts shed in the feces to become infectious — which means the litter box would have to sit unscooped for one to three days before the infection could be passed on [emphasis added]. Then, to become infected from cat feces, a person would have to touch the feces and then touch an opening in their body. (WebMD, accessed 2014)

ACR does not want to make light of the fact that if a pregnant woman does contract toxoplasmosis it can be dangerous for her unborn baby. However, those who do not like cats exaggerate this particular hazard. Many doctors are uninformed that the risk of toxoplasmosis for pregnant women is low, and exposure from cat feces is far less likely than from raw and undercooked meat.

Worms

Roundworms, hookworms, whipworms, and tapeworms can also cause disease in humans and cause malnutrition in cats if left untreated. Visceral larva migrans, a disease that often goes away on its own but can be serious in rare cases, can result from accidental consumption of roundworm eggs. Children who play in soil can be at risk, or the eggs could travel on vegetables that were in contact with infected soil (NIH, "Visceral Larva Migrans," accessed 2014).

Cutaneous larva migrans, on the other hand, is caused by any kind of contact with hookworm-contaminated soil. It is most common among travelers returning from tropical regions (Caumes, 2000).

To prevent possible worm infections, children and adults should wash their hands after playing/working outside and coming in contact with soil. Fruits and vegetables should be washed thoroughly before consumption. Travelers should wear sandals on unfamiliar beaches, and no one should go barefoot in areas that might be contaminated by dog or cat feces. Worms go away on their own or with anti-parasitic drugs (NIH, "Visceral larva migrans," accessed 2014).

Cats can be treated with a monthly topical dewormer, such as Profender, or de-worming pills can be crushed into wet food to prevent infection. Fecal exams can be performed, if possible, to detect parasites. In colonies, outdoor litter boxes should be built and regularly scooped. And remember to <u>ALWAYS wash your hands after handling cat feces.</u>

Murine Typhus

Murine typhus (*Rickettsia typhi*) is caused by fleas that are often carried by rats, but can also be found on opossums, cats, dogs, and other wild animals. Typhus occurs around the world, but in the United States, murine typhus is limited to the southern states, particularly Texas and California (NIH, "Typhus," accessed 2014). *R. typhi* does not produce disease in cats and dogs, as it does in people. Epidemic typhus, spread by lice, is generally a more severe disease.

In order to placate neighborhoods that fear this disease, some health agencies may rush in and trap and kill feral cats in the area. This is not wise, as the fleas will still exist, and may then be more prone to jump on people. In any case, the rodent population will thrive without predators to keep them in check, and rats are the primary carriers of fleas in the first place.

TNR and flea control are a far more effective solution than killing cats. Spray or dust the cats' sleeping areas with a flea preventative, especially in warm, dry seasons. Capstar pills can be crushed into canned cat food, and a monthly topical flea treatment should be applied. Clean up neighborhoods and backyards, because junk left lying around attracts rodents.

Plague

Plague is also usually carried by fleas, which in turn are transported on rodents and other mammals. Plague infects humans and animals (WHO, "Plague," accessed 2014).

People usually contract plague when bitten by a rodent flea carrying the plague bacterium, or when handling an infected animal. Millions of people in Europe died from plague in the Middle Ages, when human homes and workplaces were infested by plague-ridden, flea-infested rats. Cats were almost wiped out during this time, as they were scapegoated for being "witches' familiars." With fewer cats, there were more rats and more carriers of the plague, increasing the spread of this deadly disease (Zeugner, 2008).

Precaution should be taken in situations where exposure to rodent fleas is possible, such as when you are working outdoors or camping (CDC, "Prevention - Plague," accessed 2014). Use a repellent to keep fleas off yourself and wear gloves when handling an animal with fleas. You should also treat cats and other companion animals for fleas. To prevent flea infestations, all cat blankets should be washed regularly and sleeping places can be dusted with flea powder. Capstar pills can be crushed into canned cat food, and it is also highly recommended that cats be treated with a monthly topical flea treatment such as Advantage Multi.

Tuberculosis

Among humans, tuberculosis, or TB, is more common in regions of overcrowding and poverty. TB is a bacterial disease that is contagious and able to spread from animals to humans (CDC, "Tuberculosis (TB)," accessed 2014).

Cats are resistant to the primary strain of TB that affects humans, Mycobacterium tuberculosis, but can catch a strain that is more common in cows, Mycobacterium bovis. Dogs and humans are susceptible to both strains, but bovine TB is very rare and makes up only one percent of TB cases in the United States (McNeil, 2014).

In 2014, the first cases of humans catching TB from cats were documented in England. Four people caught bovine TB from a rare group of infected cats (McNeil, 2014). Though the other strain of TB is serious, bovine TB can be treated with antibiotics (Gray, 2014). Officials also noted that there is very minimal risk of exposure from cats and this was an unusual circumstance (McNeil, 2014).

It is not entirely known how these individuals were exposed to the disease, but it usually requires close physical contact, and most likely came from direct contact with an open wound (Gray, 2014). Cats seem to catch this disease from cows or from other animals, such as rodents or badgers, who can become infected. When dealing with free-roaming cats, you should cover any and all of your injuries and wear gloves when handling an animal who appears sick or injured.

Health Benefits of Community Cats

Despite the attention given to zoonotic diseases and claims of animals being a public health risk, there are actually more health benefits resulting from the association with cats than there is harm. Cats and dogs have been shown to lower blood pressure, relieve stress, decrease depression and anxiety, extend life expectancies, and promote overall happiness. Studies have shown that individuals who care for animals have improved immune systems and children raised around animals develop less autoimmune diseases.

A study at the University of Minnesota showed a 30 to 40 percent less risk of cardiovascular disease, including stroke, in those who lived with a cat (Qureshi et al., 2009), while a national Australian survey analyzed by Bruce Headey showed that individuals living with companion animals visited the doctor less often and were less likely to take medication for heart conditions and sleep disorders (Headey, 1999). Another study revealed that individuals who had companion animals were less likely to die after suffering from a heart attack compared to those who did not have companion animals (Friedmann et al., 2010).

Similarly, two independent studies supported the correlation between living with companion animals and a decreased risk of heart disease, particularly a decrease in blood pressure and cholesterol (Arhant-Sudhir et al., 2011; Anderson et al., 1992). Another study showed that companion animals provide for the improved health and psychological well-being of individuals (Serpell, 1991). Cat companionship has also been found to help reduce stress and anxiety while improving overall health (Jennings, 1997).

Researchers at the Columbia Center for Children's Environmental Health (CCCEH) at Columbia University's Mailman School of Public Health released findings that cat companionship has a protective effect against the development of asthma symptoms in young children at age five. The study, published by the *Journal of Allergy and Clinical Immunology*, also found that children with cats in the home were more likely to have produced allergy-related antibodies to cats (Columbia University, 2008).

Louise Holton

Feeding feral cats in Rome, Italy.

Conclusion

Although there are potential hazards for acquiring some diseases from stray and outdoor cats, the incidence is rare, and in most cases cat companionship provides improved health benefits. If common sense and good hygiene are exercised when working with colonies, transmission of infectious diseases from cats to humans can be minimized. Contact with other humans is more likely to be a source of contracting infectious diseases than contact with animals (Cornell, "Zoonotic Disease: What Can I Catch from My Cat?," 2014).

However, it is critical to be vigilant about cleanliness, especially when feeding feral cats and cleaning up cat feces. All of these precautions will help not only with potential health hazards, but will stop neighbors from complaining about dirty places due to outdoor cats.

There are millions of feral cats living in every corner of the world, and they help with the control of rodents in cities and towns. After all, this was one of the reasons they became friends with humans in the first place. One rarely hears of humans becoming ill because of the cats living among us in our alleyways and on our streets. It is a friendship appreciated on both sides, by cats and by humans. The transmission of disease from cats to humans, as a result of this closeness, can certainly be managed.

Summary

To protect yourself from cat-related diseases:

- Wear gloves and wash your hands thoroughly with soap and water after handling cat feces.
- If a cat does scratch or bite you, wash the area immediately with soap and hot running water.
- Vaccinate domestic and feral cats against rabies.
- Treat domestic and feral cats for internal (worms) and external (fleas, ticks) parasites.
- Build outdoor litter boxes and scoop frequently.
- Do not put too much food out; only supply the amount of food sufficient to feed the cats in a single day. Bring food bowls in at night to avoid attracting wildlife.

Winterizing Feral Cat Colonies

In the winter months, providing shelter for feral cats is even more important than providing food (Calhoon and Haspel, 1989). Cold, wet weather can have adverse and potentially serious effects on cats. It is very important for feral cats to stay dry. If they become wet, they will need a shelter to dry off to prevent hypothermia or freezing. In most cases, however, feral cats are able to tolerate cold temperatures and make do just as any other wild animal. They search out warm dry shelter and find any and all nearby food sources. Providing shelter, along with feeding the cats, greatly reduces any winter hardships and helps to keep the cats healthy.

Domestic cats, if left outside, probably suffer more from cold weather conditions than feral cats, who develop a winter coat in the fall. Feral cats will also huddle together in order to conserve heat. When several cats huddle together in a small shelter, their combined body heat easily raises the temperature inside the shelter.

Providing shelter is a crucial aspect of colony management. You can buy a shelter from a pet supply store, build your own shelter, or provide other types of protection against the elements. If feral

Decorated winterized shelters allow cats to escape the cold in style.

cats rely on a shed or other building for shelter, it is recommended that a smaller portable shelter be placed in the shed. As long as the cats have a dry, warm place to protect them from the elements, feral colonies can thrive during the winter.

Shelter Materials

Two key elements are needed in any good feral cat shelter. First is the material used. Material with excellent insulation qualities, such as Styrofoam or mylar, work best. Styrofoam traps the cat's body heat, turning her into a little radiator. Second is the size of the shelter; you don't want a shelter to be too big. The shelter's interior should have a minimal amount of air space, thus reducing the amount of heat the cat's body must generate to keep the space warm. Still, you do want to allow enough room for a few cats to huddle, especially if you are caring for a large colony.

A basic, winterized foam shelter is a welcome sight for feral cats in cold conditions.

Covered litter boxes (some have doors) and plastic or rubber totes work perfect for shelters. But you can also use a strong cardboard box or crate. Outdoor dog "igloos" from a pet supply store also work well (just remember to keep size in mind), and many websites sell specially-designed cat shelters. (Refer to the Helpful Resources section for more information.)

Use Styrofoam to line the containers and place straw in the bottom for bedding. For litter boxes that have vents in the roof for air flow and when using cardboard boxes, it's important to place a

tarp or plastic table cloth over the shelter to prevent water damage. The plastic barrier can be secured using bricks or other heavy objects.

Additional Tips

Ideally the shelter should have two small openings, which will allow quick escape if necessary. Make sure the openings are protected from the wind.

Use straw for bedding; it stays dry and can easily be changed. Do not use hay; it retains moisture and it is food for farmed animals. Do not use blankets or towels; they retain moisture.

Raise the shelter off the ground a few inches by placing it securely on bricks or on a wooden pallet. It's more likely to retain moisture and rot if left on the ground. Plus, this prevents water from flowing into the openings when it's raining.

Clean the shelters each spring and autumn by replacing the bedding with fresh straw or newspaper. You may even want to sprinkle flea powder or other flea deterrent in the bottom of the shelter, before adding the bedding. Do not allow cats to lay directly in flea powder and always read product instructions prior to use.

Microwavable heating pads and hot water bottles can be placed in shelters to keep cats warm. Most will stay warm for up to 12 hours, and can be especially helpful to protect against night time temperatures. Electric heating pads can be used for porch cats, and outdoor lights can be added to shelters for heat.

How to Construct a Shelter

Supplies You Will Need

- Sturdy cardboard box or plastic tote with lid (ideal size 24"L x 13"W x 15"H)

- Several thin pieces of Styrofoam (about 1/4" thick) or a small Styrofoam cooler

- Duct tape

- Utility knife

- Ruler or measuring tape

- Marker

Instructions

1. With the box or tote sitting on the ground, top up, draw a 6" circle in the center of one (or both) of the short sides of the box. Cut out the circle to create a door(s).

2. Duct tape the edges of the circle door for reinforcement and to protect the cat from being scratched by any rough edges.

3. Measure the Styrofoam pieces so they line the bottom and the walls of the box. Cut the pieces to size and use the duct tape to secure all pieces of Styrofoam to the inside of the box. You can also use a Styrofoam cooler that will fit inside of the box/tote. Cut openings in the Styrofoam to match the door(s) in the box.

4. If using a cardboard box, fold closed three of the top flaps (allowing one of the larger flaps to stand open), and duct tape the three flaps closed. One box top flap is left unsecured to allow for easy bedding changes. If using a plastic tote, simply remove the lid to change bedding.

5. For a cardboard box, run strips of duct tape lengthwise along the bottom of the box to help waterproof the bottom. This may be done to each side of the box for extra protection. Also, cover the entire box with a plastic table cloth or tarp (secured by heavy rocks or bricks) to prevent water damage.

A foam cooler and straw add insulation to a weatherproof rubber tote shelter (top removed).

Food and Water

Small bowls of dry or canned food can be placed inside the shelter. The cats' own heat will slow the freezing of the canned food and can even defrost it. NEVER place water inside the shelter; it can easily spill and cause the cat(s) to get wet. Or better yet, consider providing the cats a feeding station

A covered shelter keeps cats and food dry.

— a simple structure with a roof and floor that will keep food and cats dry.

Nutrition is especially important for outdoor cats during the winter because the cold and difficult weather conditions create additional stresses for their immune systems. Feeding them a higher quality food, if you can manage the additional expense, is also beneficial. Normally, healthy cats do not require a lot of water and can get most of their water needs from eating moist food; however, in the winter when canned food can freeze, dry food becomes a cat's staple. Therefore, providing fresh water is a necessity during cold weather. The best solution to keep water from freezing is to use a solar-powered or an electrically-heated bowl. (These are used for "porch cats" and not ideal for large colonies.) Water will evaporate relatively quickly, so the bowl needs to be filled regularly. The bowl also can be used for wet food, though it can quickly dry the food out. You can also use microwavable heating pads/disks to place under water and food bowls to keep from freezing.

The type of bowl you use in general can make a difference. Use one made of thick plastic, like a Tupperware container; it takes longer for water to freeze when in a plastic dish compared to a metal dish. Styrofoam containers lined with plastic also make great water bowls. The best bowls are deep, insulated and have relatively small openings compared to their volume. Black or dark colored bowls will absorb solar radiation better. Position the bowl so it's protected from the wind and, if possible, exposed to the sun.

Waterloo Alley Cat Project

Health Care for Feral Cats:
Guidelines for Colony Caretakers

The purpose of this chapter and its sub-chapters is to elaborate on the health care and medical side of implementing a Trap-Neuter-Return (TNR) program. In the previous chapters, we provided the how-tos of carrying out the trapping, transporting, and fostering of feral cats. Much of the following information is meant to be a guideline in assisting veterinarians when treating feral cats. However, it is also a good idea for caretakers to be familiar with this important information, so they may make informed decisions and help properly manage the health care of their colony.

Overall Health and Life Expectancy

Those opposed to TNR programs claim outdoor cats are suffering, diseased, and living a life of extreme misery. No doubt there are some *unmanaged* colonies in unhealthy condition, but more often we see managed colonies with hardy survivors who are very healthy. The Feral Cat Spay/Neuter Project located in Washington state has noted that, after treating over 30,000 cats, their euthanasia rate is 0.2 percent, or two cats out of 1,000, and "the vast majority [are] in good physical health" (Feral Cat Spay/Neuter Project, 2006).

In another study, veterinarians looked at the health of feral cats by measuring the body condition of cats *prior* to being trapped and sterilized. When trapped initially, the cats were reported to be lean but not emaciated. Veterinarians also measured the falciform fat pad, or the deposit of fat along each side of the abdomen, and found each cat to have a small amount of fat present; meaning the cats were eating enough to be able to store fat and maintain a fairly stable weight (Scott et al., 2002, web).

As for the occurrence of viral diseases, such as feline leukemia (FeLV) and feline immunodeficiency virus (FIV), large epidemiologic studies "indicate FeLV and FIV are present in approximately 4% of feral cats, which is not substantially different from the infection rate reported for pet cats" (Levy and Crawford, 2004). Furthermore, models of the transmission of the two diseases among feral cat populations "indicate that neither virus impacts overall colony size," meaning these viruses are not quickly killing infected cats, but rather cats are capable of living years with either disease (Levy and Crawford, 2004).

Personal Account from Louise Holton

In 1990, I began helping to manage a colony of feral cats living in Adams Morgan, Washington, D.C. This colony represented a typical city feral cat colony. Fed by sympathetic neighbors, these healthy black and white cats, all with great weight on them, had shiny and clean coats. We removed 32 kittens, tamed them, and placed them into homes, thereby reducing the initial size of the colony.

The major health problem facing this particular colony was the infestation of internal parasites. The cats had coccidia, a parasite that causes severe diarrhea, and they were infected with roundworms, which can cause malnutrition. Some kittens required several deworming treatments, but all recovered. The feeders told us that before our involvement with trapping and sterilization, many of the kittens also contracted upper respiratory infections (URIs) and died. Internal parasites and URIs are typically the main culprits of illness in feral cats, especially kittens. But with a few treatments of dewormer, or an antibiotic in the case of URIs, most cats and kittens recover fully.

Judy M. Zukoski

Feral cats, Adams Morgan, Washington, D.C. These cats recovered fully from parasites and infection after receiving medical care as part of a TNR program.

The life expectancy of a feral cat is still highly debated with some sources claiming a feral cat will only live to be about two years old; however, these statistics are mostly folk wisdom. A study performed on a Florida college campus over the course of 11 years reported that more than 80 percent of the cats had been residents for more than six years; which is comparable to the mean lifespan of 7.1 years for household cats (Levy, 2003).

In 2012, Alley Cat Rescue surveyed rescue organizations across the United States that provide TNR services to their communities and out of the 120 groups that responded, 25 percent reported the average age of colony cats to be around six to eight years old. Another 35 percent said the feral cats they assist are between nine and 12 years old, with more than 14 percent reporting feral cats in their communities to be 13 years old and above (Alley Cat Rescue, 2012).

Feral cats are opportunistic scavengers just like raccoons, opossums, and skunks. Though they are very resourceful animals, some individuals are going to experience times of hardship (lack of food, inadequate shelter, illness). All animal species are prone to experiencing the harshness of the natural world; however, we only choose to view feral cats differently than other wild animals because of our attachment to the idea of them being companion animals. Our emotions drive us to categorize all cats as "pets" instead of recognizing the varying degrees of domestication for these animals. As Celia Hammond explains, "We surely would not consider that other wild animals, such as foxes and badgers, should be put to sleep in their prime to save them the experience of growing old and dying" (Hammond, 1980).

Though having said that, we must also point out that despite the fact that feral cats have the *ability* to survive without human intervention, we should take some responsibility in humanely caring for them since we created their situation. We owe these animals compassion to ease some of their suffering and TNR programs do just that.

Feline Viral Diseases

The three major feline viral diseases are feline infectious peritonitis (FIP), feline leukemia virus (FeLV), and feline immunodeficiency virus (FIV). These viruses are specific to cats and cannot be transmitted to humans or other animals. As stated before, if feral cats survive to adulthood and are well fed, they are usually robust animals and largely immune to local diseases.

Nancy North

Breakfast for the feral colony at the Buenos Aires Botanical Gardens, Argentina.

Feline Infectious Peritonitis (FIP)

Feline infectious peritonitis (FIP) is a viral disease caused by certain strains of the feline coronavirus. Infected cats usually show no symptoms in the initial stages of coronavirus infection, and the virus only progresses into clinical FIP in a small number of infected cats — five to 10 percent — and only when there is a mutation of the virus or an abnormality in the immune response (Cornell, "Feline Infectious Peritonitis," 2014).

For cats who develop FIP, symptoms usually appear suddenly and increase

83

in severity, usually resulting in death. The cats often develop nonspecific symptoms of weight loss, loss of appetite, depression, roughness of hair, and fever. Tissues around the infected cells, usually in the abdomen, kidney, or brain, also become intensely inflamed (Cornell, "Feline Infectious Peritonitis," 2014).

Because the symptoms of FIP are not uniform, often manifesting differently in different cats and sometimes appearing similar to other diseases, there is no definitive way to diagnose it without a biopsy. Veterinarians often diagnose based on an evaluation of the cat's history and symptoms in combination with coronavirus test results (Cornell, "Feline Infectious Peritonitis," 2014).

FIP is not highly contagious and is transmitted through saliva and feces during acute infection. FIP most commonly affects cats in multi-cat households and is not as common in outdoor cats. This may be because outdoor cats bury their feces away from other colony members, while indoor cats usually use the same litter boxes.

There is no cure for FIP, and it is a fatal disease. Supportive care and high quality nutrition can help alleviate some of the body's inflammatory response to the disease. Corticosteroids, cytotoxic drugs, and antibiotics are often used to treat FIP, and fluid therapy and blood transfusions may also help as supportive care (Cornell, "Feline Infectious Peritonitis," 2014).

Feline Leukemia Virus (FeLV)

The feline leukemia virus (FeLV) is a retrovirus belonging to the subfamily *Oncovirinae*, which means it is a cancer-causing virus. In addition to causing feline leukemia, FeLV suppresses the cat's immune system, leaving the animal vulnerable to a variety of opportunistic diseases. The signs and symptoms of infection with FeLV are varied and include loss of appetite; poor coat condition; infections of the skin, bladder and respiratory tract; oral disease; seizures; swollen lymph nodes; fatigue; fever; weight loss; recurring bacterial and viral illnesses; anemia; diarrhea; and jaundice (Cornell, "Feline Leukemia Virus," 2014). Some cats can be carriers of the disease and show no signs of illness for many years.

Infected cats shed FeLV primarily in their saliva, although the virus may also be present in the blood, tears, feces, or urine. Other modes of FeLV transmission include mutual grooming, sharing food dishes and litter boxes, and in utero transfer from a mother cat to her kittens. A mother cat can also transmit FeLV to her kittens through infected milk.

A simple blood test can be performed in a veterinary office to determine if a cat has contracted FeLV; however, most TNR programs choose not to test feral cats for the disease. (Continue reading for more information on testing feral cats for viral diseases.) Whether a feral cat tests negative for the disease or she is not tested, we strongly recommend all feral cats receive an FeLV vaccine to reduce the risk of transmission.

Morris and FeLV

In 1991, when I first heard that one of my rescued feral cats, Morris, had tested positive for feline leukemia I was devastated. In those days, the feelings about FeLV were pretty negative and myths were prevalent.

Morris was trapped at four months of age and initially tested negative. However, he soon developed a severe upper respiratory infection that would not clear and he lost a lot of weight, so my veterinarian suggested another test, which he sent to the lab. This time it came back positive.

Fortunately, my veterinarian Dr. Pervaiz Manzoor, was always willing to work with me and to try new methods. He helped me stabilize Morris and was open to my suggestion of giving the cat Interferon to boost his immune system. After a few months of intensive supportive therapy, Morris actually started gaining weight and looking well again.

We retested Morris, and each time the tests come back from the lab with a negative result. The virus had obviously cleared from his bloodstream. We also retested several of the cats Morris had lived with for many years. These tests have all been negative for FeLV.

Unfortunately, later in life Morris developed severe gingivitis and stomatitis. It became an ongoing problem for him and it was very difficult for me to medicate him. He always retained some feral instincts and because eating hurt his mouth, he associated food served by me with pain.

My vet extracted most of Morris' teeth and this cured the stomatitis. Not having teeth is not the worst thing in the world for a cat who lives in a home or colony and is provided with food. He could still eat dry food, as well as moist. I found that chunky foods — the ones in pouches — were easier for Morris to eat than ground mashed foods, as these stuck to his gums and to his remaining teeth and caused more pain. To treat stomatitis, some recommend a combination of drugs a — "cocktail" consisting of Interferon, Medrol, and Clinadrops. But removal of the teeth is the best method to use for this disease.

Morris completely overcame FeLV and lived to the ripe old age of 17!

There is no cure for FeLV, although veterinarians can treat or at least alleviate the opportunistic infections associated with the virus. Good supportive care can also improve the quality of an infected cat's life. Nutritional support (herbs, vitamins) and other alternative treatments can help strengthen a cat's impaired immune system.

Feline Immunodeficiency Virus (FIV)

Feline immunodeficiency virus (FIV) is a retrovirus that virologists classify as a lentivirus, or "slow-acting virus." Cats diagnosed with FIV may live long, healthy lives, never showing symptoms

Adam and FIV

In 1992, Adam, a feral cat I trapped as a kitten in July 1990, escaped from my house one night. He came back the next night, bleeding from deep bite wounds to his neck. The emergency veterinarian, who treated Adam, said the wounds were probably caused by the canine teeth of another cat.

A few months later, Adam developed a high fever and a severe upper respiratory infection. Both were difficult to treat and my veterinarian suggested retesting Adam. We found that he had contracted FIV.

This wonderful, very good-natured cat recovered from the initial infection and eventually ended up weighing 14 pounds. He went on to live a happy and healthy life until June 2004. His death was not related to the FIV infection.

Adam had been living with my other rescued stray and feral cats for some time before he was diagnosed, he continued to live with them afterwards. He was very friendly and never fought, therefore I didn't separate him from the others. I randomly retested nine of my other cats a few years later, and they all tested <u>negative</u> for <u>BOTH</u> FeLV and FIV.

Adam, an FIV+ feral who lived to the age of 14.

Louise Holton

of the virus, though some cats may experience "recurrent illness interspersed with periods of relative health" (Cornell, "Feline Immunodeficiency Virus," 2014). FIV suppresses the cat's immune system, compromising her ability to fight off infection.

Common signs and symptoms of the disease include poor coat condition; persistent fever; loss of appetite; weight loss; inflammation of the gums and mouth; chronic or recurrent skin, urinary tract, bladder, and upper respiratory infections; and a variety of eye conditions may occur. FIV positive cats are also much more susceptible to various kinds of cancer and blood diseases, and some experience seizures, or behavioral and neurological disorders (Cornell, "Feline Immunodeficiency Virus," 2014).

Fortunately, FIV is not transmitted as easily as FeLV. The primary mode of transmission is through bite wounds. This explains why the cats most likely to become infected are free-roaming, unneutered males prone to territorial fighting. FIV does not appear to spread through casual contact among cats, so it is possible to keep an FIV-infected cat in the same household as a healthy cat with little risk of transmission, provided the cats tolerate each other and do not fight. There is not a danger of FIV spreading through sexual contact, and only rarely does a mother pass it on to her kittens, either through birth or infected milk (Cornell, "Feline Immunodeficiency Virus," 2014).

A simple blood test can be performed in a veterinary office to determine if a cat has contracted FIV. However, most TNR programs choose not to test feral cats for the disease. Kittens testing positive for FIV are not necessarily infected. If a kitten tests positive, the test is probably detecting antibodies passed from the mother to the kitten through colostrum, the first milk that the mother cat produces. Positive kittens should be retested between four and six months of age, when any antibodies obtained from the mother cat will have disappeared.

There is a vaccine to protect against FIV, though it is rarely administered. Any cat who receives the vaccine will then test positive for the disease, because she will be carrying antibodies. There is no cure for FIV; however, like FeLV, veterinarians can treat or at least alleviate the infections associated with the virus. Proper nutrition and good supportive care can help strengthen a cat's impaired immune system and improve her quality of life.

To Test or Not to Test?

Each colony caretaker, shelter, and veterinarian must make their own decisions about how they wish to spend their resources, and if and which tests to perform. Testing for viral diseases such as FeLV and FIV in feral cat colonies should be optional and not mandatory. Funds for sterilization programs are usually limited, so resources may be better spent on sterilization and rabies vaccines rather than on testing. The time taken to collect blood and run tests, plus the cost of testing, may be better spent on sterilization if, as a nation, we are going to reduce the feral cat population. Alley Cat Rescue does not perform testing as part of our standard TNR program; however, all cats who are placed into our adoption program or feral cats who are relocated are tested.

As discussed above, the rate of transmission for FeLV, FIV, and FIP in feral cats is very low. FeLV is primarily spread from infected mother cats to their kittens, and FIV is mostly spread among fighting tomcats through deep bite wounds. Therefore, spaying and neutering will decrease these activities and the spread of these infections. Studies have shown that "FeLV and FIV may become extinct" in cat populations with "few aggressive interactions" (Levy and Crawford, 2004). There is no reliable test for FIP, which is mainly found in catteries and crowded shelters and is less likely in feral cat colonies. Also, mass screenings of healthy cats can result in large numbers of false positives. All cats testing positive should be retested to properly confirm diagnosis, which is usually not possible in the case of feral cats, due to limited resources.

Operation Catnip's founder, Dr. Julie Levy, points out that the greatest cause of feline deaths in the United States is the killing — by humans — of unwanted stray and feral cats, which causes more deaths than all feline infectious diseases combined (Levy and Crawford, 2004). Subsequently, most TNR programs choose to focus their efforts and resources on sterilization and vaccination rather than testing.

Vaccination Protocols

Alley Cat Rescue realizes that there are numerous viewpoints concerning the topic of providing vaccinations to cats. Some people believe strongly in vaccines, some are against them or tend to provide only minimal vaccines to their cats, and others fall somewhere in between. The intention of this chapter is *not* to discuss those opinions here, but rather to provide guidance to rescuers and to those who are assisting feral cats, based on standard, accepted vaccination practices throughout the veterinary and TNR communities. Typically, feral cats receive vaccinations at the time of sterilization; however, cats can be re-trapped later to update any vaccines.

Please note: For those who are assisting outdoor cats by fostering, we highly recommend you vaccinate your indoor cats (if you do have indoor cats) prior to introducing any new cats. Even if the new cat will be isolated in a spare room or in a large cage, it is still important for your indoor cats to be vaccinated. Viruses can be transmitted through the air and through contact with improperly cleaned food and water dishes, bedding materials, your clothing, and improperly washed hands. It is much safer to take this precaution prior to bringing a new cat into the house, rather than trying to fight off an illness in multiple cats later.

Due to the rabies virus being a zoonotic disease, meaning it can be transmitted to humans, most health codes and laws require that all cats receive a rabies vaccination. (Refer to the chapter on "Zoonotic Diseases" for more information.) In some cases, if a veterinarian has not seen a particular cat before (as is the case for first time feral cats), she may insist on giving the cat a one-year rabies vaccine, over a three-year rabies vaccine. It is highly recommended that the cat receive a three-year rabies vaccine despite being seen for the first time. This helps minimize the number of times you will have to trap the cat; however, it is not necessary and a one-year vaccine is sufficient. Kittens can receive a rabies vaccine as early as 12 weeks of age.

Along with a rabies vaccine, all feral cats should receive a distemper vaccine. Distemper or feline panleukopenia virus is highly contagious and can cause high mortality in a group of feral cats, usually among kittens, who have weakened immune systems. The virus primarily attacks the gastrointestinal tract, resulting in profuse and usually bloody diarrhea, severe dehydration, malnutrition, anemia, and often death. The virus compromises the immune system by decreasing the cat's white blood cells. The distemper vaccine or FVRCP is a combination vaccine that also includes protection against rhinotracheitis, calici, and *Chlamydia psittaci*. Adult cats receive one distemper vaccine, while kittens require a series of booster vaccines spaced apart at three-week intervals in order for the vaccine to fully protect the kitten against the virus. Kittens can receive their initial distemper vaccine as early as six to seven weeks of age.

Rabies and distemper vaccines are the two main vaccinations feral cats should receive. However, we also recommend they receive a feline leukemia (FeLV) vaccine, even if you decide not to test the cat for the disease. FeLV is a retrovirus that compromises the cat's immune system, making her susceptible to other diseases. Despite the low percentage of feral cats living with feline leukemia and the low rate of transmitting the disease, we suggest feral cats also be vaccinated against the virus as a precaution. ACR's veterinarians administer a distemper vaccine that includes the FeLV vaccine; using this combination vaccine saves money in the long run over administering separate distemper and FeLV vaccines.

Please note: Several studies have found a strong association between "the administration of feline vaccines (e.g. rabies and feline leukemia virus) and subsequent development of soft tissue sarcoma at the site of vaccination" (Pet Cancer Center, 2013). Soft tissue sarcoma developed, over the range of four weeks to 10 years, at the site of vaccine administration in an estimated 0.001 to 0.0001

percent of cats. Many of these cats with vaccine-associated sarcoma, 60 percent, had highly aggressive tumors, while only six percent had mildly aggressive tumors, according to one study (Pet Cancer Center, 2013).

The risk of vaccine-induced sarcoma, a highly malignant cancer, has caused the veterinary community to look into the possibility that cats have been over-vaccinated. In 1996, the Vaccine-Associated Feline Sarcoma Task Force (VAFSTF) formed to investigate how to prevent these sarcomas. The panel made new vaccination recommendations, that booster doses of vaccines against feline panleukopenia, feline viral rhinotracheitis and feline calicivirus (FVRCP) now only be administered every three years instead of the traditional one-year booster. The panel also found that the three-year rabies vaccination provides adequate immunity, and suggested this over the annual shots to lessen the risk of sarcomas forming (American Veterinary Medical Association, 2001).

ACR strongly recommends providing a three-year rabies vaccination to adequately protect adult feral cats for at least three years, and possibly even longer. In our experience, we have found that five- to seven-year-old feral cats, who are part of managed colonies, are easier to retrap, as opposed to retrapping the cats every year. The cats will know and trust the caretaker and can be more easily trapped. Cats who are trapped too often may become trap-shy, making retrapping much more difficult.

Additional Health Concerns

While being spayed or neutered, the veterinarian will examine the cat's skin for wounds or injuries, making sure to thoroughly clean and treat accordingly. Bite wounds and minor abrasions are common. A long-acting antibiotic injection, such as Convenia, is usually administered after sterilization procedures, and will also aid in reducing and treating any infection. For severe wounds or injuries, caretakers can administer additional antibiotics in wet food, or if the veterinary hospital or the caretaker has the space and is capable of housing the cat, she may spend a few days recovering confined to a cage.

ACR colony cat, Stumpy. She was fostered for a few extra days post-surgery.

Parasite infestations are the most common transmittable health concern for feral cats (Levy and Crawford, 2004). These include internal parasites, like worms, and external parasites, such as fleas, ticks, and ear mites. As mentioned in previous chapters, it is highly recommended that TNR programs include treatments to prevent internal and external parasite infestations. Most topical applications, such as Advantage Multi, prevent and treat a wide range of parasites, so depending on which brand your veterinarian uses, each cat may only need to receive one (monthly) application in order to treat both internal and external parasites. For added protection and to treat severe cases of internal parasites, a topical dewormer such as Profender may be applied, and deworming pills and liquids, such as Drontal, can be crushed into wet food. (Refer to the chapter on "Zoonotic Diseases" for more information.)

Upper respiratory infections (URIs) are also common in feral cats, especially kittens. Signs and symptoms of URIs include nasal discharge, eye discharge, sneezing, and wheezing. Loss of appetite is also common in cats with URIs, because their sense of smell is decreased due to a stuffy nose. A long-acting antibiotic injection, such as Convenia, can be administered or daily antibiotics, such as Clavamox or Amoxicillin, can be added to wet food for treatment. For cats who can be handled, antibiotic eye ointments can also be administered. (Refer to the chapter on "Feral Kittens and Pregnant Cats" for more information.)

When they have already been trapped, cats should also receive a dental exam, because dental care is very important to a cat's overall health. Dental disease is a prevalent health concern for feral

Louise Holton

cats. In the colonies that Alley Cat Rescue manages, we have found that some older cats who lost weight and stopped eating were suffering from dental problems. We retrapped those cats and our veterinarians removed some infected or damaged teeth, and the cats started eating again and gained back their weight. Some cats, especially those infected with FeLV or FIV, are prone to stomatitis, or the inflammation of the mouth. In our experience, we have found the best treatment for this is to remove all unhealthy teeth and treat flare-up conditions with antibiotics.

Hospice Care

Hospice care for terminally ill and aging companion animals has become more popular over the years. It is similar to long-term hospice care for terminally ill humans. With the guidance of trained veterinarians, animal guardians can administer pain killers and other medications, and can nurse their sick animals until they either die naturally, or until the guardian feels the quality of the cat's life is poor enough to consider euthanasia.

ACR feels that the hospice care concept is also an appropriate one to consider for aging and terminally ill feral cats. Some feral cats, in their old age, have come to trust their caretakers, and it may be possible to trap the cat and provide in-home hospice care. However, this should not be taken lightly and all caution should be used. Even though the cat is elderly,

she is still feral and should be confined to a large cage. ACR has considered both hospice care and trap-and-euthanize for terminally ill cats in our colonies. More information can be found in the Helpful Resources Section.

If in-home hospice care is not possible and the cat can be trapped, caretakers may consider euthanasia. However, if it becomes too traumatic for a sick cat to be trapped, and you are unable to do so after several attempts, it may be kinder to leave her alone to die in peace. We feel this to be a sensible and humane approach to assisting terminally ill colony cats.

We are sure that many caretakers of animals have felt that perhaps they should have allowed their cat or dog to die in peace alone, and at other times have felt that perhaps the animal should have been euthanized sooner to prevent her from suffering further. Everyone goes through this during a time of grieving, and feral cat colony caretakers are no different in mourning when their beloved alley cats eventually die. These are hard decisions to make. However, they need to be made at some point. It is therefore worth considering ahead of time, and discussing with your veterinarian what procedures to follow.

Euthanasia

Veterinarians and colony caretakers should discuss guidelines for euthanizing feral cats prior to trapping. Most feral cats are healthy, and common illnesses and infections are easily treatable with antibiotics and parasite control measures. However, for conditions that require long-term, in-house care, but where such treatment is not possible, it is more humane to euthanize the cat than it would be to release her back outside. In extreme cases of injury or illness that exceed medical capabilities, the cat should also be euthanized. Euthanasia should only be practiced when all other options have been exhausted.

Conclusion

Please keep in mind that feral cats can be difficult to handle, especially without previous experience, and this can be a major concern for some veterinarians and their staff. However, following the guidelines laid out in this handbook, TNR programs can be implemented with minimal mishaps. Gathering as much preliminary information as possible about a feral cat colony prior to trapping and communicating openly will ensure that the caretaker and veterinarian are on the same page.

Health Care for Feral Cats:
Guidelines for Veterinarians

Alley Cat Rescue and its network of colony caretakers and veterinarians have successfully trapped and sterilized tens of thousands of feral cats. With over 30 years of experience working with feral cats, we have put together the following chapter and subchapters as guides for veterinarians and their staff, who may not have previously worked with feral cats.

The most important item to keep in mind is that the wild nature of feral cats presents a unique challenge when treating them. Therefore, the less you handle them, the safer it is for both veterinary staff and for the cats. Feral cats can be treated without mishaps by using the proper equipment and implementing these simple steps and procedures.

Preliminary Plans

When planning a colony management program, the caretaker should consult a veterinarian prior to trapping, and the veterinarian should request that the caretaker gather some preliminary information. The caretaker should note; the size of the colony (How many adults? How many kittens?); the health of the colony (Does there appear to be sick or injured cats?); and if there appear to be any tame or adoptable cats in the colony. This information is pertinent to devising a proper plan of action. It is difficult to guarantee that the cats will be trapped on an exact schedule. You may not know the exact number of cats, and you may not be able to predict either the weather conditions or your luck with trapping.

Feral cat arriving in a trap for treatment by ACR vets, Doctors Rauf Ahmad and Pervaiz Manzoor.

Most Trap-Neuter-Return (TNR) projects, especially with colonies, require flexibility and patience from both the client and the veterinarian. ACR recommends veterinarians draft a list of what they require or expect of their clients. This should include hours of operation, the procedures caregivers need to fol-

93

low (with the important message that the cats must remain in their traps), and the terms of payment, including whether some of the cost is a donation by the clinic. The caretaker should also let the clinic know if the cats will be returned to the outdoor colony or kept for possible adoption, fostering, barn homes, etc. It is important to remember that the cat's well-being is the top priority; lose sight of this and the objective of trying to help may be entirely lost. No cat should be exposed to any danger or allowed to become too stressed while remaining in the trap. Cats should have little human contact after surgery and should be allowed to recover in a calm, quiet environment, with traps or cages covered by blankets or towels.

Fundraising and Payment Plans

Payment plans should be worked out ahead of time. Both caretaker and veterinarian must remember that while clinics cannot function without adequate remuneration, a caretaker attempting to manage a colony usually has limited resources and is working to help resolve a community problem using her own personal funds. A workable plan usually can be devised to suit both veterinarians and caretakers. ACR can provide information on how to raise money to help pay veterinary expenses. There are also national low-cost sterilization programs available. Veterinarians can participate in the Friends of Animals subsidized program

(800-321-PETS), which reimburses veterinarians for part of their surgical costs, and caretakers can contact SPAY USA (800-243-SPAY), which maintains a national registry of low-cost spay/neuter service providers.

Equipment and Handling

Having the proper equipment is vital when working with feral cats. Special traps, squeeze-side cages, nets, restraint modules, and cages to house the cats after surgery are all necessary items. All equipment containing feral cats must have large notices attached that read, Warning! This cat may bite. A small transfer cage, which fits against the sliding door of the trap, can be used to move the cat if necessary.

Some veterinarians tranquilize feral cats by tipping the trap on its side. It is easier to immobilize them while they are still in their traps. Feral cats should be handled only when tranquilized. (For information on purchasing equipment, refer to the Helpful Resources listing in the back of the handbook.)

Pre-Exposure Rabies Vaccinations

As a precaution, all individuals working with feral cats should receive pre-exposure rabies vaccinations. Refer to "Steps

Surgery

Male cats who are part of a TNR program should be sterilized through castration, while female cats should receive an ovariohysterectomy. Castration is the complete removal of the testes in male cats, and ovariohysterectomy is the removal of the uterus, fallopian tubes, and ovaries in females. Vasectomies and hysterectomies are <u>NOT</u> recommended; these procedures leave the testicles and ovaries intact, meaning reproductive hormones will remain and continue to drive a cat's mating instincts and behavior, and perpetuate annoying habits such as fighting, yowling, and spraying. One of the many benefits of TNR is helping cats become better neighbors (to be more accepted by the public), and this is accomplished by eliminating those exact common complaints. Therefore, the traditional method of TNR is preferred over the Trap-Vasectomy-Hysterectomy-Release (TVHR) method.

In England, where these programs have been implemented for over four decades, flank incisions are used for females (who are not pregnant), as this could possibly lessen the chance of infection and evisceration (internal organs protruding through the incision.) However, most U.S. veterinarians perform the midline incision; proper use of inner and outer sutures minimizes the risk of evisceration when using the midline method. (Refer to "Left Lateral Flank Spay Technique" for more information on this procedure.)

While the cat is still under anesthesia, an overall physical exam should be performed so any other conditions can be addressed. The cat should be examined for wounds, and any lesions should be examined for parasitic or fungal infections and treated accordingly. Eye and ear infections should also be treated. The cat's mouth and teeth should be examined; any decaying teeth should be removed. Any matted or painfully knotted fur should also be removed.

A long-lasting antibiotic, such as Convenia, should be administered to prevent postoperative infections and to treat any other underlying infections. If antibiotics are needed after release, they should be given to the caretaker, who can mix crushed tablets or liquid medication into moist food. It is also recommended that a pain medication such as Trobutrol be administered.

Anesthetics

A number of general anesthetics, such as Telazol, Atropine, and Valium, are available for surgical procedures with a minimum of post-surgical trauma. Some veterinarians use an injectable combination of Telazol, Ketamine, and Xylazine.

Sutures

Absorbable sutures and surgical glue should be used to avoid the trauma of having to retrap cats for suture removal. Coated Vicryl or PDS (Polydioxanone) sutures are recommended for internal closure, and Nexaband S/C for external closure. This is very important as it will prevent any chance of evisceration.

Ear-Tipping

All feral cats, while still under general anesthesia, should have the top quarter inch of their left ear removed. The shape of this ear is then unmistakable, even from a distance. It must be emphasized that if too much of the pinna is removed, the ear looks cropped and may be aesthetically unacceptable to the cat caretakers. If too little is removed, the cat will not be identifiable from a distance. Also, if the cut is not straight, the silhouette is not distinctive enough. Hemostasis may be achieved in several ways: by following

Caretakers and vets know Dennis is neutered by his tipped ear.

the cut with digital pressure, electrocautery, or application of a styptic or drying antiseptic powder. Ear-tipping with a V shape is <u>NOT</u> recommended, because this can be confused with an injury from a fight.

Left ear-tipping is the preferred universal method for identifying sterilized feral cats belonging to managed colonies. Ear-tipping will easily allow the caretaker to spot a new cat entering the colony, and sterilized cats will not have to be re-trapped. Any ear-tipped cat trapped in error can easily be identified within the trap and released.

It is important that ear-tipping become common practice, because it is vital for identification and can save the animal's life. If an ear-tipped cat is caught by animal control, the staff will know that the cat comes from a managed colony and the cat can then be returned to the caretaker.

Alternatives to ear-tipping are not recommended; ear tags may fall out and collars can get caught on bushes and possibly choke or injure the cat, so neither should be used. And tattoos are hard to see by caretakers and animal control without trapping and handling the cat. Microchips, however, are a good idea, but only if used in conjunction with ear-tipping.

Vaccinations

Feral cats who are over one year old should be given a three-year rabies vaccine, along with a distemper vaccine (FVRCP) to prevent Rhinotracheitis, Calici, Panleukopenia, and *Chlamydia psittaci*. It is also highly recommended that a feline leukemia (FeLV) vaccine be administered, regardless of being tested for the disease. ACR's veterinarian administers a distemper vaccine which includes the FeLV vaccine; using this combination vaccine saves money in the long run over administering separate distemper and FeLV vaccines.

Treating for Internal and External Parasites

It is highly recommended that feral cats be treated for internal and external parasites. Topical treatments, such as Advantage Multi and Profender, can be applied while the cat is still under anesthesia. Caretakers can also be provided with pills like Capstar or Drontal, which can be crushed into food.

Testing for Viral Diseases

Each colony caretaker, shelter, and veterinarian must make their own decisions about how they wish to spend their resources, and which tests, if any, to perform. Testing for viral diseases, such as FeLV and FIV, in feral cat colonies should be optional and not mandatory. As discussed earlier, the rate of transmission for FeLV and FIV in feral cats is very low,

and sterilization will decrease the spread of these infections. Also, funds for sterilization programs are usually limited, therefore resources are better spent on sterilization and rabies vaccines, rather than on testing. (For more information, refer to the section on "To Test or Not to Test?" in the "Health Care for Feral Cats: Guidelines for Colony Caretakers" chapter.)

Kittens

Early age spay/neuter is highly recommended and can be performed on kittens who are eight- to 16-weeks-old, as long as they weigh at least two pounds. Please make sure they recover on heating pads and their body temperatures are closely monitored. To prevent hypoglycemia, kittens under four months of age should only fast for three to four hours prior to surgery, and they should also be encouraged to eat a small meal within one hour of recovery from surgery. In addition, all kittens should be examined for signs of upper respiratory infection. (Please refer to the "Early Age or Pediatric Spay/Neuter" chapter for more detailed information.)

Pregnant and Lactating Females

Colony caretakers should be advised against trapping lactating females, if possible, as her kittens could die from starvation and exposure while she is at the veterinary clinic. However, if a lactating female is inadvertently trapped, and her kittens can be located and fostered, the mother cat can be spayed through a flank incision, or even a midline incision, as long as the incisions are well sutured. Once fully recovered from anesthesia, a lactating female can be returned to the colony and reunited with her kittens to resume nursing, or she can be fostered along with her kittens.

Because healthy cats are euthanized in shelters every day and funds are usually limited, Alley Cat Rescue recommends that pregnant cats, who are not far along, should be spayed. If the caretaker wants to keep a pregnant cat, she should be fostered at the veterinary clinic or in a home until the kittens are born and have been weaned, then she can be spayed (and the kittens sterilized). Ultimately, the final decision should be made based on what is safest for the mother cat. All options should be discussed with the cat's caretaker prior to trapping, so that fostering arrangements can be made if necessary.

More information on safely fostering feral cats can be found in the "Feral Kittens and Pregnant Cats" chapter.

Postoperative Care

No cat should leave the clinic until fully conscious. Male cats need a minimum of an overnight stay in the clinic or in a home, where their recovery can be monitored. Female cats, especially previously

pregnant cats, need to be kept longer to recover properly; at least two or three days is recommended. Cats who appear to not be recovering well from surgery should be rechecked by a veterinarian prior to release. If a cat is not fully conscious after six hours, she may need fluids.

It is safest to allow the cat to recover in a large carrier or in a trap, because these can then be used for direct transportation to the colony site. This will lessen the risk of injury to humans and trauma to the cats, which can often occur while transferring cats from a cage to a carrier. Cover the trap with a sheet or towel to lessen the cat's stress.

If feral cats stay in cages at the clinic, remember they are wild. A small enclosure/den that can be secured shut can be placed inside of a cage. These boxes give feral cats somewhere to hide and will make them feel more secure. This will also prevent the cat from escaping, and make it safer and easier for staff to clean the cage. A sheet or towel should be pulled over the front of the cage. Make sure the cage is securely locked to prevent escape and label the cage card, "Warning! This Cat May Bite."

Never underestimate the ability or determination of feral cats to escape. Exercise great caution when changing cat litter or when feeding. Their sometimes docile appearance can be very deceptive, and they may lunge at the door in an attempt to escape.

What to Do if a Feral Cat Escapes in the Clinic

If a feral cat escapes from a trap or cage while in the clinic, a special net can be used to recapture the cat. Under no circumstances should anyone try to catch the cat by hand. Do not attempt to throw a towel or blanket over the cat; this is dangerous because the cat can still attack.

If the cat hides in an inaccessible place, it is best to set a trap. Cats can be left for three days without food to make them hungry enough to enter the trap. Water should be left for them outside of the trap.

Euthanasia

Veterinarians and colony caretakers should discuss guidelines for euthanizing feral cats prior to trapping. Most feral cats are healthy, and common illnesses and infections are easily treatable with antibiotics and parasite control measures. However, for conditions that require long-term, in-house care, but where such treatment is not possible, it is more humane to euthanize the cat than it would be to release her back outside. In extreme cases of injury or illness that exceed medical capabilities, the cat should also be euthanized. Euthanasia should only be practiced when all other options have been exhausted.

Conclusion

Feral cats can be difficult to handle and present certain challenges for a veterinarian and staff, but by following the simple steps mentioned above, TNR programs can be implemented with minimal mishaps. Gathering as much preliminary information as possible about a feral cat colony prior to trapping and communicating openly will ensure that the veterinarian and caretaker are on the same page.

Early Age or Pediatric Spay/Neuter

Traditionally, veterinarians sterilized kittens around six months of age. However, studies and statistics have shown that early age or pediatric spay/neuter surgery — between eight and 16 weeks of age — is safe and provides greater short- and long-term health benefits over waiting until later in development (Kustritz, 2002; Howe et al., 2000). Statistics also show that cats (and dogs) who are the healthiest and live the longest reside in states that have the highest spay and neuter rates (Banfield Pet Hospital, 2013). Early age spay/neuter is more commonly practiced than later-age procedures among veterinarians, yet some misconceptions surrounding this topic still remain.

Some individuals still think it is healthier to allow a female cat to give birth to one litter of kittens prior to being spayed, and that a female cat should not be spayed until after her first oestrus period. However, motherhood provides no extra health benefit to a female cat, and statistics show that quite the opposite is true. According to the 2013 "State of Pet Health Report" released by Banfield Pet Hospital, spaying female cats eliminates the risk of pyometra, a life-threatening infection of the uterus, and when female cats are spayed *before* their first oestrus cycle, the risk of them developing cervical, uterine, and mammary cancer is greatly reduced (Banfield Pet Hospital, 2013). Similar is true for male cats. Neutering decreases the chance of male cats developing prostatic enlargement and disease and eliminates the risk of testicular cancer (Banfield Pet Hospital, 2013).

Alley Cat Rescue

A beautiful spring kitten.

Some people also mistakenly believe that spaying or neutering a cat "too early" in development can result in behavioral problems, although once again the opposite has been found to be true. Neutering a male cat virtually eliminates spraying, or territorial urination. Neutered males also tend to be less aggressive (they fight less) and they roam less (they are not in search of mates). Unneutered cats are at four times the risk of being hit by a car than neutered cats, while unneutered cats are also three times more likely than neutered cats to need treatment for an animal bite (Banfield, 2013). In addition, decreased fighting reduces the chance of injuries and the risk of contracting a disease such as FIV.

All of these benefits add up to a much healthier life for spayed and neutered cats. On average, spayed females live 39 percent longer than unspayed females, and neutered males live a full 62 percent longer than those unneutered (Banfield Pet Hospital, 2013).

Early age spay/neuter has been endorsed by the American Veterinary Medical Association (AVMA), because it provides a solution to the overall need to stem the overpopulation of companion animals (Nolen, 2013). Further support for this procedure comes from the Association of Veterinarians for Animal Rights (AVAR), the American Animal Hospital Association (AAHA), the American Society for the Prevention of Cruelty to Animals (ASPCA), Spay USA, and the American Humane Association (AHA). There are also several statistics that create the incentive for cat rescuers and shelters to practice early age spay/neuter for kittens:

- Research shows that 40 to 50 percent of people adopting cats from rescue groups or shelters do not abide by the contracts that were signed at the time of the adoptions, including specific sterilization requirements (Hoskins, 2005).

- While some surveys show that 87 to 91 percent of companion cats have been spayed, 20 percent of those cats had produced at least one litter prior to being spayed (Christiansen, 1998).

- Cat guardians harbor serious misconceptions about the reproductive habits of cats. Eighty-four percent of 715 people surveyed believe cats cannot get pregnant before the age of six months (Christiansen, 1998).

- Euthanasia of healthy cats in shelters is the leading cause of death in cats. That is, more cats are deliberately killed for lack of homes and lack of space than those who die from feline diseases (Levy and Crawford, 2004).

With the statistics showing a low compliance rate on the agreements that the adopters have with shelters, along with the misconception that cats cannot get pregnant prior to six months of age, it has become more common for shelters and rescue groups to spay and neuter before adoption. With around three to four million cats and dogs destroyed each year in shelters, it is clear that overpopulation is the greatest killer of companion animals (The HSUS, 2014).

Some think there is an overpopulation of cats, with too many "backyard" animals being born each year, while others blame shelters, believing the shelters are not doing enough to place animals in new homes. Whatever the reasons, the bottom line is that in recent years the number of animals being euthanized has remained static at around three million (ASPCA, accessed 2014). Though current numbers are far lower than the 12-20 million cats and dogs killed each year in this country in the late 1980s (HSUS, 2014), it is unacceptable that millions are still being killed.

Overpopulation, however, is not a problem without a solution. Two important tools that reduce the number of unwanted animals without resorting to killing are early age spay/neuter and pre-adoption sterilization (spaying/neutering all animals before they are adopted into new homes.) Both factors will help not only put an end to the killing of perfectly healthy animals in our nation's shelters, but will also go a long way in stopping stray and outdoor cats from joining feral colonies.

Maggie Funkhouser

Keep kittens on a warming pad after spay/neuter surgery.

In addition to helping the greater community of cats in our country, early age spay/neuter helps the individual kittens. The procedure is safe, and kittens (as well as puppies) sterilized before they are twelve weeks old have even fewer complications from surgery than in procedures done on older cats (Lieberman, 1987). As long as veterinarians take the proper precautions, the risk to kittens receiving this surgery is minimal (Aronsohn and Fagella, 1993).

Such precautions include weighing kittens to ensure they are at least two pounds prior to undergoing surgery and closely monitoring their body temperature during and after surgery to prevent hypothermia; a warmed sheet or towel

can be placed under the surgical sheet during surgery, while a heating pad should be placed in a kitten's cage when coming out of anesthesia. To prevent low blood sugar or hypoglycemia, kittens under four months of age should only fast for three to four hours prior to surgery, and they should also be encouraged to eat a small meal within one hour of recovery from surgery. It is not recommended that litters of kittens be separated before surgery, and upon recovery from anesthesia, they should be immediately reunited to prevent unnecessary anxiety.

Alley Cat Rescue strongly believes that feral cat caretakers can be leaders in the efforts to increase early age spay/neuter of kittens. As individuals who deal directly with feral cats, caretakers are in a special position to stop overpopulation at its source. When possible, caretakers should try to trap feral kittens between eight and 16 weeks of age to be spayed or neutered. If your veterinarian does not provide early age sterilization for kittens, you can inform her of its life-saving benefits and encourage her to adopt this low-risk procedure. If we do not actively work to increase the number of cats spayed before they can have litters of their own, we are passively allowing overpopulation to continue. With early age spay/neuter, we can help cats and save lives.

Alley Cat Rescue

Feral kittens rescued by Alley Cat Rescue.

Left Lateral Flank Spay Technique

A survey of veterinarians in the United Kingdom showed that 96 percent performed ovariohysterectomies on cats using the flank laparatomy technique (side incision) over using the midline coeliotomy technique (midline incision) (Coe et al., 2006). British veterinarians prefer the flank spay, whereas U.S. veterinarians prefer to use the midline spay technique. Proponents of the flank spay technique believe there is less of a chance for infection at the wound site, and a decreased risk of evisceration occurring (internal organs protruding through the incision) should the incision break down post surgery (Remfry, 1996).

The Flank Spay Technique

A flank spay is when the incision is made on the left side (flank) of the body rather than on the midline of the abdomen. The spay procedure is the same as performed during the midline incision, and the same reproductive organs (ovaries) are removed with both procedures. However, British veterinarians also remove the entire uterus, along with the ovaries, during a flank spay to prevent future complications, such as pyometra (Remfry, accessed 2014).

As with a midline spay, the flank incision should be made as small as possible. Intradermal sutures should be used instead of skin sutures, to prevent the cat from pulling them out. And dissolvable sutures are highly recommended, as well as surgical skin glue.

Advantages of Using Flank Spay Technique

If the spay incision should break down after surgery, protrusion of vital organs through the incision is less likely with a flank incision (Remfry, accessed 2014). The flank position also helps the incision from becoming infected if the cat is not able to be kept in a perfectly clean environment following surgery.

Because the surgery is performed on the side of the body, monitoring the incision is much easier. The incision line can be seen from a distance without having to handle the cat; the midline technique, where the incision is made on the abdomen, requires the cat to be handled in order to clearly monitor its healing. Handling a feral cat less also equals less stress on the cat and less risk of injury for both cat and human.

Performing the flank incision is also beneficial if the cat has nursing kittens; however, because the approach is too small, it is not recommended for pregnant cats (Peterson, 2006). Since the flank incision is not made near the mammary glands, the female is able to be sterilized and her kittens can continue to nurse following surgery. Using the flank incision is more comfortable for the mother during postoperative recovery, and there is a lower risk of evisceration, because the nursing kittens are not pulling at the incision site like they would be if a midline incision was performed. In addition, mother cats often have large mammary glands from nursing. During a midline incision, excessive bleeding and leakage from the mammary glands can cause infection; this is avoided with the flank incision.

Disadvantages of Using Flank Spay Technique

A few disadvantages or complications that can arise from performing the flank spay have been noted as including "the possibility that the entire uterine body may be difficult to remove, a dropped ovarian pedicle may be difficult to recover, and that it may be difficult to expose the opposite ovary and uterine bifurcation" (Coe, 2006).

Also, because of the flank position, the scar will be covered over with fur once completely healed, making it difficult to identify a cat as being spayed. Occasionally the fur will regrow in a slightly different color or pattern following a flank spay, but the sure way to identify a cat as having been spayed is to ear-tip her. Ear-tipping feral cats is the universal symbol for a sterilized individual, regardless of which surgery technique was used.

adrigu via Flickr

Cat spayed using the midline approach. The incision is through the underbelly.

Postoperative Care

After all surgeries, Alley Cat Rescue recommends that both female and male feral cats receive a long-acting antibiotic to prevent infection and to help treat any underlying infections that may not be visible. All cats should be held for at least 24 to 48 hours to ensure they are fully conscious prior to being released. It is not recommended to trap lactating mothers; however, if one is inadvertently trapped, the flank surgery allows nursing felines to be released back to their litter within a 24-hour period. Most kittens around three weeks old should be able to survive in mild temperatures for about a day without their mothers.

Flank Spay in the U.S.

Despite the majority of British veterinarians preferring the flank spay, many U.S. veterinarians believe the midline ovariohysterectomy is the safest procedure to perform. Their primary concerns regarding the flank incision include limited access to the cat's abdomen should complications, such as bleeding, arise, and difficulty identifying a previously spayed cat (not all vets will know to check for a surgery scar on the flank, and not all flank-spayed feral cats will be properly identified by ear-tipping) (McGrath, et al., 2004).

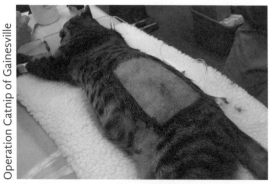

Cat being prepared for a flank approach spay procedure, often favored by colony caretakers for its visibility from a distance. The incision is through the left side.

However, some veterinarians in the U.S. do choose to perform the flank spay, citing a few advantages to the procedure over the traditional midline approach. Some feel the flank incision to be safer, as the incision is less affected by gravi-

tational forces than the midline incision, and that the overlapping musculature on a cat's flank protects against evisceration should the closing sutures fail. The flank spay can also save time for veterinarians, as the relevant organs can be easier to find through a flank incision (McGrath, et. al., 2004).

Operation Catnip in Raleigh, North Carolina and Florida, use the flank procedure for feral cats. They like the advantage of being able to view the incision through a cage during recovery so the cats need not be handled (Operation Catnip, accessed 2015). The few veterinarians who use this method claim they have not experienced excessive bleeding using the flank incision and they ensure sterile surgeries to prevent infections.

Conclusion

There is no standard surgical approach to spaying cats; both the flank and midline techniques safely sterilize female cats in about the same amount of time, with about the same amount of difficulty (Coe, 2006). In comparing the flank and midline approaches, Coe and others concluded that "neither approach has any particular advantage over the other," and "the authors consider that the midline approach is preferable, predominantly because the uterus sometimes cannot be identified from the flank approach, and it is difficult to be certain whether this is a technical problem or the cat has already been neutered, without exploring from a midline approach" (Coe, 2006).

Chemical Sterilization

History of Non-Surgical Sterilization Methods

In 1963 it was discovered that drugs called synthetic progestins could suppress oestrus (heat cycle) in female cats. Denmark was one of the first countries to try the drug progestin megestrol acetate where, in 1971, several colonies of outdoor cats were administered low doses of 2.5 to 5mg orally once per week to prevent oestrus. Out of nearly 500 females to whom the bait was available, 20 became pregnant, five aborted, one died giving birth, and 14 produced normal litters. In some instances, cats developed mammary and cystic tumors as well as pyometra (a serious and potentially deadly condition in which the uterus becomes infected and filled with fluid) (Kristensen, 1980).

In 1977, Dr. Jenny Remfry worked with the Universities Federation for Animal Welfare to carry out several field trials for megestrol acetate in the United Kingdom. At the end of the study Remfry concluded: "Even the most reliable helper may be unable to ensure that a feral cat receives her weekly dose. Therefore trap-ping and spaying is probably still the best method available to stabilize cat populations" (Remfry, 1978).

In 1984, a study conducted in Billings, Montana, used the drug megestrol acetate on cats. Approximately 70 percent of the cats did not produce kittens. However there were still some kittens born in the colony because some female cats did not receive adequate doses of the drug (Kirkpatrick and Turner, 1985).

Nancy North

Chemical sterilization is being investigated as an alternative to traditional surgical procedures, as it could provide a cheaper and less labor-intensive method of sterilizing large numbers of cats quickly in remote or hard-to-reach locations.

In 1998, news of a new contraceptive grabbed headlines. A student at the Virginia-Maryland Regional College of

Veterinary Medicine, Michelle Meister-Weisbarth, received a grant from the Geraldine R. Dodge Foundation to develop a modified strain of the *Salmonella* bacterium that can be administered to cats through an oral bait. Making use of genetic engineering and molecular biology, the vaccine (for females only) causes the cat to produce antibodies that block the attachment of the sperm to the egg (Syufy, accessed 2014).

In 2000, the Alliance for Contraception in Cats and Dogs (ACC&D) was founded by Drs. Henry Baker, Stephen Boyle, and Brenda Griffin as a program of Auburn University. The organization's mission is to develop non-surgical birth control methods for managing cat and dog populations. In many developing nations where poverty is endemic, veterinary care and population control is usually non-existent. Surgical sterilization, especially for large populations of feral cats and dogs, is not feasible in these areas. Providing non-surgical methods of sterilization would make population control easier, faster, and cheaper (ACC&D, accessed 2014).

Types of Non-Surgical Sterilization

Chemical Castration

Several methods of chemical castration exist, with some already approved by the FDA and others undergoing field trials. Chemical castration has been studied for nearly 50 years and targets the destruction of gonadal cells in males causing infertility by a lack of sperm production (Hedge, 2013).

One such chemical castration drug is Zeuterin, also known as EsteriSol. It is a zinc gluconate compound that acts like a spermicide and destroys spermatozoa in all stages of development and maturation. Only one intratesticular injection is necessary for irreversible sterility. Since the testicles are left intact, a low level of testosterone is still produced. Zeuterin has only been approved by the Food and Drug Administration (FDA) for male dogs in the U.S.; however, it has been approved for cats in other countries (ACC&D, accessed 2014).

Immunocontraception

Researchers at the USDA Animal and Plant Health Inspection Service National Wildlife Research Center (NWRC) developed a GnRH (gonadotropin-releasing hormone) immunocontraceptive vaccine called GonaCon. When the GnRH vaccine is injected, the body's immune response neutralizes the hormone's function, resulting in infertility in both males and females (National Wildlife Research Center, 2011). Scientists say the vaccine shows great promise as a wildlife infertility agent to be used instead of lethal control (Levy et al., 2011).

In 2011, scientists at the University of Florida found that a single dose of GonaCon controls fertility for at least five months and up to five years in adult female cats. Single dose vaccinations were given to 15 female cats and placebos to five others. All five cats given placebos became pregnant. Of the cats treated with GonaCon, 93 percent remained infertile for the first year, 73 percent for two years, 53 percent for three years, and 27 percent were still infertile for five years as the cats' antibodies to the vaccine decreased (Carey, 2011).

"We're hoping this research will lead to a nonlethal method of control for feral cat populations that is less expensive, labor-intensive, and invasive than current methods, such as surgical sterilization," said Julie Levy, DVM, Ph.D., lead researcher of the study and director of the Maddie's Shelter Medicine Program at the University of Florida (Carey, 2011).

Sex Steroid Hormones

Progestins are synthetic hormones designed to control fertility. "Progestins continue to be used in pet cats as well as adjunct or alternative to surgical sterilisation through TNR programs" (Romagnoli, 2015). One commonly used progestin is Megestrol acetate or MA.

MA is used as an oral contraceptive for female cats and dogs to prevent oestrus. It is available in several countries under different brand names and in generic form. In the U.S., generic forms of the drug are available; a low-dose version of the drug was previously sold as FeralStat for contraception of feral cats but it is no longer on the market. MA is also used to treat behavior disorders and skin conditions in cats (ACC&D, 2009).

MA can increase the risk of severe adverse reactions in cats, such as pyometra, developing diabetes, and an increased risk of mammary cancer (ACC&D, 2009). However 50 years of clinical research now suggests that "low doses [of MA] can be used relatively safely in cats" (Romagnoli, 2015). Proper MA dosage is vital in reducing side effects; cats are usually given too high of a dose.

Shaida Tala Sabin

Chemical sterilization could be used to treat feral cats where they are, in large, open spaces.

Conclusion

Alley Cat Rescue believes that chemical sterilants *can* have a place in controlling cat colonies in the U.S. but at this time, they cannot adequately *replace* surgical sterilization. There are several promising oral contraceptives and vaccines in existence but most are still in trial phases and are a long way from being approved by the FDA. Most of these chemical sterilants also require the cat to be trapped in order to administer the dose, and the cats need to be dosed regularly in order to be effective.

Subsequently, Trap-Neuter-Return (TNR) is still the *best* method for sterilizing feral cats in urban and suburban areas of the U.S, where veterinary services are available and caretakers are willing to pay to provide the best care for the cats. TNR not only reduces populations, but it also improves the health of the cats. Spaying/neutering greatly reduces their risk of reproductive cancers, while vaccinations, proper diet, and parasite treatments help boost their immune systems. Providing rabies vaccines also protects the public, especially in developing countries where the rate of rabies transmission is high.

ACR does, however, agree with the goals set out by the ACC&D and similar organizations for developing non-surgical methods of population control and also recognizes the urgent need for such chemical sterilants in developing countries and areas with large, extensive open space. In areas where veterinary care is already limited, surgical methods of sterilization (spay/neuter) are not feasible at this time. Furthermore, vast areas of open wilderness provides another hurdle for implementing TNR programs, so administering a chemical sterilant would be most helpful. Populations of stray cats and dogs are commonly poisoned, shot, drowned, or electrocuted to control their numbers. The newer methods of oral contraception can certainly alleviate this suffering and needless loss of life, and hopefully engender a new ethic in these places for humane control.

Guidelines for Establishing an Effective Adoption Program

This section of the handbook provides guidelines to help rescuers rehome, or adopt out, friendly stray cats and any feral cats and kittens who have been socialized. As mentioned previously, removing and rehoming friendly cats from outdoor colonies is part of a successful Trap-Neuter-Return (TNR) program, because it helps decrease the number of cats living in a colony (making the colony more manageable).

The top priority of every adoption program is the health and well-being of the cat.

Louise Holton

Plus, if the resources are available to place them into homes, it is not necessary for socialized cats to live in colonies — unlike their feral counterparts, who are not well-suited for adoption into a home. (However, some adult feral cats can be "adopted" by their caretakers and, over time, they may become assimilated to living indoors. Refer to "Adopting Adult Feral Cats" for more information, and see also "Guidelines for Safely Relocating Feral Cats" when rehoming feral cats.)

Rescuers can work on their own to place cats and kittens into homes or they may choose to work with an organization that already has an established adoption program. Depending on the number of cats and kittens one is rehoming, it might be more practical to contact a local rescue organization for assistance, since they already have the resources in place. Though please note, most rescue organization are always "full," meaning they do not have open space to accept new cats, so it is usually necessary for individual rescuers to work on their own to rehome cats.

However, many rescue organizations do have a waiting list and may offer to add individual rescuer names to the list and contact them once space becomes available to take in new cats. Therefore, it is recommended that individual rescuers have their names added to these waiting lists and work with established rescue organizations in conjunction with re-homing cats on their own. Finding suitable homes for adoptable cats can be challenging, so all available resources should be utilized.

Tips for Rehoming Cats and Kittens

In rehoming cats, word of mouth is the most useful tool one can have. Simply talking with friends, family, coworkers, neighbors, and even your local postal workers, school bus drivers, and land-scapers can lead to finding suitable homes for adoptable cats. Engaging in friendly conversation regarding com-panion animals can help one provide information about a cat or kitten who is in need of a home. And having a few cute photographs on hand to show pro-spective adopters is a bonus; remember the adage, a picture is worth a thousand words?

ACR volunteer, Victoria, at an adoption event.

To aid in conversation, creating a simple flyer for each cat or litter of kittens you are trying to rehome can be another great adoption tool. The more visibility you can provide for the cat, the increased chanc-es you will have of finding her a home. Include important information such as: the cat has been spayed or neutered; she is current on vaccinations; she has been tested for disease, treated for parasites, and microchipped; and mention if she gets along well with other cats or dogs. (It is highly recommended that all cats and kittens are spayed or neutered prior to rehoming to prevent unwanted litters. Plus, a sterilized and vaccinated cat of-fers more incentive for potential adopt-ers and for rescue organizations to work with you, because you have already done some of the hard work for them.) Also include your contact information, such as phone number and/or email address, but do not give out your home address — only provide personal information to those you know and trust.

Each flyer should include at least one photograph, though additional photos can be more appealing, and consider adding some information regarding the cat's personality or intriguing traits, such as: she is a lap cat, she is highly indepen-dent, the cat loves to sit in windows, or she is great with children. Keep in mind to only provide information that will help get potential adopters to contact you. If the cat has special needs (such as a shy cat, a senior cat, or an FIV+ cat), you can ease into these details once you have the person on the phone and you can provide more information in conver-sational form.

Adding these details to a flyer can be off-putting to some adopters, because they don't necessarily know what these details mean. Explaining special-needs cases to potential adopters via conversation and providing supplemental information can make all the difference in finding special-needs cats suitable homes. Though please make sure all important details are disclosed to adopters to prevent the cat from being returned or abandoned.

Supply flyers to those you speak with and ask them to share with their friends and family. Contact local businesses and see if they would be willing to hang your flyers for clients to see. Think animal-friendly businesses like veterinarian hospitals and pet-supply stores; though other businesses may be willing to help if the owner and/or staff likes animals.

Take advantage of social media to help find homes for adoptable cats and kittens. With countless individuals having access to the Internet, using social media sites like Facebook, Twitter, and Instagram will greatly increase visibility and the potential of finding the perfect home. These sites offer quick and easy sharing with the click of a button! Or consider creating your own blog or website. With numerous how-to videos and tutorials available online, following a few simple steps can help you create your own online adoption site.

You can also ask local rescue organizations if they would be willing to post your cats on their website or to their Petfinder.com and Pets911.com accounts, if they utilize those sites. Again, rescue organizations might not be able to physically house cats you are trying to rehome, but they might be willing to provide you with online assistance, so it never hurts to ask. Please note, we do not recommend using websites like Craigslist to rehome cats, for they can attract individuals who may not have good intentions for animals.

Another great idea for rehoming cats is to give potential adopters the option of first fostering a cat or kitten. Providing a trial period is a great way to help some individuals get over the fear of commitment. When a person is permitted to foster a cat for a month or two, to see if the cat will be happy in her new home and to see if the cat will get along with other cats, dogs, or even children, this can help relieve some of the initial hesitation and reservation. This is also a great way to see if this is the right home for the cat; some cats have a more difficult time adjusting to new surroundings and to new people and animals. In addition, fostering can serve as a way to screen potential adopters to ensure they will be responsible guardians. An initial foster period is beneficial for both parties involved and ensures a better fit for all.

Lastly, be creative, persistent, and patient! Think outside of the box when trying to rehome a cat. Share cute stories or stories of triumph and use great photos to pull on the heart strings of people. Explain why a particular cat is so special and how wonderful it would be if she was adopted. Paint a picture for people. And don't give up! Rehoming a cat can be challenging, so remember to be persistent (utilizing all available tools) and be patient. You might not rehome a cat overnight, but with some time and some effort you will find the right home for her.

Four-day-old kitten fostered by ACR.

Adoption Guidelines and Forms

These next few paragraphs and accompanying forms, which can be found in the back of the handbook, are meant to help guide individual rescuers who are rehoming cats and kittens on their own. If you are working with a rescue organization to place cats, they will most likely have their own guidelines and forms to use, so be sure to inquire about their specific formalities.

Prior to rehoming a cat or kitten, Alley Cat Rescue provides all potential adopters with an adoption application and a list of guidelines they will be expected to follow. ACR wants to see our rescued cats placed in homes where they will be treated as a member of the family for the rest of their lives which, with care, can be from 15 to 20 years. Therefore, if some potential adopters do not feel they can appropriately adhere to our guidelines, then we suggest they reconsider whether or not adopting a cat at this time is right for them.

As part of an initial screening for adopters, you may also want to consider requesting a few references, including their veterinarian. This will allow you to ask a few friends, family members, or colleagues about the potential adopters' previous companion animals, if they had any, and to gauge if the individual has the appropriate time and space to devote to a new companion animal. You could either call the references or email them a short questionnaire.

Upon adopting a cat from ACR, individuals must sign a legal contract stating compliance with our requirements, which are in the best interests of the cat. Again, in reading over the adoption contract, if any potential adopters do not feel they are able to comply fully, it is recommended that they abstain from adopting a cat at this time. ACR would rather an individual be upfront about their reservations and possible non-compliance with our guidelines and contracts, than adopt out a cat only to have her returned or abandoned.

To ensure a recently adopted cat is adjusting well to her new environment, ACR highly recommends conducting a

114

post-adoption follow-up. This can be in the form of an email, a phone call, or a pre-scheduled visit. Following up with recent adopters not only gives you peace of mind, but it also allows for individuals to ask questions or express any concerns. Most adopters are happy to hear from you and are excited to share news regarding their new family member.

Important Notes

- Work in conjunction with a rescue organization, even if it is just for advice or online posting assistance. It never hurts to ask.

- Offer a foster period to potential adopters to help alleviate any initial hesitation and/or reservations. Be willing to work with adopters.

- Ask potential adopters for a few references (including their veterinarian), so you can better ensure the cat will be adopted by a responsible, caring individual.

- If possible, offer adopters the ability to contact you post-adoption with questions or concerns.

- Please note that only some rescue organizations have a no-kill policy, meaning they do not euthanize healthy animals, and all animals are kept until adopted. County-run shelters in particular usually do NOT operate under a no-kill policy, meaning they will euthanize healthy animals if they need to free up space for incoming animals. Most county-run

shelters have a time limit of a few days to adopt out animals, but once that specified limit is reached, the animal is killed. In one sampling of shelters and other organizations, shelters were found to euthanize 71 to 72 percent of all cats who enter (The NCPPSP, 1997). So before you agree to work with an organization, ask them specifically if they operate under a no-kill policy.

- It is highly recommended that all cats and kittens who are up for adoption are spayed or neutered prior to being rehomed. Remember, these cats and kittens came from outdoor colonies with unsterilized cats. The key to a successful TNR program and to ending cat homelessness is through spaying and neutering.

- It is highly recommended that all cats and kittens are properly vaccinated prior to rehoming. Providing vaccines prevents disease and other health conditions, some of which can be fatal. It is always best to ensure a cat or kitten receives her initial vaccinations, so her immune system can build up antibodies to resist potential future exposures.

- It is highly recommended that all cats and kittens are treated for internal and external parasites prior to rehoming. These parasites can cause health issues and should be prevented.

- It is highly recommended that all cats and kittens are tested for FeLV and FIV prior to rehoming. Testing a cat prior to adoption can prevent cats from being returned, abandoned, or killed, should she be later tested and found to be positive for either disease. Some veterinarians still recommend to their clients to euthanize FeLV and FIV positive cats, which is not necessary. Therefore, it is safer to test the cat prior to rehoming so potential adopters are aware of her special needs.

- Always keep safety in mind. Never give out your personal information, such as your home address, whether it be listed on a flyer, a website, or to someone you recently met. Instead only provide your phone number and/or email address as the primary method for contacting you. And suggest meeting potential adopters at their house, so you can inspect the home and gauge if you think it is a safe environment for the cat; take a friend with you or let someone know

where you will be.

- Never use the words "Free to good home" on flyers or online sites. Advertising "free" animals can attract individuals who may not have good intentions for the animals. Unfortunately, some people who are looking only to make money and do not care for the well-being of animals are drawn to such ads, particularly those looking to sell animals to research laboratories or breeding facilities. Sometimes it can be helpful to mention an adoption fee to dissuade these individuals and to only attract those who are truly interested in adoption. Plus, asking for a small adoption fee can help recoup some of your veterinary costs, and allow you to rescue more cats. Avoid using websites like Craigslist when rehoming cats; there have been reports of individuals with bad intentions adopting cats from such sites.

Adopting Adult Feral Cats

More than 30 percent of individuals acquire their cat(s) by feeding a hungry stray cat who shows up at their door (ASPCA, accessed 2014). The cat probably became lost or was dumped outside to fend for herself. At first, the cat may be shy and somewhat afraid of people, but usually with lots of love, shelter, and food, she will start to trust people again and can be reintroduced to indoor life.

On the other hand, even though a feral cat may frequent porches and be regularly seen sleeping in garages and sheds, she probably has lived her entire life with minimal human contact and will most likely remain feral. She knows that humans can provide food and shelter, but she will keep her distance and may run and hide if approached too closely. This behavior is true for most feral cats, though some individuals may become comfortable with their caretaker (to varying degrees) and be able to adjust to life indoors. So while adopting a stray is more likely, it is not impossible to adopt a feral cat.

There are two different scenarios in which an adult feral cat can be socialized. In the first scenario, the cat is living outdoors and you simply build on your current relationship through regular encounters. The second scenario involves socializing a feral cat who is confined to a cage in your house. Please note, the first scenario is safer for both parties and is recommended over the latter. In cases where a feral cat requires indoor confinement (if she sustained an injury and requires constant care and medication or you are fostering a pregnant or nursing feral cat), it is possible to socialize the cat while practicing extreme caution. In either case, patience, persistence, and positive reinforcement can help build trust in the relationship.

Nancy North

Feral cat in Buenos Aires.

If it is necessary to confine a feral cat indoors, you will need a large cage and a

Personal Account from Louise Holton

In dealing with thousands of feral cats over the years and listening to stories at conferences where I have spoken about Trap-Neuter-Return (TNR), someone usually stands up and tells a story about a feral cat they took inside, who after some time, sat on their lap and purred.

On the other hand, I could tell you the story of Katie, who came to me as a young four-month-old kitten. She was very wild and arrived with four other feral cats. After sterilizing them, I sent the four others to a barn home, as people were threatening to poison their small colony. Initially, Katie suffered from chronic conjunctivitis that simply would not clear for the first seven years of her life. Because of this, I decided not to let her go to the barn home with the other feral cats.

Despite being a kitten when she came to me, Katie resisted every attempt to be socialized. Katie passed on in 2014 at the ripe old age of 21, but always remained independent. In her later years she slowed down a lot, and lived mostly on the top of a cat tree near my desk, where I work all day. If I tried to touch her, she would turn around and hiss and spit at me. If I got too close, she would strike out with her claws.

Although she never lost her feral personality, I know she lived happily alongside my other cats. She ate well, used the litter box, and fortunately, she was never sick much in her life after the initial conjunctivitis cleared up. She was not socialized as a kitten and was determined to keep it that way her whole life. I know Katie mostly trusted me, as long as I continued to provide her food and did not mess with her!

I know some caretakers get frustrated when they cannot pet or cuddle a rather wild cat. But, if you can stand it, and have other cats to pet, a feral cat like Katie who is content living in your home and does not want contact, can be quite happy!

cat den for her to hide in to feel safe. It is highly recommended that you keep the cage in a spare bedroom or other room that has limited foot traffic. Line the cage with newspaper, provide plenty of fresh, clean blankets, and cover the top of the cage with a folded sheet. Prior to bringing a feral cat into your home, make sure you read over the chapters which discuss proper handling and fostering guidelines to prevent any mishaps.

Building Confidence and Trust

Building confidence and trust with a feral cat is the most important part of the relationship. It also requires a lot of patience and persistence, for socializing a feral cat takes time. At first a feral cat will be terrified of you. A bond will not form overnight; it may take months or years for a feral cat to trust humans. And even then, each cat is different, having her own personal degree of comfort with human closeness and contact. Some feral cats may only bond with their caretaker(s) and hide from new people.

It is important not to rush or push a feral cat into trusting you. Forcing the issue will not help, but rather could hinder or set back any progress you have made. Sudden movements and forced contact can scare the cat and reinforce her wariness of humans. Building a relationship must be done at her pace. And always keep in mind that you may never gain a feral cat's trust enough to where you can pet her, let alone bring her into your house. It is helpful to have a plan in mind if you are able to socialize a feral cat; however, it is not wise to become overly obsessed with any preconceived notions you may have about your relationship — only time will reveal the level of human closeness and contact the cat will tolerate.

Working with a Feral Cat Outdoors

It is most common for an individual to socialize a feral cat by working with her while she is in her outdoor home. Providing a reliable food source and shelter will help build a trustful relationship. It is also important to establish a permanent feeding area and a set schedule; most animals find security in routine. Make sure the feeding station and shelter are in an area with limited foot traffic and keep the area clean. Do not leave excess food available, especially overnight, to prevent other animals like raccoons, skunks, and opossums from hanging

around. And try to provide a shelter that does not draw attention.

Feral cat Mango, trapped by ACR in Los Angeles, CA.

Desireé Stapley

Once a regular feeding schedule has been established and the cat seems to realize this is her new home, you can start to socialize with her by sitting nearby while she is eating. (Sitting helps to reduce the appearance of you being a large threat; get down on her level.) Sit as close to her as she will allow without running away. At first you may need to be quiet, not making any noise, and just be in her presence. Eventually you can start to talk to her in a soft, soothing voice, and make your way closer to her. Allow her to smell your hands and become familiar with your scent. Some feral cats will permit petting while they are eating, for it provides a happy distraction; again, just use caution when trying to make physical contact. It may take several weeks or months to reach the point in your relationship where she will seek out your affection and allow physical contact. Remember to take things slowly and try not to let her sense any frustration if this process is taking some time.

Moving Her Indoors

Either before or after you have made physical contact with her, you can begin to coax her into your house. It is much easier to help a feral cat become accustomed to being indoors when you have an enclosed porch area, basement, or other room that is closed off from the rest of the house, where you can safely leave a door cracked open to the outside. At first, she will need to know that she can escape if she feels frightened. Use food to entice her into the new area and set up an additional shelter, using blankets that already have her scent on them. You will also want to set up a litter box. It can be a balancing act when transitioning a feral cat from one area to another. You do not want to completely remove her original food source or shelter until she is comfortable with the new set up. Making drastic changes suddenly can make her uneasy and can harm the trust you have established, so take it slowly. It is recommended that once she becomes comfortable living in her new area, that you close the door during the night to increase her safety. Cats, like many animals, are nocturnal and most active at night.

Once she has become comfortable with living on the porch or in the basement, you can decide if you want to introduce her to the rest of the house or if you want to simply call this space her home. There are quite a few additional items to consider when deciding whether to introduce a feral cat to living in a house. You will need to take into account your house's dynamics (other animals, small children, how busy and loud), and it will depend on the cat, if she will want to live fully indoors. Many caretakers have "porch cats" or "basement cats" who are content living on their porches and in their basements with no desire to live in the house. And there is no reason to force the issue. Providing her a warm, safe place she can live for the rest of her life is more than most feral cats have.

If you do decide to try to introduce her to the rest of the house, you can use the same steps of transition as before. Allow the door adjacent to the porch or basement to remain open at first, so she can escape back to her area where she is most comfortable. It is helpful to keep bedrooms and other spare rooms closed to help minimize the amount of new space she has to explore and the amount of hiding places available. When feral cats are introduced to new areas they tend to hide. You need to be careful not to allow her to hide for long periods of time, because going without human contact for too long could cause her to revert back to her wary self. Remember to use caution, only allowing her in the house when supervised. As you and her become more comfortable with her being in the house, you can allow her to have free-range with less supervision. This method of transition is recommended when no other animals live in the house. (However, if you do decide to use this method to introduce her to the rest of the house and you have other animals, it is highly recommended that they be confined, so she can explore the house without intimidation.)

<u>If other animals live in the house, it is best to first confine her to a single room for a short time</u>. This will allow her some time to get comfortable with her new surroundings and living indoors, before the added stress of being introduced to new animals. Adapting to a new territory and adapting to new animals at the same time is not recommended. Introducing too many new elements at one time can be overwhelming and may hinder any progress you have made in building trust with her. The more comfortable she feels around new cats and dogs, the easier it will be to introduce her to the rest of the house; eliminating one stress at a time is very beneficial to her progress. The following two sections go into greater detail on the process of helping a feral cat become accustomed to living indoors and how to safely introduce new animals to one another.

Please keep in mind, whichever method(s) you use to transition a feral cat to living indoors, be very cautious that any sudden and dramatic changes can be especially frightful. You do not want to traumatize her. So take your time, be patient, and use baby steps when working to gain her trust and grow your relationship.

Working with a Feral Cat Indoors

For a feral cat who is confined to a cage indoors, the routine of providing fresh food and water, scooping the litter box, and changing the newspaper and bedding will help aid in gaining the cat's trust. These regular visits reinforce to the cat that you are not there to harm her but rather to provide for her. Always remember to be especially cautious when opening the cage door; cats are fast and she may attempt to escape. Move slowly, without any sudden movements, and use a quiet, soothing voice. Also, it is highly recommended that a cat den be added to the cage to give the cat a place to retreat to when you are in her space; providing a den will help her feel more safe.

Allow her to smell your hands, either through the bars of the cage or inside the cage, so she becomes familiar with your scent. You can also feed her meaty human baby food on your fingers. Over time, if she is starting to warm up to you, she may rub her face against your hand and begin to invite physical contact. Again, only proceed to the next step of the relationship when the cat cues you to do so. Reaching into the cage and trying to engage in physical contact before she is ready will most certainly result in a defensive behavior (scratching or biting) and can set back any progress you have made. With time and patience, hopefully she will show signs of interest in receiving your contact.

To ease any stress or tension, you can leave a radio or television playing softly. The constant chatter can help a cat get used to human voices and help her to not feel alone when you are not in the room. Utilizing products, such as sprays and plug-in diffusers, that simulate natural cat hormones can aid in relaxation. And lighting lavender scented candles or wearing lavender essential oil, while you

121

are in the room, can help ease anxiety. Still, never leave a burning candle unattended and do not wear too much oil, as to completely cover your natural scent.

Another option is to allow a friendly cat to hang out in the room with you, while visiting the feral cat. Cats are "copycats" and if another cat is purring and being friendly to a human, the feral cat will see this and may become more trusting. Just be sure to keep the feral cat confined and do not allow the friendly cat to be in the room without supervision; this will prevent any inappropriate behavior such as bullying. And always make sure all cats have been vaccinated and neither cat is showing signs of illness (sneezing, running nose, or eyes) prior to making introductions.

Alley Cat Rescue

Denise, an ACR "office" cat, is guarded around humans when alone, but becomes friendly and affectionate when other feline friends are close by.

To increase your engagement with the cat and also ease stress, you can begin to play with her. Wand-like toys (the ones with strings attached to long sticks) are perfect for prompting play. Again, use slow, non-threatening motions and only continue these actions if she seems interested in responding; do not force the issue if she seems agitated. You may want to adhere a wand toy to the cage or leave a ball in the cage, so she can play on her own, and try giving her small amounts of catnip. Remember to provide positive reinforcement for any and all good behavior, such as giving her a few treats and praising her.

As she becomes more comfortable with you playing and petting her, you can slowly allow her to venture out of the cage. To prevent her from hiding and reverting back to her wary nature, keep her confined to that room. Make sure all doors and windows are closed and, if possible, make sure there are not too many pieces of furniture for her to hide under (though having a cardboard box or two in the room, where she can "hide" for a bit to feel safe can be helpful.) You just do not want her to be able to hide somewhere that you will not be able to coax her out. Take some time to build on this stage, allowing her plenty of time to settle into her room, and remember not to push her too fast onto the next step.

After she has sufficiently settled into her room, if you have other companion animals, now is the perfect time to slowly introduce them to one another. As stated in the previous section, the more comfortable she feels around new cats and dogs, the easier it will be to introduce her to the rest of the house; eliminating one stress at a time is very beneficial to her progress. If you allowed another cat into her room, as suggested to help with socialization, she may already be familiar and partially comfortable with your other cat and that is a great step. The animals should also be able to smell each other and perhaps even reach each other under the door, which helps.

When introducing another cat or dog to the feral cat, it is safest to re-confine her to a cage to make initial introductions. It is difficult to determine how each animal will react to one another, so it is best to have a barrier at first. Only allow one additional animal in the room with her at a time; you do not want to overwhelm her or make her feel threatened. After a week or so of introductions through a barrier, you can work up to allowing more intimate interactions. (The next section will go into greater detail on how to introduce new animals safely.)

Once she has made introductions with her other housemates and they seem to get along for the most part (some initial minor fighting is to be expected until everyone has reached an understanding), you can slowly introduce her to the rest of the house. Allow her to explore the remaining rooms for short periods of time, while supervised of course, and confine her back to her room so she can feel safe. It is helpful to keep bedrooms and other spare rooms closed to help minimize the amount of new space she has to explore and the amount of hiding places available. At first, you might also want to confine your other companion animals to allow the feral cat to explore; this can be a delicate balance, so use your best judgment of the situation. Continue with periods of exploration and periods of confinement until you and her feel comfortable with her having free-range of the entire house.

Tips for Introducing New Cats Safely

The most important tip to remember when introducing new cats to one another, is to <u>ensure all individuals are spayed or neutered and vaccinated prior to initial contact</u>. You do not want to contribute to the cat overpopulation problem due to accidental pregnancies, nor do you want to transmit any disease, so please take all precautions. It is also highly recommended that all cats are tested for disease prior to making any new introductions. And cats should be treated for internal (worms) and external (fleas) parasites to prevent transmission. (Please refer to "Health Care for Feral Cats: Guidelines for Colony Caretakers" for more information.) Make sure there are no visible signs of illness in either cat, such as an eye infection or upper respiratory infection, prior to making introductions; it is much easier to treat one cat over having to treat two or more cats for an illness. And, again, take it <u>SLOWLY</u> when introducing new animals to one another.

As mentioned above, the best way to introduce a new cat to another cat (or dog) is to confine the new cat to a single room for a few weeks. This will allow her some time to adjust to her new environment without any intimidation from her housemates, while also providing her a place where she can feel safe. The new cat can make her initial acquaintance with a protective barrier in place. It is highly recommended, especially when introducing a feral cat to other animals, that you also use a large crate to help facilitate introductions. <u>Always supervise and only allow one additional animal in the room with her at a time</u>.

Initially, the animals should show interest in wanting to smell each other and they may even reach through the bars to bat at each other. Hissing, growling, and some swatting is to be expected. Promote good behavior and help keep the cats calm by offering treats (meaty baby food, without onion, fed on a spoon or your fingertip is a particularly tasty snack), petting them, and using a soothing voice to praise. Use a wand toy to coax them to play together through the bars. Be consistent in training them on what actions are viewed as acceptable and which are not.

After a week or two of getting acquainted through a barrier, you can slowly allow more intimate interactions. It is advised to have a spray bottle of water on hand to correct any bad behavior and to safely break up any fighting. It may take some time for the cats to work out their hierarchy of who is "top cat." Sit on the floor in front of the cage and gently coax the feral cat out into the room, while keeping an attentive eye on your other cat.

At this stage, they should be fairly familiar with each other and engage in a nose-to-nose greeting. As they continue to thoroughly smell each other, some hissing and swatting may occur. Be prepared to correct any behavior before it escalates into fighting. A few squirts from a water bottle should defuse any fighting or you can make a loud noise, such as clapping your hands, to startle them. <u>Never use your hands to break up a cat fight</u>; this is very dangerous and could result in injury. Allow the cats to interact with each other for short periods of time, building up to longer visits. Use your best judgment to gauge each cat's ability to tolerate the other in deciding how long each visit should last.

Utilizing products, such as sprays and plug-in diffusers that simulate natural cat hormones, can help alleviate stress and tension and aid in relaxation. In addition to a pleasing lavender scent through candles or oils, adding a few drops of a calming agent to the cat's water can also help. Always read the labels before using any products and provide supervision during initial use to make sure your cat(s) do not have any allergic reactions. (Refer to the Helpful Resources section for a list of companies who make such products and where you can purchase them.)

Again, toys can be a great way to facilitate interaction between cats, while relieving stress. Most cats can be easily coaxed into playing with one another, because it creates a distraction that is positive. When both cats are enjoying themselves and having fun, they are less likely to be bothered by the other's presence. Wand toys and laser pointers are especially helpful in directing joint play sessions, as well as the circular cardboard scratchers that have a track for a ball; get the ball spinning and watch as the cats dart after it! Use treats, catnip, and praise to reinforce positive behavior.

Things to Consider

Never forget that a cat's wild nature is always there, under the surface, and can kick in at any time. Even a feral cat who has been socialized and welcomes human contact will still retain some of her wild instincts. When she feels scared or threatened, she may go into attack mode as her survival instincts take over, so you must always keep this in mind.

If you are not especially careful and do not take into account the wild nature of the cat, you could become injured. A visit to an emergency room for a cat bite, especially from a feral cat, can get you and the cat into quite a predicament. The anti-cat folks have made careers of telling everyone that feral cats carry rabies and are sick and diseased (which we have discussed as not being true). So, unfortunately, most doctors are always suspicious of cat (and dog) bites.

When first introducing a feral cat to a room in the house, she may try to climb the curtains or the blinds, so it is advised that you remove these at first, until she settles down. Cats do feel safer when they are elevated off the ground, so it can be helpful to add a cat tree in front of a window so she can look out. Just be sure that if you have drop ceilings (the type where the tiles can be lifted up), cat trees and other furniture are not elevated so high that she is able to get into the ceiling.

Most feral cats will use a litter box right away. They have a natural instinct to relieve themselves in material that is easy for them to dig in, such as soil, sand, or mulch. At first, use a material that is similar to what she has been used to outdoors. Play sand works well. Do not use construction sand, which may contain harmful additives. You can then slowly transition to a standard cat litter, but make sure not to use one that is scented. Some litters have special cat attractants in them to help entice the cat to use it, so those may be helpful.

If you have a dog(s) in the house, it can be helpful to provide an area of the house that is just for the cat. Creating a dog-free zone can really aid in her feeling comfortable living indoors, especially if your dog is very active and/or highly interested in the cat. You might consider installing a cat door so she can access a particular room or use a baby gate to help define particular boundaries for your dog. Use this dog-free space to set up her feeding area, litter box, and a bed or two. Having separate areas for your cat(s) and dog(s) can also help reduce tension and fighting in the house, as well as help to keep them from eating each other's food and to keep dogs out of litter boxes.

Trips to the veterinary clinic can be a challenge. For most cats, it is not that easy to get them into a carrier, especially when they learn a carrier means a trip to the vet; but for a feral cat, a carrier could mean this is going to be her last day on earth. Therefore, it is helpful to acclimate a feral cat to a carrier before needing to actually use one. Place an opened carrier in the cat's living area with a blanket inside, as an inviting place to sleep. Put treats in the carrier to help entice her inside and practice simply shutting the door while she is in there. Be careful not to scare or traumatize her, but slowly help her get used to the idea of being in there without any threat of danger.

If you are unsuccessful at helping her to get comfortable being in a carrier, you can use a net specially designed for catching cats. You can either use the net to help assist in dropping her into a large carrier or you can place her into the carrier while she is still trapped in the net. I have transported cats to the vet many times in these special nets.

You can also use a cat den or transfer cage to safely transport a feral cat. Most feral cats find these small boxes comfortable and prefer to sleep and hide in them. Place a towel or blanket and a few treats inside the den to help entice her.

If a feral cat is especially difficult to transport, you can ask your veterinarian for a light sedative to put in the cat's food. This will make the cat easier to handle. The veterinarian may have to tranquilize the cat before treating her anyway, so this might be something worth discussing.

The last thing to remember is that not all feral cats are able to be socialized. Every cat responds differently to humans and you should always keep the cat's best interest as a top priority. In the case where you are unable to successfully socialize a feral cat, whether she is outdoors or indoors, you must make the decision as to where it is best for her to continue living. Do not keep a feral cat in your house if she has been hiding under the bed for a year and you never see her. Even though she may be eating and drinking, what kind of life is it for a cat to live under a bed for her entire life?

If she is outdoors and there is no immediate danger to her (no one is threatening to trap or kill her and she does not live next to a busy highway), then allowing her to remain living in her outdoor home is her best option. Again, you can see if she would be comfortable living on your porch, in your basement, or in another enclosed area of your house for added shelter and security. But if she does not want to do that, provide her with a makeshift shelter. (Refer to "Winterizing Feral Cat Colonies" for instructions on building simple shelters.) You could also build her an outdoor enclosure to help provide her with some added protection in the case she might be in danger/threatened living outdoors.

Another option is to find her a barn home. It is not usually advised to relocate a feral cat, but if she is in danger and it is not possible for her to continue living in the current location, relocating her would be a more appropriate option. Keep in mind, there are vital steps that must be taken in order to safely and successfully relocate a feral cat. You cannot just release a feral cat at a new site and believe she will stay put. She must be provided with a proper transition period of confinement in order for her to stay put and consider the new site her home. For more information on finding suitable barn homes and safely rehoming a feral cat, refer to the chapter, "Guidelines for Safely Relocating Feral Cats."

Conclusion

If you want to give an adult feral cat an indoor home, with lots of patience, persistence, and tolerance this can be achievable with some cats. It's not impossible to adopt a feral cat. Just remember, a feral cat may allow you to pet her when she is living outdoors and wanting food, but this does not mean she will not act wild if you bring her indoors. Every cat acts differently. While you might be able to tame one cat, another one might be a different story. And always remember to be cautious, take the relationship slowly, and keep the cat's best interest in mind when deciding what living arrangement would be most appropriate.

Personal Account from Louise Holton

One feral cat I lived with was fascinated by my eyes for some reason. He would walk right over to me when I sat down on the floor; he would not let me touch him but he would look closely at my eyelashes! So I started blinking a lot when I was near him. Wild cats often do not like you to stare directly at them; they take this as a sign of aggression. But Nelson loved to watch my eyes.

He was a beautiful black cat, with a silky coat. Over time, he eventually became completely tame and enjoyed being petted. His twin brother Sammy, on the other hand, never became tame. After two years of him constantly trying to escape my house, I decided it was better for Sammy to live outdoors. He was much happier out there.

It can take months or even a year or two for a feral cat to become tame. A friend of mine, who took in a one-year-old feral cat from me, called me at midnight a year after she took her in. She was very excited. "Louise!" she yelled over the phone, "Callie just let me pet her for the very first time!" Making such a connection with a feral cat can be extremely rewarding.

Indoor/Outdoor Cats

The indoor/outdoor cat debate is very controversial among animal caretakers and humane societies. Unlike most European countries where the majority of cats spend their days outdoors, Americans are increasingly keeping their cats permanently indoors. In 2008, 65 percent of survey participants said they keep their cats strictly indoors (Rowan, 2012). As we continue to move into the cities, life in high rise apartments makes it difficult for cats to access the outdoors. There's also an increased concern for a cat's safety living in a busy city as compared to living in the suburbs or out in the country.

Up until the 1950s, caretakers didn't have much of a choice in the matter, as they had to allow a cat out to go to the bathroom. Thanks to the invention of litter, caretakers now have the ability to restrict their cat's outdoor activities.

In South Africa, where I was born, it would have been almost impossible to keep your cat indoors because most homes are built for the pleasant temperate weather; the mostly-sunny winter days in Johannesburg reach the mid- to upper-sixties. Homes are built with large windows and sliding glass patio doors. In Johannesburg summers, it used to be that homes were cooled by keeping doors and windows wide open, even at night. And about 30 years ago, cat litter was almost impossible to find in Johannesburg stores.

In talking with British friends and colleagues, most cats living in England have access to the outside via a cat flap (cat door). If an individual wants to adopt a cat and keep her strictly indoors, the shelter won't refuse the adoption; however, most shelters *prefer* that cats have access to a garden. In the U.S., the situation is reversed and most shelters will *refuse* a home unless the cat is to be kept strictly indoors; the majority of shelters do not support permitting cats outdoors.

Maggie Funkhouser

Mama Cat, who lives solely outdoors and has made this garden her home base.

Risks for Cats Who Live Strictly Indoors

Cat caretakers must take into consideration that indoor cats can sometimes suffer psychologically and develop behavioral problems. Dr. Nicholas Dodman of Tufts University School of Veterinary Medicine and Roger Tabor both note that American cats sometimes have higher rates of anxiety-related problems, which may be related to cats living indoors with little effort being made to find outlets for their natural instincts (Tufts, October 1995; Tabor, 1997).

Author Patricia Curtis makes a similar note in her 1997 book, "The Indoor Cat:"

> This is not to say that confinement can create no problems at all. The indoor cat of an uninformed and negligent owner may be neurotic, extremely unhappy, and in poor health. Some owners have unrealistic expectations of their cats; some are just indifferent. It is known that among zoo animals confinement can be a powerful stress factor. A domestic cat confined to a house or apartment will, in certain circumstances, develop stress symptoms. It may tend to chew up houseplants when it craves grass, sharpen its claws on furniture for lack of tree bark, and climb the draperies or leap to the top shelf of a cabinet of breakable treasures to achieve the lofty vantage point cats enjoy.

And holistic veterinarians Dee Blanco and Don Hamilton feel that most cats confined indoors will not attain their healthiest and happiest state. In their practice, these veterinarians have noticed an increase of urinary tract problems, vomiting, and stress-related problems, which can be attributed to the indoor-only existence (Hamilton, 2010).

When confined indoors without access to stimulation and activity, some cats suffer from mental health issues as well as physical health issues. Some cats become overweight and suffer from heart disease, thyroid issues, and diabetes, while other cats develop behavioral issues from anxiety and stress. Sadly, behavioral issues is a main reason why caretakers relinquish cats to shelters; that's why it is so important to provide entertainment for indoor-only cats.

Alley Cat Rescue's Position

Our position at Alley Cat Rescue is <u>not</u> that everyone should open their doors and allow their cats out to roam around outside! We <u>do</u> believe that many cats, especially if given a stimulating environment, can live quite contentedly indoors, especially in areas where outdoor living is unsafe. For caretakers who want to allow their cats outdoors, ACR strongly advises the use of specialized fencing designed for confining cats, and we promote outdoor cat enclosures or catios. This way cats have a nice balance of indoor and outdoor living without risk.

VCA Animal Hospitals reports that "in general, cats will live healthier lives if they are kept indoors, however, owners will have to pay special attention to their needs so they stay happy and fulfilled." They go on to say "outdoor cats are often happier because they roam freely and are able to hunt and get plenty of exercise" (VCA, 2012).

They also state that: "Indoor living, however, is not without potential problems. Although cats living inside are less affected by trauma and infectious diseases, indoor confinement can lead to behavioral problems. It is important that indoor cats have plenty of resources for perching, scratching, water drink-ing, and eliminating. Appropriate toys and activities are necessary to stimulate them mentally in order to keep them happy and to get the required amount of daily exercise" (VCA, 2012).

The general message out there is that outdoor cats only live for about two years; however, as we discussed earlier, the lifespan of an outdoor cat is comparable to that of an indoor cat. And as you can see in the ACR survey (which is printed in the back of the handbook), neutered cats in colonies can live long, healthy lives.

There are pros and cons for both indoor and outdoor environments:

INDOOR ISSUES

- boredom can cause behavioral issues
- indoor cats can become overweight due to lack of exercise
- bored cats can become overly dependent
- escape from home — accidents like this happen when someone leaves a door open; the indoor cat then has no experience with the outdoors
- consuming poisons in the house
- eating poisonous house plants
- getting stuck in the washing machine or dryer

OUTDOOR ISSUES

- stray dogs can attack cats
- diseases from other cats
- eating poisoned rats (can happen to indoor cats as well)
- fleas, ticks, worms
- traffic — some outdoor cats do become "street wise," but some cats do get hit by cars
- coyotes can attack cats
- cats living outdoors can become lost
- become accidentally trapped in sheds or vehicles

Countless fencing products are available today that make it safe and convenient for cats to access the outdoors, yet still remain confined. There's cat fencing that connects to the top of an existing fence, and there's fencing systems that can be installed for entire yards. You can buy several different cat enclosures or you can build your own. Most porches and patios can easily be enclosed by using screen material. (Refer to the Helpful Resources section for companies that sell cat fencing.)

Whether a cat is secured in an enclosure or she can freely roam, any cat who has access to the outdoors should also have access to a covered shelter, especially during cold winter months. Even if a cat comes in during the evening, it is still a good idea to have an outdoor shelter just in case she does not come inside before you go to bed; some cats will insist on staying outside over night. (Refer to "Winterizing Feral Cat Colonies" for more information.)

Personal Account from Louise Holton

One day many years ago, a woman named Loretta called me from a rural area on the Maryland/Pennsylvania border, where her and her husband owned a small farm. They both enjoyed spending time with cats; however they were allergic to them. The solution — they lent their barn space to a few feral cats!

After the last two cats died of old age, Loretta went to her local animal shelter and asked to adopt a few feral cats or any cats with behavioral problems who were likely to be euthanized, to live in her barn. Her offer was rejected. She was told quite pointedly the shelter would rather euthanize the cats than allow her to take them to be barn cats.

A few weeks later, Loretta read about Alley Cat Rescue needing barn homes for feral cats and she called me. I took my disabled father with me for the four-hour journey (along with four feral cats), and we spent a wonderful day with these two very good people. They had a perfect setting for outdoor cats, complete with a large barn and a large playpen/cage for the confinement period.

The couple spent a lot of time during the next three weeks talking to the cats and getting to know them. They sent me weekly updates about the progress being made! In fact, we became good friends and we are still in touch today. Loretta loves sharing the latest stories about her barn cats!

Tiger and Squeezy enjoy their outdoor catio.

Maggie Funkhouser

beds and couches because they are too stressed from being confined. These cats are impossible to medicate and trips to the veterinarian are difficult, if you are even able to catch the cat. This is no way for any animal to live. Not to mention, with the sheer number of feral cats living in colonies, it would simply be impossible to find enough homes or sanctuaries for all of them.

ACR does have difficulty, however, with accepting policies that would rather euthanize feral cats than allow them to live a good life under responsible care in an outdoor home, and when policies do not allow nonlethal control of feral cats on the basis of "no-outdoor-cats." One of the major reasons that nonlethal control of feral cat colonies is so contentious in the U.S. is because of the prevailing attitudes towards outdoor cats. While the public is embracing the outdoor life of feral cats, most shelters still find it difficult to accept *any* cats being outdoors, even feral cats.

Feral cats are not meant to live indoors. They are wild animals and they are already living in their home — outdoors. Most adult feral cats are very unhappy living in homes. Some do adjust and become comfortable sharing space with their caretaker(s); however, others will spend their entire lives hiding under

Authorities must begin to accept outdoor feral cats as part of the urban landscape, so the millions of volunteer feeders and caretakers can quickly and expediently sterilize the feral cat population to help make them healthier and safer. As policies progress to support TNR efforts for outdoor cats, the needless killing of healthy cats in our nation's shelters will dramatically be reduced, along with wasteful taxpayer spending.

Yes, it can be dangerous living outdoors and yes, some feral cats get hit by cars or attacked by dogs or other animals; but to kill millions of feral cats, as many authorities advocate for, in order to "protect" them from the possibility of experiencing something bad — when so many thousands of feral cats live in managed, safe colonies for many years — is just too extreme a measure to be ethically acceptable. The same thing could be said of you, your children, or any other animal.

Any one of us could get hit by a bus or sustain an injury simply by conducting our daily routines, but that is not a reason to avoid venturing outdoors. And it is certainly not a reason to advocate for the killing of healthy, sentient beings.

Conclusion

When it comes to deciding whether or not to allow a cat access to the outdoors, please take some time to weigh all the pros and cons. The benefits of keeping a cat away from possible dangers outdoors have to be weighed against the effects on a cat's behavior. Obviously safety is a main concern for any caretaker, but one must also think about a cat's natural behaviors. If a cat is kept strictly indoors, it is imperative that the caretaker provide adequate stimulation to help the cat express her energy and instinctual activities, so that she does not develop mental and/or behavioral issues.

Again, if one does choose to allow a cat outdoors, there are countless fencing and enclosure options available that permit cats the freedom of outdoor living while keeping them safely confined. And some cats, like dogs, enjoy taking walks on a leash. It may take some practice and coaxing, but with time (and treats) some cats will get used to being outdoors while on a leash.

Also, when adopting a new cat, it is always best to keep her indoors at first. She will need time to get used to her new family, as well as her new surroundings.

Once she has settled in, you can gauge if she seems interested in going outdoors. Some cats are perfectly content with not venturing outside and some are downright terrified of being outdoors. Either way, it is much easier to go from an indoor to outdoor cat than to go from an outdoor to indoor cat. Once cats have had that first taste of freedom, it's tough to convince them to go back inside. And always make sure cats who have access to the outdoors are up-to-date on all vaccinations and parasite prevention, and it's a good idea to bring an outdoor cat indoors at night.

Louise Holton

Outside enclosures can give an indoor cat safe exposure to the outdoors.

As for feral cats, they are already living in their home. Whether they were born to a feral mother cat or became lost or abandoned, these cats are accustomed to living outdoors and their natural, wild instincts help them survive. Felines have been living on this planet, as part of the landscape, for millions of years as solitary hunters high on the food chain. Feral cats have been found living in a

133

variety of climates and environments, including some of the harshest places on the planet.

And even though feral cats are capable of living without human support, as we began domesticating cats thousands of years ago, so, too, came the obligation to care for them. We created their current situation, so it is our responsibility to ensure their populations are managed in a humane manner. TNR not only reduces the number of cats by stopping the breeding cycle, but it also improves the cats' health because dedicated caretakers look after their safety.

Atticus and Leo lived as porch cats for many years.

Cats and Predation

Felis catus, the domestic and feral cat, is a predator and carnivore. Like any predator, the cat is equipped with sharp teeth and claws, and highly developed sensory capabilities, such as heightened eyesight and sense of smell, and an extensive range of hearing. The cat also has very sensitive whiskers and guard hairs that increase its sense of touch. Along with being classified as a predator, cats are also considered scavengers; meaning they will eat whatever food is available, including human handouts, garbage, and carrion (dead animals).

Roger Tabor

Cats are opportunistic feeders and will eat where food is available.

To date, the diet of cats has been studied on four continents, including 16 studies in Europe, 12 from North America, 15 in Australia, and one study was performed in Africa. Thirty-one studies have been conducted on islands, with most occurring on remote oceanic islands (Fitzgerald and Turner, 2000). And although these studies have helped identify the most common prey cats feed on and the many contributing factors as to why they feed on certain prey, few studies have examined the *impact* of cat predation on such prey populations.

There simply is not sufficient information available to determine if cat predation has any detrimental effects on the overall populations of prey animals, including birds; yet environmental and bird groups, like the American Bird Conservancy, continue to push for the eradication of feral cats, claiming cats are in fact contributing to the decline of bird species and other wildlife. The few studies that have been conducted on cat predation are from remote islands with closed ecosystems, where local bird populations have not evolved with predators. Because cat predation on continents is very different from island environments, it is inaccurate and inappropriate to extrapolate data from these particular studies to predict predation on continents. (Continue reading the next chapter "Debunking the Myths and Misinformation" to learn more about the "bad science" these environmental groups are using to advocate for the banning of TNR and the eradication of outdoor cats.)

Rodent Specialists and Scavengers

Scientists often categorize predators based on their prey preferences (are they generalists or are they specialists) and their mobility (are they residents to one area or are they more nomadic). The domestic cat (both house and feral) is considered to be a "generalist resident predator, exploiting a wide range of prey, and able to switch readily from one prey to another;" however, some also classify cats as "partially migrating generalists" because they will travel in order to scavenge for food (Fitzgerald and Turner, 2000).

Cats use two different types of strategies when hunting: mobile or the "M-strategy" and stationary or the "S-strategy." When using the mobile strategy, cats are observed moving between two points and stopping when potential prey is detected. For the stationary strategy, cats will sit and wait for any signs of prey movement and then ambush or pounce (Fitzgerald and Turner, 2000).

German zoologist and cat behaviorist, Paul Leyhausen has concluded that the cat has a preferred sit-and-wait strategy, which is much better suited to catching burrowing rodents (Leyhausen, 1979). Cats will wait for hours outside of burrows for these animals to come out. This preferred hunting method, says Leyhausen, is "definitely detrimental to success in bird hunting" (Berkeley, 2001). "Small songbirds are more mobile (faster and in three dimensions) and less predictable when they move than rodents" (Fitzgerald and Turner, 2000). Birds fly in any direction and make it more difficult for cats to catch them.

In her 2001 book, "Maverick Cats," author Ellen Perry Berkeley examines almost 50 years of studies conducted on the stomach and fecal content of feral and rural cats in the U.S. The results confirm that small mammals make up the largest percentage of the cat's diet. Listed below are some of the examples presented by Berkeley:

- 1940, Oregon: A study on the stomach analysis of 80 feral and rural cats concluded: mammals made up 61.8% of the stomach contents by volume; birds, 18.9%; carrion, 10.7%; garbage, 6.3%; cereal, 2%.

- 1941, Oklahoma: The examination of 107 cat stomachs concluded: mammals, 55% by volume; garbage, 26.5%; insects, 12.5%; birds, 4%; reptiles, 2%. Frank McMurry and Charles Sperry state "the data do not justify the common belief that every roadside or field-roaming cat is in search of avian food."

- 1949, Michigan: "In his article 'Farm Cat as Predator,' the head of a wildlife experiment station described exactly that: one farm cat and the total prey it brought home over a period of eighteen months – 1,628 mammals and 62 birds. With restrained triumph, the article suggested that this 'positive statistical record,' while perhaps not typical, casts doubt on the negative reputation of the domestic cat, 'a scapegoat with few to speak up on his behalf.'"

- 1951, California: Food habits of the feral house cat of the Sacramento Valley were studied and the results found: "mammals were clearly the primary source of food (64.1% by volume), although birds were substantially represented (25.2%)."

- 1957, Missouri: "The stomachs of 110 cats killed on highways, away from towns or farm dwellings, showed that the primary foods were 'injurious rodents' and that 'the house cat's feeding is largely beneficial to man's interests.' These hunting house cats were found to feed upon small rodents 'more than four times as often as upon rabbit, the second most important food, and nearly nine times as often as upon birds.'"

A fecal analysis conducted in New Zealand's Orongorongo Valley of feral house cats found that mammals accounted for 93 percent of the food by weight, and birds 4.5 percent (Berkeley, 2001). And a study by Coman and Brunner, in Australia, found (by stomach analysis) that mammals made up 88 percent of cats' diets by volume, and birds made up 5.2 percent (Berkeley, 2001). A more recent study conducted around Lake Burrendong in central eastern North South Wales, Australia, found that 68 percent of the volume of cat scats was composed of rabbit, and a further 11 percent of carrion; which consisted of kangaroos killed by shooters and sheep who had died or been killed by a larger predator (Molsher et al., 1999).

In "The Domestic Cat: The Biology of Its Behavior," Fitzgerald and Turner conclude that dietary studies carried out by Leyhausen, Fitzgerald, and others support the findings that the domestic cat living on continents primarily preys on small mammals. The "remains of mammals were present in 33 to 90 per cent of guts and scats (on average 69 percent frequency of occurrence) whereas, contrary to the widely held view that cats prey heavily on birds, remains of birds were found on average at 21 per cent frequency of occurrence" (Fitzgerald and Turner, 2000).

And when cats are not hunting rodents, they are scavenging for food. Cats are opportunistic feeders and will eat what is most readily available. Cats will dig through trash, eating the leftover food that humans have tossed out. They hang outside of cafeterias at colleges, behind convenience stores, and hotel kitchens. Food scraps and discarded grease and cooking oils from restaurants provide high-calorie meals for cats. Dumpsters also provide a steady source of food for rodents, making them easy prey.

Through the years, cats have learned to recognize dumpsters and humans as potential food sources. Biologist and cat behaviorist, Peter Neville says, "A deliberate strategy of scavenging has enabled many feral cats almost to give up hunting altogether. They may learn instead to lie around waste bins of hotels for fresh supplies or to cadge from well-meaning human providers in urban areas" (Neville, 1992). This behavior is one of the primary reasons cat domestication began more than 10,000 years ago.

Roy Pederson via Shutterstock

Cats are resourceful and can often find sustenance in human refuse.

In the above dietary studies, garbage was included in the data for two of the studies. In the Oklahoma study, behind mammals, garbage was listed as the second main source of food (26.5 percent) (Berkeley, 2001). Roger Tabor, states, "Although cats are superb hunters, it is their scavenging ability that allows them to survive as feral-living animals and live with us eating food off a saucer" (Tabor,

1995). Feral cats are very resourceful and have been able to survive on garbage and food scraps for centuries.

Old, Sick, and Young Prey

Cats, like any predator, tend to feed on the most vulnerable prey, because they are the easiest to catch. These individuals include those who are young or old and those who are sick or in a weakened state. One study conducted by Liberg shows that cats preyed heavily on young, weakened, and dying rabbits, while another study revealed that cats living in a New Zealand forest "methodically hunted" a population of rabbits, targeting young individuals as they emerged from burrows (Fitzgerald and Turner, 2000). Studies by George and Carss also show that most of the prey brought home by cats was young animals (Fitzgerald and Turner, 2000).

In ecosystems that lack populations of rodents and rabbits, cats tend to focus their diet on birds; however, Paul Leyhausen says cats "almost always catch only old, sick or young specimens" (Berkeley, 2001). Research has shown that most birds caught by cats are a "doomed surplus" who would have died anyway. According to one study, researchers found that songbirds killed by cats tend to have smaller spleens than those killed through non-predatory events. They concluded that "avian prey often have a poor health status" (Møller and Erritzøe, 2000).

And the UK's Royal Society for the Protection of Birds (RSPB) states, "It is likely that most of the birds killed by cats would have died anyway from other causes before the next breeding season, so cats are unlikely to have a major impact on populations." Every year, many millions of birds die naturally due to starvation, disease, or other forms of predation. And most of the millions of baby birds hatched each year will die before they reach breeding age (RSPB, 2014).

Ground-Feeding Birds

In examining the diet of birds on continents, Mead looked at records of banded birds in the U.K. and found that 31 percent of the birds recovered were caught by cats, whereas 69 percent died of other causes (Fitzgerald and Turner, 2000). He noted that all species of birds recovered "feed on the ground or low vegetation and regularly live in gardens" (Fitzgerald and Turner, 2000). Mead suggested that "cats did not affect the overall population levels of these birds, and because the birds in suburban and rural parts of Britain have coexisted with cats for hundreds of generations, they may now be under less pressure from cats than they were from the assorted natural predators in the past" (Fitzgerald and Turner, 2000).

Several other studies have also concluded that most species of birds eaten by cats on continents are ground-feeding ones. In Liberg's study, he recorded that mostly starlings and pheasants were caught, whereas Bradt and Borkenhagen recorded house sparrows, and Farsky, Hubbs, and Niewold recorded pheasants (Fitzgerald and Turner, 2000).

Diet is Determined by Available Prey and Seasonal Cycles

Once again, cats are opportunistic feeders and will eat whatever food is most available. Dietary studies have revealed invertebrates (insects, spiders, isopods, crayfish, and molluscs) are frequently consumed by cats, but they provide little sustenance. More reptiles are eaten by cats living at low latitudes; whereas household food is highly common in the diet of cats at higher latitudes. Fitzgerald and Turner (2000) report that "in much of Europe it may be difficult to find places where cats do not have access to household food."

Several studies have been conducted that show how changes in the number of prey species available in a particular area are reflected in the diets of cats. One study conducted by Liberg revealed that cats preyed heavily on rabbits when the rabbit population was high, and as the rabbit population declined, cats began eating more rodents (Fitzgerald and Turner, 2000). Young rabbits were favored between May and September, because they were easy prey; just as weakened, dying, and dead rabbits were favored during the winter months. Another study carried out in the Netherlands showed a similar

139

correlation. When the vole population was high, most cat stomachs contained remnants of voles and more voles were counted per stomach. The converse was also true; when the vole population was low, fewer were eaten by cats (Fitzgerald and Turner, 2000).

After examining the stomach contents of 128 feral cats in Australia, Coman and Brunner concluded, "It appears that feral cats are opportunist predators and scavengers and the level of predation of any one prey type will depend largely on its relative availability" (Berkeley, 2001). Earl Hubbs made a similar discovery noting how the seasonal variability of a particular geographic location is reflected in a cat's diet. Hubbs remarked, "This seasonal variability of the cat's diet suggests a constant adjustment to availability of various types of prey and is not necessarily a direct reflection of preference" (Berkeley, 2001).

Cats are adaptable predators, and will consume the food or prey most readily available.

Other Factors that Affect Diet and Hunting

As cats grow older in age their hunting tends to decrease. This makes physiological sense, since senior cats do not have the physical ability to hunt as they did when they were younger, and their sensory skills have been reduced. Several studies support this conclusion, including one conducted by Borkenhagen that found that cats less than five years old brought home the largest number of prey (Fitzgerald and Turner, 2000).

Another important factor that drives hunting and affects diet is whether a female cat is eating only for herself or for a family. Several studies have shown a correlation between female cats with kittens and increased hunting. Studies conducted by Meister reveal that females with kittens are more efficient hunters than non-mother cats (female and male). In one of the studies, six mother cats captured more rodents than 17 non-mother cats, despite having spent much less time hunting than did the non-mother cats (Fitzgerald and Turner, 2000). Leyhausen also reported that mother cats catch considerably more prey when they have kittens, for "it is assumed that the kittens themselves provide the stimuli that promote carrying prey home" (Fitzgerald and Turner, 2000).

Predators Do Not Destroy Prey

No matter who the predator or the prey, it is <u>not</u> part of the natural balance of life for a predator to *destroy* its prey. Oliver Pearson, who studies the complex interaction between predator and prey, said it's "absurd" to assume that predators cause permanent damage to prey populations, even when they kill almost every last prey specimen. Pearson told Ellen Perry Berkeley that "Feral cats have been terrorizing my study area for one hundred years and haven't done any noticeable damage yet" (Berkeley, 2001).

One of the few studies that actually looks at the effects of cat predation on prey, cautions the use of extrapolated estimates. Author of the study, D. G. Barratt says:

> Predation estimates alone do not necessarily reflect relative impacts on different prey types. Nor do apparently high rates of predation prove that prey populations are detrimentally affected, particularly in highly disturbed and modified environments. For birds, at least, habitat-related factors may be substantially more important in determining communal structure in suburbs than predation by house cats. (Barratt, 1998)

As seen in the above study by Liberg, when the local population of rabbits began to decline, cats switched over to eat-ing rodents. The same was true with the mentioned Netherlands study, where cats fed on voles when the population was high, and less so when the population had decreased. Paul Errington, considered an international authority on predation, said:

> Preying upon a species is not necessarily synonymous with controlling it or even influencing its numbers to any predictable degree. Predation which merely removes an exposed prey surplus that is naturally doomed anyway is entirely different from predation the weight of which is instrumental in forcing down prey populations or in holding them at given approximate levels. (Berkeley, 2001)

Naturalist and ornithologist Roger Tory Peterson also remarked on surplus prey being taken when he said:

> Most thought-provoking of all is to discover the balance of nature: the balance between a bird and its environment ... that predation harvests only a surplus that otherwise would be leveled off in some different way; hence putting up fences and shooting all the hawks and cats will not raise the number of Red-eyed Vireos to any significant degree. (Peterson, 1996)

Nature always keeps animal populations in check; when a surplus of one species exists a shortage of another species will also exist. The number of each species will fluctuate up and down as nature works to find balance between the two populations.

Native Species Vs. Alien Species and Filling Empty Niches

The definition of a native species is an organism that is indigenous to a particular region. The definition of an alien or exotic species is an organism that is introduced either accidentally or deliberately by human actions into places beyond its natural geographical range. Famous examples of alien species include house sparrows, starlings, pigeons, several species of rats and mice, kudzu (a vine), and numerous bacteria and viruses, such as HIV, smallpox, influenza, and plague.

In today's world, most alien or exotic species come labeled as noxious, pests, vermin, invaders, introduced species, or invasive species. They are considered to have no beneficial place within the environment and many are said to compete with or out-compete native species for a place within local ecosystems. These "pests" are also considered not to have any monetary value, and in some cases they are said to cause monetary damage or profit loss when they interfere with livestock and farming operations. Lethal management practices are implemented to control the majority of these species. Feral animals fall under this label of "alien" and are often considered pests. Eradication programs exist for many of the planet's feral cats, dogs, rabbits, pigs, goats, sheep, horses, and camels.

Humans have been distributing animals, plants, and viruses around the world since their beginning. Thanks to their ability to travel, organisms are easily relocated to new parts of the world where they either survive and take up residence in their new habitat, or they succumb to their new environment and die. In the past, ships sailing to discover new lands carried stowaway rats and disease, but they also intentionally took with them pigs, sheep, rabbits, and crop seeds for food, as well as horses for transportation. As disease became a growing concern, sailors kept cats aboard their ships to eat rats. And as people began to colonize new lands, the animals, plants, and disease carried upon these ships, too, took up residence.

Today's landscape looks nothing like it did hundreds of years ago, let alone thousands or millions of years ago. Species have travelled to all corners of the globe with and without assistance from humans, meshing into new habitats and creating all new ecosystems with all new food webs. It is difficult to ascertain the origin of all of the species on the planet. The landscape is constantly changing, which makes it hard to label species as either native or exotic. Scientist James Carlton coined the term "cryptogenic" to label organisms that cannot with assurance be defined as either native or exotic (Low, 1999).

As travel and trade continue to increase exponentially, it is naive to deny the inevitability of globalizing the world's ecology. Even the utmost of precautions used by the travel and trade industries cannot prevent the distribution of animals, plants, and disease across the planet. And as the line between native and exotic continues to blur, a new era will come to light. Biologist and author, Tim Low speaks of this phenomenon as a "cryptogenic future" where exotic species become accepted as native wildlife (Low, 1999).

New habitats are being created all the time, and not all native species are negatively affected by exotic species. Some native species become dependent on introduced species, and in most cases, exotic species are simply filling niches that have been vacated by native species because humans have driven them to extinction. Coman and Brunner state:

> Whether feral cats have been responsible for the decline in numbers of some native mammals is open to question. The once common Eastern Quoll, a carnivorous marsupial locally known as the eastern native cat (*Dasyurus viverrinus*) is now either rare or extinct in most parts of Victoria [Australia], and introduced feral cats may be doing little more than filling an ecological niche left vacant by the near disappearance of the indigenous carnivore. (Berkeley, 2001).

Feral cats are also filling the niche of natural predators who are not present in urban environments. Not many foxes, coyotes, hawks, or owls reside in cities, so feral cats fill that void and feed on rodent prey, which is abundant in urban areas.

Cats on Islands

The dietary information just listed was derived from studies conducted on continents. In this section, we will examine the diet of cats living on islands, where birds have not evolved with mammalian predators. Island ecosystems are very different from continental ecosystems; however, the findings from these few island studies have been inappropriately applied to continents and this misinformation continues to be much publicized by conservationists and the media.

Cats were intentionally transported to islands around the world to control rodent stowaways, and rabbits were brought for food. "Although the islands where cats have been introduced differ enormously in size, climate, and native fauna, they tend to have the same few introduced mammals as prey and few, if any, native mammals" (Fitzgerald and Turner, 2000). House mice, black rats, brown rats, Polynesian rats, and European rabbits can be found on islands where cats have also been introduced.

Dietary studies of cats on islands that also have an introduced rabbit population have shown that rabbits, "usually form a large proportion of the [cats'] diet, on average 55 percent frequency of occurrence," and on islands without rabbits, "rats are usually present in more than 70 per cent of gut contents or scats" (Fitzgerald and Turner, 2000). On islands located at temperate latitudes, house mice are common in the diet of cats. However, on islands with no rabbit

143

populations and small rodent populations, birds are an important food source for cats. "On islands where seabirds are recorded in the diet, birds are present on average at 60 per cent frequency of occurrence" (Fitzgerald and Turner, 2000). And for islands that completely lack mammalian prey, cats survive by feeding on birds, skinks, and invertebrates.

Seabirds who have evolved on islands void of mammalian predators have not developed any "defensive behaviours," making them easy prey for introduced species (Fitzgerald and Turner, 2000). These birds are not used to living with nor defending themselves against predators, so many of them easily become prey. Most island birds who fall prey to cats also build their nests on the ground. Petrels, penguins, and terns "usually comprise a large proportion of the birds eaten on the smaller oceanic islands" (Fitzgerald and Turner, 2000). Van Aarde's analysis of the prey remains found in cat stomachs on Marion Island revealed that feral cats "feed mainly on nocturnal burrowing petrels" (Berkeley, 2001).

Island birds are not only eaten by cats, but they are also largely consumed by introduced rats. Rats destroy nests, eating eggs and feeding on fledglings. As illustrated previously, the removal of cats from islands subsequently results in the rapid increase of rat populations, which cause more damage to the very birds conservationists intended to protect. In the book, "Trophic Cascades: Predators, Prey and the Changing Dynamics of Nature," (2010) John Terborgh and Dr. James A. Estes include studies that further support the counterproductivity of eradicating feral cats and point out how cats actually protect birds from rats:

> Mesopredator release has also provided management lessons for eradication efforts that target both an invasive apex predator and an invasive mesopredator. Using multispecies models that accounted for the presence of two invasive predators (cats and rats) on native islands, for example, Courchamp et al. (1999), conclude that the eradication of cats alone could result in a release in the rat population and ultimately intensified bird declines. More sophisticated models, such as Fan et al. (2005) similarly predict that as an apex predator, cats offer birds some degree of protection from rats.

Removing cats from islands also leads to an increase in rabbit populations. When cats were eradicated from Macquarie Island, the rabbit population quickly increased, destroying the island's vegetation. This resulted in decreased plant materials for birds to build nests and left the native penguin population more susceptible to predators. Again, the very birds conservationists were trying to protect ended up being more vulnerable.

The fact is that whether cats live on continents or on islands, their diet consists mainly of small mammals (i.e., mice, rats, and rabbits); however, on some islands, particularly ones with low or no mammalian prey populations and high bird populations, cats tend to feed more frequently on seabirds. (This makes sense since we discussed earlier how a cat's diet depends on what prey is available.) Island environments are closed systems, meaning they are shut off from surrounding areas and no new organisms enter the system. When a new species is introduced to an island ecosystem, there is great risk of upsetting the entire system, for island ecosystems are highly sensitive to change. Unfortunately, many conservationists use these few island studies that show high predation rates on birds to give the false impression that the same conditions exist on all islands and even on continents.

Conclusion

As presented by the evidence here, cats mostly prey on rodents and rabbits, while relying on their scavenging skills to help supplement their diet. Cats provide an invaluable service of preventing the spread of disease by controlling rodent populations, and they have been protecting food storage from rodents for thousands of years. Their predation on rodents and rabbits, particularly on islands, has also been shown to protect vulnerable bird populations.

Again, there is currently not enough information available to even begin to predict how cat predation affects the overall populations of prey, in particular birds. Based on today's research, it is also difficult to estimate on average how many birds a cat kills each year, and organizations continue to disagree on the estimate of how many feral cats there are living in the U.S.

After extensively examining studies on the hunting and dietary behaviors of cats, Fitzgerald and Turner (2000) conclude, "Any bird populations on the continents that could not withstand these levels of predation from cats and other predators would have disappeared long ago ..." And Meade points out, as noted above, that birds living in England today are under *less* pressure from cats than they were in the past from natural predators.

Some of the planet's bird populations are in great decline and we support the need to increase protection for these birds and other threatened wildlife. However, it is not only irresponsible and a misuse of power to blame cats for decreased bird populations, but morally unacceptable — especially when conservationists advocate for total eradication of cats. National reports and world reports continue to provide evidence which points to human activity as the true culprit of declining bird populations. (We will go into more detail regarding the loss of bird populations in the chapter, "Where Have All the Birds Gone?")

Furthermore, we do not deny the island studies that record high levels of bird predation from cats, and we recognize that birds on islands are particularly vulnerable to cats because they lack the defense mechanisms possessed by birds living on continents. However, as stated previously, we disagree with conservationists extrapolating the results from these studies across continents when these ecosystems and fauna are vastly different. Unfortunately, this "bad science" has only muddied the waters on cat predation and has made some conservationists dislike cats very intensely; like former Smithsonian bird researcher Nico Dauphine, who was convicted of attempted animal cruelty after she was caught on camera trying to poison a feral cat colony in Washington, D.C. (Cratty, 2011).

And while conservationists continue to spread this misinformation without offering any viable solution to the feral cat problem — nor to protecting birds — animal organizations across the U.S. and around the world, are implementing Trap-Neuter-Return (TNR) programs every day, which aim to benefit both cats and birds. Sterilizing outdoor cats stops the breeding cycle and prevents countless litters of kittens. Reduction in colony size not only reduces hunting pressures on local wildlife, but as depicted in the above studies, cats who do not have kittens to feed tend to kill less prey.

TNR programs also remove kittens and cats who can be socialized from colonies and any stray cats who have become lost, further reducing colony size. Mature and senior cats become the remaining colony residents, who studies have shown hunt less. Cats also consume whatever food source is most available and the easiest to procure; providing regular meals is part of a successful TNR program and aids in reduced hunting.

Eradication attempts for feral cats are highly counterproductive and inhumane to not only the cats being culled but to other animals who are simply considered "collateral damage." It makes no sense to kill one species in order to save another based on a classification system (native vs. exotic) that is clouded with uncertainty, and when there is no denying our planet is headed towards a cryptogenic future. Conservationists and cat rescue organizations <u>must</u> work *together* in order to protect both cats and birds.

Debunking the Myths and Misinformation

Report after so-called report, study after so-called study, cats are being blamed for the decline in bird populations and other wildlife, and depicted as enemies of the environment. Just as cats were hunted during the late Middle Ages under falsified pretenses, bird conservancy groups and wildlife organizations, like the American Bird Conservancy (ABC), the National Audubon Society, and the National Fish and Wildlife Service (NFWS), are creating a "witch-hunt" for modern times. The information these organizations are providing on cat predation and the effect cats have on the environment is beset with errors, exaggerations, glaring omissions, and inexcusable bias — as is most of what passes for "research" on this issue.

The research and data these organizations offer can be traced back to a handful of deeply flawed studies that have become the "holy grail" of statistics. Not to mention, they completely ignore statistical information regarding the effectiveness of Trap-Neuter-Return (TNR), which has been gathered by countless highly accredited veterinarians and cat organizations through years of research and rescue.

As seen in the previous chapter, the relationship between cat predation and prey populations is highly complex and very little research has been conducted on this hot topic. For conservationists to advocate for the killing of a species based on a lack of information and *mis*information is irresponsible and unethical. In this chapter, we will expose this "bad science" that organizations continue to promote as evidence for the justification of killing cats.

Infamous Studies and Extrapolated Numbers

It cannot be emphasized enough that *few* scientific studies have been conducted to accurately portray cat predation on prey populations. Most studies have been performed on the dietary habits of cats, with little research dedicated to the overall effects of predation. And some of these studies are based on flawed, unpublished information with small sample sizes, poor data gathering techniques, and results that are being extrapolated across continents and different types of environments (as presented with the island studies in the previous chapter).

One of the most infamous studies highlighted by conservationists to falsely accuse cats of killing billions of birds every year was conducted by Peter Churcher and John Lawton; the study has become known as the "English Village" study. Churcher asked his neighbors to collect any prey their cats brought home, and over the course of a year, 70 cats returned home with over 1,000 prey specimen. These findings were then extrapolated across all of Britain, based on the cat population at the time, and it was derived that cats in Britain were killing an estimated 100 million birds and small mammals each year (Tabor, 1991).

This beautiful, ear-tipped feral disproves the misconception that community cats are unhealthy and diseased.

In analyzing this study, one can see some of its glaring mistakes. First, this study is based on a very small sample size — 70 cats over a period of one year. Secondly,

recording the number of prey brought home by cats is not a very accurate method of collecting data. As we have seen, cats are known to scavenge and eat carrion, so simply bringing prey home is not indicative of the number of prey actually *killed* by the cats. Also, cats do not always bring every prey item back home, and the data is based on the fact that all cat guardians collected every prey specimen brought home. A lot of variables were at play in collecting data for this study, so how accurate can one say the results are?

Another error in conservationists citing this study is the extrapolation of data across an entire country. Roger Tabor examines this study in his 1991 book, "Cats: The Rise of the Cat," and says, "It is not realistic just to multiply the number of catches of these [70] rural cats by the entire cat population of Britain. Most cats are town cats with small ranges, and catch fewer items of prey than the village cats of this survey." Tabor continues on to explain that even though a high number of house sparrows were consumed by cats, their population doubled the following breeding season, and because most people assist birds (feeders, nesting boxes), their populations are "kept at well above 'natural' levels. Even if there are a lot of cats in built-up areas, there are also a lot of birds" (Tabor, 1991).

In 1994, a reporter for the *Sonoma County Independent*, Jeff Elliott, investigated the growing claim that cats are responsible for killing millions of birds and the push for eradicating cats. In his article, "The Accused," Elliott remarked on the infamous English Village study saying, "Rarely are projections made with such limited data, except in junior high science projects." Later in 1995, Churcher himself cautioned against such projections stating, "I'd be very wary about extrapolating our results even for the rest of Britain, let alone America." He continued by saying, "I don't really go along with the idea of cats being a threat to wildlife. If the cats weren't there, something else would be killing the sparrows or otherwise preventing them from breeding" (Tufts, 1995).

Another study that is often presented as "evidence" by conservationists is the "Wisconsin Study," performed by John Coleman and Stanley Temple. The study is a survey of rural residents of Wisconsin performed to estimate the number of free-ranging cats living in the entire state. The results from this survey were published in the *Wildlife Society Bulletin*, where submissions are subject to a peer-review process. This survey in no way measures cat predation, but only estimates the number of cats in Wisconsin.

Subsequently, the authors published several additional articles in an attempt to predict the potential impact of free-ranging cats on the bird population in Wisconsin; however, these articles were never peer-reviewed and some of the estimates are based on unpublished data. One such article appeared in 1996, in the *Wisconsin Natural Resources Magazine*, where Coleman and Temple make their "best guesses" (as referred to by the researchers themselves) of the number

of birds killed by cats in rural Wisconsin. They concluded: 7.8 million birds as the low estimate, 38.7 million as the intermediate estimate, and 219 million birds each year for the highest estimate. In 1999, the authors published another article in *Wildlife Control Technologies*, extrapolating those guesses yet again stating, "Nationwide, rural cats probably kill over a billion small mammals and hundreds of millions of birds each year" (Coleman et. al, 1999).

Flashy headlines about cat predation should be regarded with skepticism. Many have flaws and rely too much on estimation.

Cara Frye

It wasn't until Jeff Elliott interviewed Temple that the truth was revealed. "The media has had a field day with this since we started. Those figures were from our proposal. They aren't actual data; that was just our projection to show how bad it might be," replied Temple (Elliott, 1994). Yet, almost 20 years later, these exaggerated and "guesstimated" numbers are still being used and they are becoming more and more accepted as fact.

149

Sticky Numbers

Peter J. Wolf, the voice behind *Vox Felina*, examines just how these sticky statistics have come to be viewed as actual data. In his 2010 blog post, "Repeat after Me," Wolf recalls a National Public Radio broadcast where *Wall Street Journal* columnist Carl Bialik describes the process whereby such slippery figures gain traction:

> An interesting phenomenon of these numbers is that they'll often be cited to an agency or some government body, and then a study will pick it up, and then the press will repeat it from that study. And then once it appears in the press, public officials will repeat it again, and now it's become an official number.

Unfortunately, this is exactly what has happened with the data from both the English Village study and the Wisconsin study. Along with major newspapers, such as the *New York Times*, the *Los Angeles Times*, and the *Wall Street Journal*, conservation organizations like ABC, the National Audubon Society, and the NFWS continue to repeat these sticky numbers as solid evidence.

Roger Tabor addressed this concern in regards to the English Village study saying, "The mesmeric effect of big numbers seems to have stultified reason" (Tabor, 1991). And Gary J. Patronek, VMD, Ph.D. of Tufts University said this about cat predation statistics in a letter to the editor of the *Journal of Veterinary Medicine* (1996):

> If the real objection to managed colonies is that it is unethical to put cats in a situation where they could potentially kill any wild creature, then the ethical issue should be debated on its own merits without burdening the discussion with highly speculative numerical estimates for either wildlife mortality or cat predation. Whittling down guesses or extrapolations from limited observations by a factor of 10 or even 100 does not make these estimates any more credible, and the fact that they are the best available data is not sufficient to justify their use when the consequences may be extermination for cats.
>
> If asking for reasonable data to support the general assertion that wildlife mortality across the United States attributable to cat predation is unacceptably high can be construed as 'attempting to minimize the impact,' then I am guilty as charged. What I find inconsistent in an otherwise scientific debate about biodiversity is how indictment of cats has been pursued almost in spite of the evidence.

As demonstrated here, it is very easy for a small scientifically valid, peer-reviewed study to be manipulated — thanks to the media and anti-bird groups — into a much larger, broader statement which is being used to push an agenda to kill cats.

Conclusion

As we've seen throughout the previous chapters, the few cat predation studies that have been carried out on continents have resulted in countless biologists stating that (1) cats are no more harmful a predator than any other predator, (2) cats have been a part of the landscape for thousands of years, therefore birds and wildlife who could not withstand such predation from cats would have died off long ago, and (3) human activity is more devastating to birds and wildlife than any cat predation. Unfortunately, conservationists continue to cherry-pick studies, citing unpublished, unreviewed data and guesses as reliable, scientific research in order to falsely accuse outdoor cats for declining bird and wildlife populations.

In March 2013, George Fenwick, president of ABC, clearly stated his position on outdoor cats and TNR programs, when he wrote in a *Baltimore Sun* opinion piece called, "House Cats: The Destructive Invasive Species Purring on Your Lap:"

> The only sure way to protect wildlife, cats and people is for domestic cats to be permanently removed from the outdoor environment. Trap-neuter-release programs that perpetuate the slaughter of wildlife and encourage the dumping of unwanted cats is a failed strategy being implemented across the United States without any consideration for environmental,

human health, or animal welfare effects. It can no longer be tolerated.

Local governments need to act swiftly and decisively to gather the 30 million to 80 million unowned cats, aggressively seek adoptions, and establish sanctuaries for or euthanize those cats that are not adoptable.

Dr. Julie Levy from the University of Florida's Veterinary School and co-founder of Operation Catnip was quoted in *Best Friends* magazine (2013) as stating, "There are much more important pressures on bird populations [than cats] — primarily pollution and habitat destruction. And those are harder areas for bird groups to be effective in." Levy said:

> The problem is that part of the campaign is an attack on humane control of homeless or feral cats. Most of us love song-birds as much as we love cats, so we are not trying to choose one species over another. We're trying to come up with a solution that benefits everybody in the picture.

Levy concludes that the goal is to reduce the feral cat population saying, "we can do it in a humane way that respects the animals rather than in a 50-year-old vision of animal control, in which the only way you can help animals is by killing them" (Best Friends, 2003).

Alley Cat Rescue agrees that outdoor cat populations need to be controlled. But we also believe that because nonlethal

Porch cat, sharing a shelter with an opossum. Feral cats usually live alongside most wildlife quite safely, except for coyotes. Although it has been found that coyotes and feral cats often avoid each other.

Louise Holton

fix" of killing does not work. Never has and never will. And more importantly, eradication will cause even more devastation to birds if these conservation groups ever convince the U.S. government to agree to such a plan.

For too long cats have received a bad rap and been blamed for the destruction of birds and wildlife. It is time for conservation groups to stop using exaggerated numbers and bogus studies to base these claims upon. Yes, cats kill birds, but for agencies, especially government-supported ones, to push for the eradication of cats based on such falsehoods and deception is horrifying and tragic ... and it could have devastating consequences. Removing all outdoor cats — a meso-predator and a highly specialized rodent hunter — would be an unimaginable disaster for the American environment.

methods exist and work, they should be used. This seemingly attractive "quick-

Killing Outdoor Cats is a Dangerous Game

One only has to look at the history of eradicating cats from small islands to see the countless flaws and devastating effects associated with this management approach: (1) it took many years to remove all or most of the cats (19 years in one case); (2) each case required several methods of control, including poisoning, shooting, trapping, and releasing a virus and predatory dogs; (3) after the cats were removed, rodents and rabbits took over and destroyed the environment, putting at risk the very animals conservationists were trying to save.

Where Have All the Birds Gone?

According to the 2014 "State of the Birds" report, populations of birds living on prairies, deserts, and at sea have declined between 30 and 40 percent, in the last 40 years; nearly one-third of U.S. birds are endangered, threatened, or in significant decline (North American Bird Conservation Initiative, 2014). Conservationists and government agencies continue to blame outdoor cats as a major cause for the decline in bird and wildlife populations, despite the fact that national and world reports clearly conclude that <u>human activity</u> is the true culprit. As we approach the planet's sixth mass extinction event, scientists warn that human activity is the driving force behind this current state. Conversely, previous mass extinction events were caused by natural planetary transformations or catastrophic asteroid strikes. In the past 35 years, the human population has doubled, and it is projected to reach over 8 billion by the year 2030 ("Population Growth," accessed 2015).

"More than 6.8 billion human beings are now demanding ever greater quantities of material resources, decimating the world's richest ecosystems, and dumping billions of tons of heat-trapping gases into the atmosphere each year,"

> "According to a 2000 study published by a global alliance of conservation organizations called BirdLife International, almost 1,200 species — about 12 percent of the world's remaining bird species — may face extinction within the next century."
>
> -Worldwatch Institute, "Winged Messengers" (2003)

concludes the 2010 "State of the World" report published by the Worldwatch Institute. And even despite a significant increase in our resource efficiency, "global resource use has expanded 50 percent over the past three decades" (Worldwatch Institute, 2010). Human activity such as habitat destruction, pollution, climate change, and the use of toxic chemicals, is the cause of declining bird and wildlife populations ... <u>not</u> cats.

Habitat Loss, Climate Change, Pollution, and Pesticides

The 2013 "State of the Birds" report says the primary cause of declining bird populations is due to habitat loss, agricultural expansion, climate change, and pollution (North American Bird Conservation Initiative, 2013). The survival of migrating birds highly depends on the planet's forests. Without available tracts of forestland, countless bird populations lose their nesting sites and food sources. Songbirds use these forests to fly back and forth with the changing seasons, returning every year to the same areas to lay their eggs and raise their young; however, more and more of these birds find themselves returning to sites where forestland has been bulldozed, leaving them with little to no available resources for survival.

The Council on Hemispheric Affairs says, "experts estimate that each minute, 11 football fields of forest are cleared." What is truly frightening about this figure is how world governments continue to support such actions.

> With all the environmental and ecological consequences, one must question the motives of not only the Brazilian government [referring to clearing the Amazon rainforest], which has tolerated such a destructive development model, but also its endorsement by the international community which has jeopardized the future of mankind. (COHA, 2009)

With this tragic rate of clear cutting of forestland and the rapidly growing sprawl of cityscapes, habitat destruction is obviously the number one reason for declining bird populations, as well as other wildlife. Professor of biology at Stanford University, Rodolfo Dirzo says, "We tend to think about extinction as loss of a species from the face of Earth, and that's very important, but there's a loss of critical ecosystem functioning in which animals play a central role that we need to pay attention to as well" (Carey, 2014). All animal and plant species on this planet are connected; the loss of any one species can affect an entire ecosystem, sending out a ripple effect to surrounding environments.

> "The global environmental crisis has caught up with migratory birds. There are simply too many people making ever increasing demands on a fixed supply of resources. It is inconceivable that we can continue on the same reckless path for very long."
>
> -John Terborgh, "Why American Songbirds are Vanishing" (1992)

One of the major driving factors behind deforestation, besides the reliance on paper products, is the increased consumption of animal products. According to a 2006 U.N. report, "Livestock now use 30 per cent of the earth's entire land surface." Animal agriculture has been turning lush forests and grassy prairies into barren deserts since the beginning of human history, but thanks to the advent of factory farming in the 1950s, this pace has exploded dramatically. It is hard to believe that much of North America was once covered by luscious forest, seeing as how today that land is home to livestock production. The devastation of clear-cutting forest for animal agriculture is now continuing in Latin America, especially the Amazon River Basin, where 70 percent of forestland has been turned into pastures for livestock grazing (United Nations, 2006).

The Food and Agriculture Organization of the United Nations (2014) says, "greenhouse gas data show that emissions from agriculture, forestry and fisheries have nearly doubled over the past fifty years and could increase an additional 30 percent by 2050 ..."

Raising animals for food also contributes substantially to global warming and is responsible for more water pollution, topsoil depletion, and wildlife destruction than any other human activity. Senior U.N. Food and Agriculture Organization official Henning Steinfeld reported that "Livestock are one of the most significant contributors to today's most serious environmental problems. Urgent action is required to remedy the situation" (United Nations, 2006). Raising animals for food is one of the largest sources of carbon dioxide and the single largest source of both methane and nitrous oxide emissions (EPA, accessed 2015). "Livestock and their byproducts account for at least 32,000 million tons of carbon dioxide (CO2) per year, or 51% of all worldwide greenhouse gas emissions" (Goodland and Anhang, 2009).

Along with deforestation and global warming, birds are also in decline due to increased air, water, and soil pollution and the use of toxic chemicals. Again, the major contributor to both of these problems is animal agriculture. In 1997, the USDA estimated that animals raised for food produced 1.4 billion tons of waste, which is 130 times the nation's volume of human waste, or five tons of animal waste for every U.S. citizen (Horrigan et al., 2002). The waste, containing vast amounts of nitrates, pathogens, and hormones, winds up in the air, the water, and the soil. Air pollution causes respiratory problems, and water pollution kills large portions of marine life either directly or through formations of algal blooms; decreased marine life is bad news for birds, especially seabirds who rely on fish and other aquatic life for food.

The use of toxic chemicals such as pesticides, herbicides, fungicides, and fertilizers poses a severe risk to birds, killing them directly or by causing decreased breeding success, physical malformations, or impaired ability to migrate or to avoid predators. Globally, the U.S. uses one-fifth of the five billion pounds of pesticides used each year, with the agricultural sector accounting for the majority of that use (Grube et. al, 2011). The application of pesticides and fertilizers on the estimated 14,136 golf courses worldwide, adds to the problem. On average, each golf course uses around 150 acres of land, with each acre being treated with 18 pounds of pesticides annually (Cox, 1991). In the 1991 *Journal Of Pesticide Reform*, Caroline Cox writes:

Is 'an oasis of burbling creeks, swaying trees, and rolling seas of shimmering green' an appropriate description of a golf course? Or would 'a toxic waste dump, a destroyer of wetlands, and a misuse of farmland and water' be more correct? What does pesticide use on golf courses mean for golfers, nearby residents, wildlife, and the environment in general?

According to reports since 1971, because of "exposure to the organophosphate insecticides diazinon, chlorpyrifos, and isofenphos, blackbirds, blue jays, Brant and Canada geese, coots, grackles, gulls, mallards, robins, starlings, and widgeons have all been killed on golf courses" (Cox, 1991).

Cats are talented tree climbers and love to be up high, yet prey primarily upon ground dwelling animals like rodents.

Magnus Johansson/CC BY-SA 2.0

A 2013 study led by Canadian toxicologist Dr. Pierre Mineau identifies acutely toxic pesticides as the most likely leading cause of the widespread decline in grass-land bird numbers in the U.S. (Mineau and Whiteside, 2013). The indirect effects of pesticides mediated through a loss of insects as a food resource also takes a toll on birds, while eagles, owls and hawks accumulate high chemical concentrations in their bodies from ingesting poisoned prey; farmers poison any animal viewed as a threat to their operation, including rodents, rabbits, and foxes. Unfortunately, it is almost impossible to find any place on the planet where chemical residues are not detectable.

Windows, Communication Towers, Power lines, and Wind Turbines

Millions of birds, worldwide, die each year when they collide with man-made structures, like glass windows and buildings, communication towers, power lines, and wind turbines. Ornithologists estimate that between 100 million and 1 billion birds are killed each year from building strikes, particularly with windows (Loss et. al, 2014). Birds simply cannot differentiate a reflection from reality. Even if a bird flies away after striking a window, she may die later as a result of internal injuries.

Communication towers (radio, television, cellular) are very tall structures usually located on elevated land, and their supporting guy wires are extremely dangerous for migratory birds. Fast flying birds do not see these loose wires and birds who are not very agile have difficulties avoiding them. Scientists estimate that 6.8 million birds are killed every year in the U.S. and Canada due to flying into communication towers (Longcore et. al, 2012). Collisions with power lines are estimated to kill up to 175 million birds annually, with tens to hundreds of thousands more birds being electrocuted (Manville, 2005).

Although wind turbines are an important form of clean technology for renewable energy production and an important tool in combating climate change, they can be dangerous for migratory birds. Their blades rotate at speeds of up to 200 kilometers per hour and, when placed along the major migratory routes of birds, like coastlines and mountaintops, wind turbines can become obstacles for birds causing both injuries and fatalities. It is estimated that 573,000 birds are killed every year in the U.S. from collisions with wind turbines (Smallwood, 2013).

Other Causes Contributing to Declining Bird Populations

Although the above mentioned issues are the main culprits of declining bird populations, other important factors also play a significant role and should be taken into consideration. According to newly released data, the federal Wildlife Services, a branch of the U.S. Department of Agriculture (USDA), killed more than 2.7 million animals during fiscal year 2014; nearly 60 percent of animals killed were birds, including bald and golden eagles, blackbirds, bluebirds, cardinals, cormorants, cranes, doves, ducks, egrets, falcons, finches, geese, hawks, herons, ibises, meadowlarks, ospreys, owls, pelicans, ravens, robins, sparrows, swallows, wild turkeys, vultures, and woodpeckers, just to name a few (USDA, 2015). Along with birds, numerous other animals (including 300+ mountain lions and nearly 800 bobcats; 700+ feral cats; 16 pet dogs), are killed intentionally or unintentionally every year by the government to protect powerful agricultural, livestock, and other special interests. Since 1996, our country's Wildlife Services has shot, poisoned, and snared more than 27 million animals. "It's sickening to see these staggering numbers and to know that so many of these animals were cut down by aerial snipers, deadly poisons and traps," said Amy Atwood, a senior attorney at the Center for Biological Diversity in a press release (Center for Biological Diversity, 2015).

> "Human-related factors threaten 99 percent of the most imperiled bird species, and bird extinctions already far exceed the natural rate of loss. At least 128 species have vanished over the past 500 years, 103 of them since 1800."
>
> -Worldwatch Institute, "Winged Messengers" (2003)

The 2014 "State of the Birds" report says that one of the main causes of declining sea birds is oil spills, while some populations of birds are in decline because of oil and natural gas extractions. The report also cites mountaintop coal mining as a contributing factor, for entire mountain peaks of forestland are cleared to extract mineral resources (North American Bird Conservation Initiative, 2014).

It is best to rise above the "sticky numbers" and sloppy statistics, and work toward humane solutions for feral cat management.

Longline fishing is another danger to birds, which claims hundreds of thousands of seabird lives every year, when birds are inadvertently hooked on baited lines and drowned. Sadly, at least 23 species face extinction from this industry. The Worldwatch Institute reports, "more than 30 countries have longline fleets, yet little has been done to address the problem despite findings that simple mitigation measures can drastically cut bird bycatch" (Youth, 2003).

Humans also exploit birds through hunting and the pet trade industry. Poorly regulated or illegal hunting and capture contributes to the killing of millions of birds. In nations such as Malta and China, "deep-forest birds such as Neo-

tropical curassows and Asian pheasants quickly disappear when hunters invade pristine areas" (Youth, 2003). If birds are not being hunted, then they are being captured and sold into the exotic pet trade. "A third of the world's 330 parrot species are threatened with extinction due to pressures from collecting for the pet trade, combined with habitat loss" (Youth, 2003).

Some Bird Populations are on the Rise

Even though birds may be killed by cats and other predators, many experts have said repeatedly that this does not mean the birds preyed upon are declining in number. In fact, although some songbird populations are declining, other bird populations such as blackbirds, greenfinches, blue jays, and brown-headed cowbirds are exploding. Many birds have been faring well in the U.S., especially birds living in urban environments. "Birds are increasing and that's good," said Kevin McGowan of the Cornell Laboratory of Ornithology (Bryner, 2009).

The 2009 "State of the Birds" report states, "The urban/suburban indicator, based on data for 114 native bird species, shows a steady, strong increase during the past 40 years." The report continues on to say:

American Robins can thrive in many habitats, including lawns with abundant earthworms. California Quail and Abert's Towhees find suburban plantings a suitable substitute for native aridland habitats. Gulls, vultures, and crows seek abundant food at garbage dumps and along roadsides. Hummingbirds, chickadees, sparrows, finches, woodpeckers, and other birds take advantage of bird feeders. Even hawks and owls find increasingly safe nesting sites and abundant prey in our towns and cities. (North American Bird Conservation Initiative, 2009)

So while reports indicate a decline in some bird populations (mostly songbirds who migrate and depend on forestland), those species who take up residence in urban and city landscapes are increasing in numbers. These birds find nesting sites in tall buildings and backyard sanctuaries. They scavenge through human garbage and frequent garden bird feeders. Ironically, the highest concentration of feral cats can also be found in these same landscapes; most cats tend to congregate in cities and urban areas because more people live there, and because that is where food and shelter is most available. If bird populations are rising in our cities and urban areas, while living alongside feral cats, then how can conservationists blame cats for their demise?

Conclusion

At this time in history, when the burgeoning human population is causing so much destruction to the Earth, we need to remind ourselves of our species' responsibility and consider our *double*

standards. We often excuse or ignore the devastation done to the environment by humans and the results of this destruction to the wildlife we share this planet with. Urban sprawl, shopping malls, roads, golf courses, and most of all, the use of harmful pesticides, all play a part in reducing habitat and food sources, which have negative effects on wildlife.

Roger Tabor, one of the world's leading experts on cats and one of the few biologists who has studied feral cats for over 30 years, had this to say to Estelle Munro in her 2003 article, "Living in the Gray Zone:" "The clear leading animal that's really putting wildlife at risk is the human population. We just don't like to acknowledge that it is our fault. It's not a case of the cat being the worst offender. It isn't even remotely the worst offender. It's us."

Conservationists state they are not saying cats are the number one cause of bird deaths, but they also say that it is too late to find solutions to stop, or at least slow down, land development, and it is easier to kill cats, so let us take that approach. The former director of the American Bird Conservancy's "Cats Indoors!" campaign, Linda Winter puts it simply, "We may not know the exact numbers of birds that cats kill, but we know cats kill them, and it's an unnecessary and easily avoidable loss" (Ridgley, 2003).

Humans have the largest effect on the environment and all living things on the planet Earth. Unfortunately, not until politics, money, and personal agendas

159

are set aside will the devastation on the planet halt. Blaming cats for songbird decline is a facile and simplistic "solution" to a complex problem. Alley Cat Rescue invites conservation groups to work *with* us and the many other cat rescue groups across the country to implement humane, nonlethal management programs for feral cats. That is how we will get a handle on reducing the number of outdoor cats, so that cats, birds, and other wildlife will all benefit.

We ALL want the same thing: fewer feral and outdoor community cats. We, Trap-Neuter-Return (TNR) advocates, have a solution, where the conservation groups do not. We want fewer cats, using humane, nonlethal methods. They would like to ban our work. This will only cause more colonies to form, and more kittens to be born, to suffer, and in many cases to die. Again, time spent blaming cats for our environmental ills is time wasted. If we really want to save birds and other wildlife, then we need to work together and focus our energy on tackling the big-picture issues, like habitat loss, climate change, and pollution, that are the *true* culprits of wildlife devastation.

Double Standards: Humans are Pests

"If there is a world's worst pest, an exotic invader that surpasses all others, surely it is the human species," biologist and author Tim Low notes in his 1999 book, "Feral Future: The Untold Story of Australia's Exotic Invaders." "No other animal has swarmed across the globe in such numbers or displaced so many other life forms in the process. Our ability to invade new habitats is unsurpassed." (Low, 1999)

TNR: Past, Present, Future

TNR Timeline in the U.S.

1980 Annabell Washburn, often credited as being the first advocate to bring TNR to the U.S., establishes Pet Adoption and Welfare Service (PAWS). PAWS begins practicing TNR on feral cats living on Martha's Vineyard in Massachusetts.

1982 Ellen Perry Berkeley writes, "Maverick Cats: Encounters with Feral Cats," the first book about feral cats to be published in the U.S.

1986 Washburn works with Tufts University School of Veterinary Medicine staff and students to sterilize feral cats in the British Virgin Islands, marking one of the first collaborations between veterinarians and activists.

1988 Founding the program Alliance for Animals, Donna Bishop introduces TNR for feral cats in Boston.

1989 The Stanford Cat Network (now the Feline Friends Network), the first TNR program for a large college, begins on the Stanford University campus. Within 15 years, a population of 1500 is brought down to 85 feral cats.

1990 Louise Holton co-founds Alley Cat Allies (ACA) as the first U.S. national organization to promote and implement nonlethal control for feral cat colonies. Holton based ACA on the Cat Action Trust (U.K.).

1991 *Animal People* magazine staff Merritt Clifton and Kim Bartlett begin a seven-month trial of TNR in Fairfield County, Conn.

1992 Merrimack River Feline Rescue Society establishes a TNR program in Newburyport, Mass.

1992 Tufts University's School of Veterinary Medicine sponsors a feral cat workshop organized by Dr. Andrew Rowan, with Merritt Clifton, Louise Holton, and Donna Bishop as presenters.

1992 Feral Cat Coalition located in San Diego, Calif. starts the first mash-style TNR clinic.

1993 Ocean Reef, Fla. resident, Alan Litman, with the cooperation of the Ocean Reef Community Association, establishes and launches ORCAT.

1993 San Francisco SPCA, under the direction of Richard Avanzino, creates the "Feral Fix Program."

1994 Lynda Foro creates the first national No Kill Directory and the first No Kill Conference.

1994 San Francisco becomes the nation's first no-kill city when the San Francisco SPCA, under Rich Avanzino, establishes an adoption pact with the Department of Animal Care and Control.

1994 Operation Catnip in North Carolina opens a mash-style spay/neuter clinic.

1994 PetSmart Charities begins to provide grants towards TNR programs for free-roaming cats.

1994 Jeff Elliott's article "The Accused" is published in *The Sonoma County Independent*, shedding light on the misinformation and twisting of study results to frame cats as killers of wildlife.

1995 The American Veterinary Medical Association (AVMA) Animal Welfare Forum focuses on the welfare of cats and includes discussions about feral cats

and their management. Louise Holton is called upon by Dr. John Hamil of The California Vet Medical Association to answer questions about feral cats and rabies; he calls Holton an expert in the field.

1995 Doing Things for Animals (founded by Lynda Foro) holds the first national no-kill conference, "No-Kills in the '90's;" it has since been discontinued.

1996 American Humane Association and The Cat Fancier's Association sponsor a conference, "A Critical Evaluation of Free-Roaming/Unowned/Feral Cats in the United States."

1997 Louise Holton founds Alley Cat Rescue (ACR) to focus her efforts on establishing a shelter to rescue homeless cats and offer subsidized spay/neuter services to support local TNR in Maryland; to date, this program has spayed or neutered over 40,000 cats. ACR also established a national network of Cat Action Teams across the U.S. to assist people with cats in their neighborhoods.

1998 Dr. Julie Levy opens a second chapter of Operation Catnip in Alachua County, Fla.

1998 Feral Cat Coalition of Portland receives a grant to build a mobile vet hospital, and they change their name to Feral Cat Coalition of Oregon to serve feral cats across the entire state.

1999 Neighborhood Cats in New York City is created thanks to Bryan Kortis, Ruth Sharp, Shirley Belwood and a colony of feral cats living on the Upper West Side of Manhattan.

2001 Best Friends Animal Society holds its first "No More Homeless Pets" Conference, and continues to hold national conferences yearly.

2001 A third chapter of Operation Catnip opens in Virginia.

2004 The No Kill Advocacy Center is created by Nathan Winograd, listing TNR programs for feral cats as part of the No Kill Equation.

2005 The first "No Kill Conference" (organized by the No Kill Advocacy Center) is held and continues to operate annually.

2006 The Humane Society of the United States (HSUS) advocates TNR for feral cats.

2012 "The Outdoor Cat: Science and Policy from a Global Perspective" conference is hosted by The HSUS and co-sponsored by the Humane Society Institute for Science and Policy, the Found Animals Foundation, and the Humane Society Veterinary Medical Association.

2015 Madrid, Spain becomes a no-kill city, after adopting legislation that bans "the slaughter of stray animals."

2015 28 U.S. states have local governments with laws and/or policies that support TNR for community cats.

*See page 195 for source list.

Late 1960s and 1970s in England

There were several TNR pioneers during these years, one being former model Celia Hammond, who started trapping and sterilizing feral cats and returning them to their outdoor homes. Celia pressured the Royal Society for the Prevention of Cruelty to Animals (RSPCA) to change their policy away from catch-and-kill, which lead to the creation of the Feral Cat Working Party. Celia became the first chairwoman of the National Cat Rescue Coordinating Committee (NCRCC), a British group organized in 1975 by animal activist Ruth Plant.

Ruth, another TNR pioneer, was certainly ahead of her time, being one of the first individuals to question animal control's lethal methods for managing stray cat and dog populations while suggesting that suppressing the reproductive cycle could provide a more effective and humane solution. In treating hard-to-handle feral cats, Ruth naturally turned to contraceptive pills; which lead Dr. Jenny Remfry to carry out some of the first field trials of administering synthetic progestins to free-roaming cats in the U.K. Ruth

163

also strongly believed that education was key to ending pet homelessness and encouraged an open dialogue between animal control and the public, rather than simply killing animals (Remfry, 2001). "Ruth Plant believed firmly — heretically, in those days — that animal welfare work shouldn't be limited to pets but should also serve stray and feral animals" (Berkeley, 2004).

Alley Cat Rescue

Mother cat Smokey.

In 1977, two members of the NCRCC created a new organization, the Cat Action Trust (CAT). Celia Hammond was appointed a patron, Ruth Plant became Honorary Secretary, and Roger Tabor and Dr. Jenny Remfry served on the Advisory Panel (Remfry, 2001). Today, the Cat Action Trust has several branches of volunteers neutering feral cats throughout England and has become a model organization.

Feral Cat Symposium Held in 1980

Universities Federation for Animal Welfare (UFAW) invited 14 speakers for their symposium, "The Ecology and Control of Feral Cats," held in London, England. "It is fair to say that UFAW's symposium was a defining event, a watershed occurrence. Before 1980, feral cats were considered vermin; after 1980, they were beginning to be considered worthy of humane treatment," notes Berkeley (Berkeley, 2004).

Dr. Jenny Remfry, who worked with UFAW, deserves immense credit for this change in attitude, along with veterinarian Roger Ewbank who became director of UFAW in 1979. Ewbank became interested in Remfry's work with feral cats and "thought the time was ripe to put the ecologists in touch with the people advocating population control" (Berkeley, 2004).

Tom Kristensen, a veterinarian from Denmark's Society for the Protection of the Cat, spoke at the symposium about the wonderful results they had with TNR in the mid-1970s. Dr. Remfry had visited Denmark in 1976 to find out what they were doing and brought her findings back to Britain. Her recommendation was to implement TNR for all feral cats (Berkeley, 2004).

Roger Tabor also spoke at the symposium sharing data from his study of neutered cats in London's Fitzroy Square. His study included a group of black and white cats similar in coloring to T.S. Eliot's famous "Jellicle Cats." Tabor noted that the resident cats, "even a few years after neutering, still maintain their tight family cohesiveness and still continue to exclude other cats" (Tabor, 1981).

Biologist and author Peter Neville spoke of similar neutering programs in France, Israel, Italy, Kenya, and South Africa, and he himself was going off to establish official programs in Greece and Tunisia (Neville, 1992).

Ellen Perry Berkeley reported on all of this in her book "Maverick Cats: Encounters with Feral Cats." She also noted that the Feral Cat Working Party "gives its highest recommendation to the neutering of whole colonies, 'provided that their long-term welfare is ensured'" (Berkeley, 2001).

Dr. Jenny Remfry, with the help of Peter Neville, wrote "Feral Cats: Suggestions for Control," published by UFAW in 1982. The booklet became a bestseller and the third edition was published in 1995. Remfrey reported that attitudes were continuing to become "more enlightened" (Remfrey, 1989).

South Africa in the Mid- to Late 1970s

I discovered a small colony of feral cats living behind an accounting firm I founded in Braamfontein, Johannesburg. An-

other woman who worked in the building and myself put out food for them on a regular basis. I had called the Johannesburg SPCA about the cats, and they told me to trap them and bring them in for euthanasia. I was not going to do this, as the cats seemed fine to me, other than having litters of kittens running around, so I continued to feed and look after the cats.

Billie, rescued by Alley Cat Rescue.

Then one day, I opened the local Johannesburg newspaper, the Rand Daily Mail, and read that the local SPCA had changed its stance on feral cats saying that decades of trapping and removing had not worked and they would try TNR instead. I was overjoyed at the progressive change and started doing some TNR work with them in Johannesburg. The article also mentioned Britain and the humane work they were doing for feral cats, so I contacted UFAW's Roger

165

Ewbank, as well as Jenny Remfry to get more information.

Harry William Liam, feral kitten rescued by Alley Cat Rescue.

Sadly, over the next decade, TNR fell off the radar in South Africa. It wasn't until 1990, when Kim Bartlett published an interview with me in the Animals' Agenda, that a few forward-thinking folks in South Africa picked up on TNR again. It was then that several groups were formed across South Africa to provide TNR services to feral cats; most of these groups continue this work today.

Late 1980s and Early 1990s

In Boston, Mass. in 1984, AnnaBell Washburn, who was working on Martha's Vineyard with PAWS, an organization she had founded a decade earlier, had at-tended a conference of the World Society for the Protection of Animals and heard Peter Neville speak about the worldwide success of neutering schemes for feral cats. Later in 1985, while vacationing at her house on Virgin Gorda in the British Virgin Islands, she discovered several colonies of feral cats, so for the next decade, she took Tufts veterinary students to the island each year to conduct TNR (Slater and Shain, 2005).

In the July 1990 issue of Cat Fancy, author Ellen Perry Berkeley wrote the article "Feral Cats," highlighting a few ground-breaking programs tackling the feral cat issue throughout the U.S., including AnnaBell Washburn's dedicated work. Both Annabell Washburn and Kim Bartlett were instrumental in encouraging me to start an organization, to bring TNR as the preferred method of managing feral cats to the national stage. Subsequently, in October of 1990, after caring for a colony of cats in the neighborhood of Adams Morgan in Washington, D.C. since that summer, I co-founded Alley Cat Allies; which has given community cats, especially feral cats, the much-needed voice they deserve.

Later in 1991, I was introduced to Alan Litman, the founder of ORCAT. Alan had a vacation home in the exclusive Ocean Reef community located in Key Largo, Fla. and in the late 1980s, started Ocean Reef's Trap-Neuter-Release (TNR) program for the community's cats.

Ocean Reef was initially a fishing village and had many introduced rats, so a good-

Alley Cat Rescue

intentioned groundskeeper brought in five unneutered cats to help solve the problem. The cats did their job of course and the rats were under control, but the cats began to multiply and eventually more than 2,000 of them were patrolling the area.

Ocean Reef's residents had been trying to control the cat population through killing, but as we know, this is not a long-term solution. Alan stepped in with a unique plan. He had read somewhere about TNR and, being an avid cat lover, he believed the cats should be trapped and sterilized, rather than killed. And although he lived in Pennsylvania, he would visit his Ocean Reef home for one week every month, during which time he started trapping cats and taking them to a local vet to be sterilized.

In 1993, Litman and a group of home-owners opened their own clinic, the Grayvik Animal Care Center, and sterilized 500 cats. Today the population is down from the initial 2,000 cats to 350, of which around 100 now reside at the care center (Grayvik Center, accessed 2015). ORCAT is recognized as a model TNR program throughout the country. I have seen thousands of cat colonies around the world, and quite frankly I have never seen any colony of cats living in such luxury, with clean feeding stations hidden discreetly behind or beneath the luxurious foliage, as the cats of Ocean Reef.

I recall spending a week there with Alan and his crew, and every day we toured the grounds by golf cart with the feeder conducting routine rounds, including feeding, watering, and cleaning up any messes the cats may have made. The feeding route around the area took about four hours, as there were 70 colonies and feeding stations set up. Some colonies were just four or five cats, whereas some consisted of around 12 cats.

All the cats without exception, were in the greatest of health. They were monitored carefully, and if any appeared sick they were trapped and taken to the clinic for treatment. I even met some older cats who were 19 and 20 years old! And every year, the community comes together for a fundraiser for the cats.

After I co-founded Alley Cat Allies, TNR took off on a national scale and several major groups were formed to implement TNR in their cities. In 1991, Randi Fairbrother incorporated Catalysts for Cats as a nonprofit organization in Santa Barbara, Calif. (Catalyst for Cats, Inc., accessed 2015). This group has achieved a lot for feral cats in the area, and to date, they continue their dedication to alleviating the suffering of cats and reducing their populations through TNR.

Another forward-thinking individual of the time was a dear friend of mine, Sally Mackler. Sally was one of the first to incorporate mash-style operations in providing TNR services to communities. Sally, along with Dr. Rochelle Brinton, formed the Feral Cat Coalition in San Diego, Calif. in 1992. Since inception, they have TNR'd over 40,000 cats and they

167

continue to provide free TNR services to the residents of San Diego county (Feral Cat Coalition, accessed 2015).

In 1994, San Francisco, Calif. became the nation's first no-kill city, marking a historical achievement in the evolution of the no-kill movement. Under the direction of Rich Avanzino, the San Francisco SPCA established an adoption pact with the Department of Animal Care and Control. The agreement guarantees a home to every adoptable dog and cat in San Francisco.

Late 1990s and Early 2000s

In 1997, a local rescue group, including well-known veterinarian Julie Levy, founded Operation Catnip in Raleigh, N.C. to assist stray and feral cats. This was the first and largest program of its type in the southeastern United States. Later in 1998, Dr. Levy moved to Gainesville, Fla. and opened the second chapter of Operation Catnip. A third chapter was soon opened in February of 2001 in Richmond, Va. Operation Catnip provides a monthly, one-day TNR clinic for stray and feral cats; the program is free of charge to the public (Operation Catnip, accessed 2015).

Also in 1997, the Feral Cat Coalition of Portland (FCCP) received a grant making it possible for the group to build a mobile veterinary hospital to provide TNR services to feral cats. In doing so, the group decided to change their name to the Feral Cat Coalition of Oregon

(FCCO) to better reflect their assistance to feral cats throughout the entire state. This mobile clinic was the first of its kind in North America and it remains the only mobile hospital exclusively serving feral cats (Feral Cat Coalition of Oregon, Accessed 2015).

Another highlight of 1997, and a milestone for me, was the founding of Alley Cat Rescue (ACR) in Mt. Rainier, Md. I decided to dedicate my efforts to rescuing homeless cats from the streets and providing sterilization services to the local community; therefore, I created my second cat organization. ACR proudly follows a no-kill policy, where cats and kittens remain in our care until appropriate homes are found; this includes hospice care for sick and elderly cats. We operate an adoption program and provide low-cost spay/neuter services to low-income residents of Maryland, Washington, D.C., and Virginia, as well as run a TNR program for feral cats. ACR has sterilized over 40,000 cats since our inception.

In 2001, under the leadership of Nathan Winograd, Tompkins County, N.Y. became the second no-kill community in the U.S., "saving 100 percent of healthy and treatable animals, and 100 percent of feral cats" (Winograd, 2009). Later in 2004, Nathan founded the No Kill Advocacy Center, listing TNR programs for feral cats as part of the No-Kill Equation. That following year, the No Kill Advocacy Center held its first No Kill Conference, which continues to be held annually. (No Kill Advocacy Center, accessed 2015).

As the complexity surrounding outdoor cats continues to increase, so does the need for stakeholders to come together on one platform to review all available science so more adequate policies can be created. In doing so, The HSUS and co-sponsoring organizations the Humane Society Institute for Science and Policy, the Found Animals Foundation, and the Humane Society Veterinary Medical Association, hosted a conference called "The Outdoor Cat: Science and Policy from a Global Perspective" in December 2012. Dr. Kate Hurley, Dr. Julie Levy, Laura Nirenberg, Andrew Rowan, and Dennis C. Turner were among the presenters. In concluding the conference, participants acknowledged the lack of information and the need for further studies in order to more effectively combat the issues, while also recommending the "optimization of existing management tools and greatly expand[ing] public education to increase awareness and encourage more responsible pet ownership" (The HSUS, March 2013).

TNR is now endorsed by some of the largest animal organizations in North America.

Conclusion

Managing feral cats through spay/neuter started with a handful of compassionate individuals, who saw a more humane way of reducing cat populations. Today, TNR programs are implemented in thousands of cities across the United States and in several countries around the world. Pioneers like AnnaBell Washburn, Celia Hammond, and Ruth Plant paved the way for TNR and helped change the public's view of feral cats.

TNR is endorsed by some of the largest animal organizations in the country, including the American Society for the Prevention of Cruelty to Animals (ASPCA), The Humane Society of the United States, and The American Humane Association. In Canada, the Canadian Federation of Humane Societies supports TNR, and the U.K.'s Royal Society for the Prevention of Cruelty to Animals (RSPCA) supports the "trapping and neutering of feral cats where local charities have the capacity to do so" (RSPCA, accessed 2015). With countless studies and research supporting the effectiveness of TNR in reducing cat populations and the public's commitment to nonlethal methods, TNR programs will continue to increase and save the lives of millions of community cats.

International Programs
for Feral Cats

Years ago, at a conference on animal protection, I spoke of a campaign to help feral cats in Australia. I referred to two campaigns in Australia to kill feral cats. The first campaign was when a member of the Australian Parliament suggested wiping out cats in Australia by the year 2020 through the use of a lethal feline virus (panleukopenia or feline distemper). And the second campaign was in 1999, when Robert Hill, the Federal Environment Minister, announced that the Australian government would begin field trials of the experimental poison FST-2 to kill feral cats. The designers of the new poison claimed that it specifically targets cats and would not kill other animals. Other so-called "safe" poisons are now known to cause birth defects, cancer, and additional problems in both animals and humans.

FST-2 works by slowly suffocating cats by depriving their blood of oxygen. The RSPCA in Australia has "cautiously accepted the results of the laboratory work." The July 3, 1999, *New Scientist* magazine stated: "The effects of FST-2 are very similar to carbon monoxide poisoning. Cats given a fatal dose are dead within an hour" (Bonner, 1999).

The article goes on to quote Clive Marks of the Victoria Institute of Animal Sciences: "It is very important that we do not have cats eating a sub-lethal dose, which leaves them debilitated." Hugh Wirth, a veterinarian and president of Australia's RSPCA, stated in the article that "he is satisfied that the poison is humane" (Bonner, 1999).

A young Australian woman in the audience got very upset with me and thought I was singling out Australians, making them out to be cruel and inhumane towards animals. I told her that most countries have tried killing feral cats as the first option, and that actually it was scientists from my home country of South Africa who first used the lethal feline distemper virus on the feral cats of Marion Island. (Refer to the chapter "The Effectiveness of TNR Programs" for more information.)

In truth there is no utopia for animals anywhere in the world. I wanted to start this chapter on international campaigns by making it very clear that the goal of Alley Cat Rescue is to bring nonlethal control, specifically Trap-Neuter-Return (TNR), to feral cats everywhere in the world. Feral cats are considered by many to be "introduced" or "alien pests." Feral cats were introduced by humans hundreds of years ago, and killing them will not miraculously wipe them out. We should be ethically bound to treat all sentient beings with compassion, and whenever proven, nonlethal methods are available, we should be morally bound to use these instead of resorting to killing. When we have made these statements, the anti-cat folks have said, "What about all the birds and small mammals that cats prey on?" The answer to this is:

1. We are controlling and reducing the number of stray and outdoor cats, using acceptable and effective programs. Killing does not work. In fact it is counterproductive, allowing for unneutered cats to enter the vacated territory and the breeding to continue.

2. Cats prey mostly on rodents — they are rodent specialists — and they help society by keeping rodent populations in check.

3. Predation on rodents helps birds, as studies show that rats do far more damage to birds than cats do.

4. The birds preyed on by cats are mostly young, old, or sickly and would not survive to see the next breeding season.

5. Most feral and domestic cats live in urban areas. According to the 2009 "State of the Birds" report, "114 native urban birds species show a steady, strong increase for the past 40 years."

6. ACR asks all cat advocates to help birds and other wildlife by making simple changes to their lifestyles that will protect the habitat of birds. Take steps towards creating bird-friendly gardens, not using pesticides and fertilizers, and reducing the consumption of animal products, which contribute substantially to habitat destruction, climate change, and pollution. This is the single most important thing any of us can do to help birds survive.

Feral cats are under attack in almost every part of the world. The same myths that exist in one country about feral cats exist in other countries as well, with the possible exception of England. One and a half million feral cats live mostly harmoniously in England (most live in crowded London), without being considered a major health hazard to local humans. And TNR programs for feral cats have been implemented for a long time. As part of our dedicated work to help cats, ACR will continue to bring communities from around the world together, so we can humanely manage feral cat populations and reduce their suffering. For more information on any of our international programs, please visit our website.

ACR Helps Cats in South Africa

From an early age, I rescued a variety of animals; my family always shared our home with countless companion animals. In the mid 1970s, I worked with the Johannesburg SPCA to TNR feral cats, which lead to my wanting to assist feral cats after moving to the United States. Years later, I've come full circle, dedicating part of my work to helping cats in South Africa, with the African wildcat project.

African wildcats (*Felis silvestris lybica*) are the ancestor of today's domestic cats. Unfortunately, like so many cat species (cheetah, leopard, tiger), the African wildcat (AWC) is in danger of extinction. Human encroachment is one reason for their decline. Land development forces AWCs to live on smaller tracts of land. Their habitats are fragmented, making migration from one tract of land to the next dangerous. Plus, habitat loss decreases the number of prey animals, making finding food more difficult. There has also been an increase in conflicts with humans; farmers shoot the cats, believing they kill livestock.

Alley Cat Rescue

African wildcat in South Africa. This wildcat's numbers are in decline due to habitat loss and interbreeding with ferals and strays. Alley Cat Rescue has a TNR project in South Africa.

Besides the dangers imposed by humans, hybridization is also a threat to the African wildcat. Local domestic cats (whether they are family pets, strays, or feral), breed with AWCs, which dilutes the species' gene pool, decreasing the number of purebred wildcats. Currently, the African wildcat is considered endangered and is protected under CITES (the Convention on International Trade in Endangered Species of Wild Fauna and Flora) Appendix II. Unfortunately, this protection is limited (hunting is only regulated and/ or prohibited in a few countries) and in South Africa, there is no legal protection for them. Farmers routinely kill African wildcats out of fear that they will kill farmed animals and livestock.

Adding to the problem, veterinarian clinics are sparse and locals do not have the transportation nor the money to take their cats to the vet. This means fewer companion cats are sterilized, which increases the probability of domestic cats breeding with the AWCs. ACR saw this first hand while visiting South Africa, when we spotted stray and feral cats in several of the cities on the outskirts of game reserves; the cats who were being "cared for" we were told were NOT being sterilized. It was clearly evident that interbreeding between wildcats and stray/ feral cats is easily occurring and the need for TNR is critical for both cats.

In 2009, ACR visited with the Faculty of Veterinary Science of the University of Pretoria in Ondersterpoort, South Africa to discuss the possibility of a partnership that would include operating a mobile clinic on the borders of Kruger National Park to spay and neuter community cats. Due to the U.S. economic downturn, sadly this has not been possible. This campaign would go a long way in keeping unneutered feral cats under control, and help keep the African wildcats in the park free from hybridization.

ACR has also been working consistently with a group in Sun City, the Las Vegas of South Africa, to provide TNR to feral cats living at the resort, as well as cats living on the perimeter of Pilanesberg Game Reserve. Again, our efforts are to prevent the interbreeding of feral cats and African wildcats. To learn more about our program to save the African wildcat, please visit our website.

ACR Helps Cats in Mexico

In March of 2007, ACR visited Puerto Vallarta, Mexico along with four veterinarians and two vet techs to hold a free spay/neuter clinic. Over two days, we spayed and neutered 100 cats and dogs, including several feral cats. Many generous animal lovers helped with the clinic by volunteering, organizing, and donating supplies.

Laura Gelezunas, a Banderas News video journalist living in Puerto Vallarta, had seen the problem with her own eyes and contacted us for help. When Laura first called me, she explained that she was an American working in Mexico, and she had a passion for animals. She told me the plight of animals she had seen in Mexico and asked if we could send any help to curb the overpopulation problem. Of course we jumped at the opportunity to take our expertise in working with stray and feral animals to help in Mexico.

This was the first mash-style spay/neuter clinic that ACR had organized, and the largest clinic for Puerto Vallarta. Vets joined us from all over the U.S.: Dr. Pervaiz Manzoor and Dr. Javaid Manzoor came from Maryland, Dr. Ajaz Alvi came from Chicago, and Dr. Bill Pearce came from Texas. Dr. Pearce was the only vet who had previously participated in spay/neuter clinics in Mexico. When asked why he volunteered at spay/neuter clinics, Dr. Pearce said, "Why do you do this? Because it's the right damn thing to do. And what brings me out? Because I can."

Along with sterilizing 100 cats and dogs, our veterinarians shared vital surgery techniques, postoperative care treatment, and tips for working with feral animals to the dedicated vets working in Puerto Vallarta, who now run their own spay/neuter clinics. There are an estimated 45,000 stray dogs and 100,000 stray cats living in the Puerto Vallarta area. The success of this clinic will prevent hundreds of thousands of unwanted animals from being born and is the first step in the fight against pet overpopulation.

Israel

For many years, both The Cat Welfare Society of Israel (CWSI) and Arad for Animals have been working tirelessly to stop the cruel poisoning of cats in Israel. In 1998, after one attack by a rabid dog in an isolated area nine kilometers outside of Arad, the city announced that it would eradicate all stray cats and dogs in Arad. After the discovery of one rabid fox in the city of Arad in 1999, officials responded by ordering the poisoning of all stray and feral cats in the area (Friedman, 1999).

The Israeli government used alpha-chloralose to poison cats. This poison causes convulsions and consequently a slow, painful death. It does nothing to stop the spread of rabies. Israel's Ministry of Agriculture and Veterinary Services used to authorize municipal veterinarians to put out food laced with strychnine in the streets and fields. Stray animals along with companion animals would eat the poisoned food and die of asphyxiation over a period of 24 hours.

Israeli Veterinary Services claimed that the mass poisonings were necessary to protect the public from rabies (Friedman, 1998). Many scientific experts and world agencies, such as the World Health Organization (WHO), have stated that poisoning animals is not only cruel but also ineffective in controlling rabies. In fact, it increases the spread of the disease by creating vacuums into which rabid animals can then enter.

WHO claims that the oral vaccination of wildlife is the only effective means to eliminate and control rabies (WHO, 2013). And the National Academy of Sciences stated as long ago as 1973 that, "[p]ersistent trapping or poisoning as a means to rabies control should be abolished. There is no evidence that these costly and politically attractive programs reduce either wildlife reservoirs or rabies incidence" (National Research Council, 1973).

In the late 1980s, Rivi Mayer was one of the first people to suggest spaying and neutering street cats in Israel. Again, prior methods of population control meant poisoning. Fortunately this has changed and poison is now illegal. Mayer says neutering cats is not part of Israel's culture yet. More education needs to be done to get people to spay and neuter pet cats and the strays they feed.

In January 2000, CWSI, with the help of several veterinarians, trapped 70 feral cats at a kibbutz and neutered and vaccinated them in one weekend. This event lead to the establishment of a TNR program for feral cats in that area.

The municipality of Tel Aviv has good intentions, but they don't keep up with the amount of cats being born on the streets. They have to do at least 100 spays and neuters a day to keep up with the rate of cats giving birth. "We can do 10 cats today, so 10 cats are going to reproduce less kittens," says Dr. Zvi Galin, Tel Aviv's chief veterinary officer. Dr. Galin contends, "It's something. For me if I can help one, I can help one. It would be good to help thousands, but I can't do it" (Rosen, 2012).

The citizens of Israel are becoming more interested in companion animals and in supporting humane, nonlethal control of animal populations. A lot of credit for these changes must go to the tireless work of people like Rivi Mayer from CWSI and Ellen Moshenberg, who have never given up the struggle for humane care of animals.

Gambia

As is the case with many resorts throughout the world, hotels in the tiny African country of Gambia have colonies of stray and feral cats. Often hotels, which do not consider any other possibility, kill the cats. But the problem does not go away, and the hotels must keep killing.

A group of concerned people in the U.K. got together and found two Gambian hotels willing to let them use their facilities for a neutering project. The Gambian Livestock Services gave permission for a veterinarian to bring medical supplies and equipment into the country to help the cats. Funds were raised through appeals to airlines, pet food companies, travel agencies, and trap manufacturers. Veterinarian Jenny Remfry, who has had a tremendous amount of experience setting up international neutering programs, went along to help set up the program.

Monarch Airlines provided transportation for the 12 large containers carrying the equipment. Many of the hotel guests were interested in the procedure. Some German tourists even adopted three kittens and took the kittens back with them to Germany. As a result of these efforts, a former Gambian government employee has organized the feeding of the hotel cats and will help coordinate future TNR projects.

Peter and Frances Miller, who initiated the project, have obtained non-profit status in the United Kingdom. They have obtained permission from seven hotels to neuter their cats and are working on training people in Gambia to help with trapping and feeding.

The Cats of Lamu

A unique population of cats lives on the island of Lamu, off the coast of Kenya. Cinematographer and film director Jack Couffer believes that the cats are the descendants of the cats of Egyptian pharaohs. Couffer spent 20 years on this island observing and caring for the cats.

In 1998, Couffer wrote "The Cats of Lamu." He and his wildlife photographer son, Mike, took all the photos. Dr. Jane Goodall had this to say about the book:

> This is more than a book about cats — it brings to life a little known corner of Africa, with its age-old way of life and the fascinating relationship between the people and the cats themselves. The photographs are stunning, capturing the essence of Cat: They complement and add a great deal to the text. (Couffer, 1998)

The cats were mostly left to their own devices, with plenty of fish scraps to live on, although many people fed the cats as well. Often, Couffer found that some residents were feeding anywhere from 20 to 50 cats each day.

Couffer writes:

> The cats play an important role in the ecology of the town. Despite several centuries of frequent visitation by trading ships — the chief means of dispersal of rats and their diseases — there has never been bubonic plague in Lamu. Sharing duties with marabou storks, the cats provide the best the town has to offer as community sanitation crew and vector control department. (Couffer, 1998)

Unfortunately, he goes on to explain a time when the cats of Lamu were portrayed as disease carriers and killed. He says, "In spite of the record that the cats help in suppressing the plague, the possibility of the cats spreading the plague was used as a scare tactic to try to get public acceptance for killing off the cats" (Couffer, 1998). Finally, realizing that there was no way they would be allowed to kill the cats of Lamu, the KSPCA sent in teams from the World Society for the Protection of Animals who trapped and sterilized around 6,000 cats.

In recent years, a nonprofit trust, The Lamu Animal Welfare Clinic (LAWC) formed on the island to provide treatment, vaccinate, and neuter the cats. Since it started its operations in 2004, the clinic has cared for more than 10,974

animals all over the Lamu Archipelago. Lamu cats are famous — believed to be a preserved gene pool of the long-legged, fine-boned Egyptian cats of ancient times — honored rat-catching passengers on the dhows of the Arab traders of centuries ago. On the ships and in the shops and houses they are appreciated for efficient work in keeping the rodent population down. Their position in Lamu, a predominantly Muslim town, has been enhanced by the fact that the Prophet Muhammad was particularly fond of cats.

England, France, Italy, and Greece

All of these European countries have had TNR programs in place for many years. In England, the two larger and well-known groups are Cats Protection and the Cat Action Trust. However, several other groups such as SNIP (Spay/Neuter Islington's Pussies) have neutered cats in part of London, and they also have established an international team of veterinarians who will travel to foreign countries to implement spay/neuter programs.

Another group in England is The Celia Hammond Animal Trust (CHAT); which was founded in 1986. Over the years, CHAT has sterilized thousands of feral cats, and now has two veterinary clinics where they provide low-cost surgeries, as well as a dedicated rehoming/sanctuary center. Celia Hammond, who, over 30 years ago gave up a lucrative modeling career to help cats, told *Your Cat* magazine that she thinks she has helped rescue over 50,000 cats over the years.

In France, another famous model, actress, and singer, Brigitte Bardot, became known for her animal rights activism. In 1986, she established the Brigitte Bardot Foundation for the Welfare and Protection of Animals, which has helped thousands of feral cats through spay/neuter programs.

The Torre Argentina cat sanctuary in Rome, Italy, has about 250 cats living among the ruins.

A remarkable law was adopted in 1998 in Rome. It guarantees cats the right to live where they are born. This means that they are allowed to live in their homes whether these may be in the Coliseum, the Teatro di Marcello, Trajan's Market, or the Caius Cestius Pyramid. It has been estimated that Rome has around 10,000 cat colonies. Many of the cats are now sterilized thanks to the efforts of a few caring individuals (Natoli et al., 2006).

Torre Argentina, Rome's Cat Sanctuary, is one such organization helping to care for around 250 cats, who find shelter in some of the oldest temples in Rome (400-300 BC). Everyday volunteers from different countries feed, clean, and care for the cats. Tourists are welcomed to wander the ruins, visiting with the cats and stopping by the gift shop. Patrons are also encouraged to "adopt" a cat to help continue their life-long care.

And Venetians believe that their city was saved from the devastating plague of 1348 by their cats who killed the diseased rats. After visiting Venice, an English tourist, Helena Sanders, formed a group in 1964 called DINGO, to spay and neuter many of the cat colonies. Venice also adopted a law to guarantee cats the right to live in freedom (Natoli et al., 2006). DINGO helped to stabilize and reduce colonies using TNR. Thirty years ago the cats numbered around 12,000. The success of DINGO in Venice, using nonlethal control, is a model for other cities to emulate. Venice has been very successful at controlling its cat population, which was down to 5,000 in 1999 (Stanley, 1999).

Many visitors to Greece (me included) immediately see the many cats roaming the streets, laying around archaeological sites, and of course loitering around tavernas looking for a handout. On my visit to Greece, I thought the cats were in better condition than the dogs. I saw many dogs with open wounds from fighting and some were really skinny. We also

177

were struck by the many puppies walking around everywhere, some without mothers. I saw six Labrador-mix puppies sleeping under a sparse fig tree right near the Acropolis on a very hot day in Athens.

Many of the problems facing dogs and cats in Greece are worldwide problems; abuse, neglect, and abandonment. In Greece, it seems worse to travelers who live in countries that closely regulate pet ownership and licensing. And even though there is abuse and cruelty in other countries, the fact that there is some retribution for animal cruelty, could be a deterrent to those abusing animals.

Poisoning is very common. Thousands of stray dogs and cats were poisoned to "clean up" the streets and parks before the 2004 Olympic Games in Athens, as is done in most cities prior to hosting the Olympic games. Government-run shelters are always full and animals live there in appalling conditions. Veterinarians are hard to find, especially on the islands, as I can attest to; I could not find a single veterinarian on the island I was staying on to treat an injured cat. I had to buy supplies and treat him myself.

After being included in the European Union, pressure was placed on the Greek government to bring its animal policies in line with other countries in the EU. But in 2007, they were reported to the European Court of Justice for "continuing lack of action for animal welfare." The statement read:

The decision to take this action against Greece follows persistent shortcomings identified in the field of animal welfare over a number of years. The standard of animal welfare in Greece remains below par and the necessary legislation has not been adequately implemented. Therefore, the commission has no alternative but to refer the case to the Court of Justice. (European Commission, 2007)

Singapore

"Saving lives through enriching more minds."

This great statement is the mantra of The Cat Welfare Society in Singapore. It works closely with town councils, housing boards, environmental agencies, and the Veterinary Authority of Singapore to resolve cat issues effectively and humanely. The Cat Welfare Society of Singapore wishes to cultivate a community outreach movement to reach people with the message of responsibility and tolerance. The group helps communities resolve issues related to community and outdoor cats.

China

Beijing is infamous for rounding up and killing thousands of feral and abandoned cats in preparation for the 2008 Summer Olympics. Four years later reveals a typical round-up-and-kill outcome — the cats are back (Bruno, 2012).

Mary Peng, co-founder of the International Center for Veterinary Services in Beijing says China does not have the tradition of neutering pets. Peng is a Chinese-American native New Yorker who has lived in Beijing for the last 20 years. She has taken on the mission of convincing Beijing's residents that the best solution to the feral cat population is TNR. Peng says Beijing learned in the recent past that exterminating cats just leads to a new colony eventually moving back in. Of course the mass killing of adorable kittens usually causes an uproar.

Peng offers clinics in English and in Chinese on TNR. She helps identify care providers, or cat feeders, to help get them involved with TNR. Cats are sterilized and given rabies vaccines. (China has a high human rabies problem; around 3,000 people die of rabies each year.)

Peng has a good example of a reduced, TNR'd colony. In 2006, 23 cats in a colony were trapped. As with every colony some were taken in and adopted, and today only five cats remain. "We proved to the community it can be done here," she says (Bruno, 2012).

Hawaii (U.S. State Worth Special Mention)

The English explorer James Cook brought cats to the islands of Hawaii in the late 18th century. Cats were valued members of the early sailing ships because they helped control the rodent populations. Mark Twain toured the island of Kauai in 1866 and said: "I saw cats: Tom cats, Mary Ann cats, long-tailed cats, bobtail cats, blind cats, black cats, tame cats, wild cats, platoons of cats, companies of cats" (Twain, 1975).

Today, with a population of 50,000 residents who have made cats their most popular companion animal, Kauai has a large population of feral cats. Several Kauai natives such as Dottie Beach, a retired board member of the Kauai Humane Society, take care of many of the community cats. Islanders also feed cats at the beach and at the many hotels and resorts. Unfortunately, not all hotels show compassion towards the cats and some call in "bounty hunters" who often use cruel methods to kill the cats.

Other islands like Oahu and Maui have groups such as The Feline Foundation, Hawaii Cat Foundation, and AdvoCATS, all implementing TNR programs for feral cats. The Hawaiian Humane Society has spayed and neutered over 11,000 feral cats for 1,417 feral cat caretakers since 1993. In total, these groups have neutered over 75,000 cats through their low-cost spay neuter programs.

The Feral Cat Task Force of Kauai says the answer to the feral cat problem is to step up education efforts and strengthen local laws. The group is working hard to reach its goal of "zero feral, abandoned and stray cats on the island by the year 2025" (Moriki, 2014).

At the beginning of the year 2000, Hawaii's Department of Health came up with a plan to amend the Vector Control policy and to implement a ban on the outdoor feeding of free-roaming cats. ACR joined with several groups on the islands and rushed letters, faxes, and emails to the Health Department and the Governor opposing the feeding ban and expressing support for properly managed, well-fed colonies of cats.

After the public outpouring of support for the caretakers and the cats, the state agreed to look at legislation allowing them to study the feral cat issue. There are at least 18 groups in Hawaii implementing TNR on the different islands.

Conclusion

If you are an animal lover and cannot stand seeing neglected animals anywhere, there are several international organizations you can contact, before you travel, for information on how to get help for these animals. Please refer to Addendum 5 in the back of the handbook for a list of organizations.

And when you hear the environmental groups vilify cats and use them as scapegoats for the damage done to the planet, remind them to take heed of the United Nations-sponsored Millennium Ecosystem Assessment. The report states that humans are rapidly transforming the environment, converting more land into farmland since the end of World War II than in the 18th and 19th centuries combined. The report continues, noting that even these new farmlands have been exploited and polluted to meet the rising demands of humans for food, water, and raw materials, and that up to 30 percent of mammal, bird, and amphibian species are at risk of extinction due to habitat loss and human action (Blua, 2005).

There are community cats living all across the world. As they did centuries ago, they still play a vital role in controlling rodent populations. Rodents do far more damage to birds and other wildlife than cats and are also vectors of diseases, such as the plague, to humans. Let us keep pushing for humane, nonlethal management of feral cat populations.

Alley Cat Rescue's commitment is to help stray and outdoor community cats in the United States and worldwide, and to implement humane care to help improve their lives, put an end to cat overpopulation, and reduce the number of feral cats living in colonies.

Addendum 1: Wildlife Organizations

Unfortunately, many species of wildcats are listed as "endangered" or "threatened," with some even listed as "critically endangered" and "extinct in the wild," meaning they are only found in captivity. Some species of wildcats have become extinct — not even existing in captivity — being lost from the Earth forever. If we do not take sufficient steps now towards protecting and preserving the remaining species of wildcats, they, too, will soon become extinct. Below is a list of organizations around the world, that work to save wildcats, if you wish to support their efforts.

Alley Cat Rescue
www.saveacat.org
Mt. Rainier, Maryland

Big Cat Rescue
www.bigcatrescue.org
Tampa, Florida

Carolina Tiger Rescue
www.carolinatigerrescue.org
Pittsboro, North Carolina

Cat Conservation Trust
www.karoocats.org
South Africa

Emdoneni Cat Rehabilitation Centre
www.emdonenilodge.com
South Africa

Endangered Wildlife Trust
www.ewt.org.za
South Africa

Exotic Feline Rescue Center
www.exoticfelinerescuecenter.org
Center Point, Indiana

Hoedspruit Endangered Species Centre
www.hesc.co.za
South Africa

The Ann van Dyk Cheetah Centre
(formerly the DeWildt Cheetah Centre)
www.dewildt.co.za
South Africa

The Cat Survival Trust
www.catsurvivaltrust.org
United Kingdom

International Society for Endangered Cats
www.wildcatconservation.org
Alberta, Canada

Jaguar Rescue Center
www.jaguarrescue.com
Costa Rica

Kruger National Park
www.sanparks.org/parks/kruger
South Africa

Lion Rescue
www.lionrescue.org.za
South Africa

NABU's Snow Leopard Conservation Programme
www.nabu.de
Kyrgyzstan

Pilanesberg National Park
www.pilanesbergnationalpark.org
South Africa

Shambala Preserve
www.shambala.org
Acton, California

Wildcat Haven
www.wildcathaven.org
Sherwood, Oregon

Wild Cat Sanctuary
www.wildcatsanctuary.org
Sandstone, Minnesota

Addendum 2: TNR and the Law

While TNR programs are increasing in number and becoming more widely accepted, there are still few laws or regulations that specifically govern it; however, more and more cities are adopting TNR policies. So before you begin trapping, you might want to look into local laws.

You may be required to obtain a permit or register with a local rescue group, or gather statistics about and maintain health records of the cats in your colony. Also make yourself aware of any local laws concerning the feeding and sheltering of free-roaming animals, rules defining animal ownership, and vaccination requirements (especially in regard to rabies.) Some areas have enacted feeding bans in a misguided attempt to manage feral cat populations through starvation, while others have chosen to define anyone providing food or shelter to a feral cat as her "owner."

By knowing the laws in your area, you can be confident in understanding your rights and responsibilities as a cat caretaker. And if you encounter roadblocks to TNR in your community, get creative. A passionate person with fresh ideas has immense power to make positive change, especially at the local level. Use our sample letter to send to local city council members and the sample petition to gather names of your community residents in support of cats and TNR programs, to convince city council and other local government groups to take the humane approach to managing feral cats. And if you are experiencing particular difficulties, please contact us, so we may be of assistance.

Addendum 3: Foster Guidelines

The below information provides more detailed instructions on how to safely foster cats and kittens in a home environment. Guidelines for establishing a foster care program have also been included, as well as an example foster parent agreement form, which can be found in the back of this handbook. We recommend supplying any potential foster parents with a sheet of guidelines, similar to the one below, prior to having them sign an agreement form, so they are fully informed.

Foster Care Program Guidelines

A foster care program can allow staff and volunteers a chance to provide care in their homes for cats/kittens who are currently not in an adoptable condition or cats/kittens who need special care. For cats who would have difficulty surviving in a shelter environment or need special care, such as very young kittens or sick or injured cats, it is the only alternative to euthanasia. Foster homes are able to provide an environment where cats/kittens can thrive until they are ready to be adopted.

The decision to foster a cat/kitten should be considered carefully and foster agreements should be taken seriously. Fostering should be a positive experience for the cat/kitten. The decision to place a cat/kitten in foster care should be made carefully and only after considering the following questions:

1. Will this cat/kitten be able to be placed up for adoption, after he/she has been fostered?

2. Does the foster applicant have proper housing and adequate time available to foster the cat/kitten(s)?

3. Does the foster applicant meet all of the requirements and agree to all terms in the foster agreement? (Please see foster agreement.)

Additional Considerations

Foster parents who have other animals under their care need to understand the risks of bringing a new foster animal into their home and the risks of animal-to-animal disease transmissions. Foster parents who have cats living in their household should make certain their cat(s) has tested negative for feline leukemia (FeLV) and feline immunodeficiency virus (FIV), and the foster cat/kitten going into their care has been tested as well. Foster parents who have other dogs and cats under their care should have these animals current on all vaccinations and all animals within the household should be spayed/neutered.

New foster cats/kittens should be kept separate from other animals living in the household for at least a week, even if each animal appears to be healthy. Foster parents should also practice good hygiene when caring for foster animals, such as washing hands between contact with each animal.

Foster parents should understand that many animal-to-animal disease transmissions can occur from animal to animal via direct contact or via indirect contact with hands, clothing, bedding, food dishes, and other items that may have been contaminated with disease.

Zoonotic diseases are diseases that are transmitted from animals to humans. Common zoonotic diseases include ringworm, mites, and fleas. Less commonly transmitted zoonotic diseases are tapeworm, coccidian, toxoplasmosis, or giardia. Foster caretakers should be educated about possible zoonotic diseases and what precautions to take to help prevent transmission.

Caring for Foster Cats and Kittens

Sanitary living conditions are very important for cats/kittens under foster care. Carriers should be wiped out with a diluted bleach solution (four ounces of bleach mixed with one gallon of water) before each use. This diluted bleach solution should also be used to clean litter boxes, food and water bowls, and other items as needed, and before use with a new animal.

The food that is chosen for the foster cat/kitten should be appropriate for the species, age, and size of the individual cat/kitten. Do not feed cats/kittens food meant for dogs, and only feed food that is age appropriate (i.e. only feed kittens with food specified for kittens). Also, make sure all special-needs cats, who require a particular diet, are fed with food suitable to their needs (i.e. cats with UTI issues should be fed special urinary food).

Any diet changes should be made gradually over the course of several days, mixing the new food with the old food. The amount of new food added to the mixture should be increased each day, until the diet consists only of the new food. By making dietary changes slowly and in stages, this will lessen any digestive discomfort that can often occur when changes are made abruptly.

It is very important to keep areas where kittens are being fostered extremely clean, because their immune systems have not fully developed during their first few weeks of life. Take care to change bedding material if soiled, using a mild detergent.

Boxes in which the kittens will be staying should be lined with several layers of clean towels and old clothes. Please take care to put fleece, flannel, or cotton material on the top layer that will be in contact with the kittens. For the first few weeks of their lives they cannot retract their claws and they may get stuck in the loops of towel material.

Kittens cannot maintain their own body temperature for at least the first two weeks of their life, so it is very important they are kept away from drafts and additional warming may be necessary. To keep kittens warm, a large bottle of water can be warmed in a large container of hot water, then wrapped with a towel or cloth to help provide warmth. Similarly, uncooked rice can be put into a large sock and tied at the end, then microwaved to create a heat source for the kittens. This should also be wrapped in a towel or cloth before placing with the kittens to make sure that it is not too hot.

If you choose to use a heating pad, it should be used on the lowest setting. Never place the heating pad across the entire bottom of the box; the kittens need to be able to move away from the heat if it becomes too hot for them. Heating pads must be covered with a waterproof material and they should be placed in the box in such a way that the kittens cannot crawl under the heating pad. Whenever you are using a heat source, please monitor the kittens closely to avoid burns.

Feeding Kittens, Newborn to Two Weeks of Age

Neonatal kittens need to be bottle fed using a milk replacer specifically designed for kittens, such as KMR (Kitten Milk Replacer); these products can be purchased at most animal supply stores. Follow the guidelines on the label of the milk replacer to determine the amount to feed each kitten. Be careful not to overfeed, as this may cause diarrhea which leads to dehydration. Make sure you hold the kitten up right and do not force too much milk into her mouth or the fluid will go into her lungs and she could aspirate.

When feeding orphaned kittens, they will reject the milk replace when they a full. However, please keep track of how often they reject the milk replacer. If the

kittens miss two consecutive feedings, please contact your veterinarian immediately as this could be an indication that something is wrong with the kittens.

If diarrhea develops upon increasing formula, return to the previous feeding level for at least three to four days. After this period, you may increase the amount of formula. If diarrhea persists for more than 24 hours, please see a veterinarian immediately.

The eyes of newborn kittens open between seven and twelve days. Once the kittens have opened their eyes, encourage them to lap the milk replacer from a shallow bowl. Leave the bowl in the box with the kittens for one hour to allow ample time for the kitten to lap the milk replacer. If after one hour, the kittens will not lap from the bowl, then go back to bottle feeding. After three to five days of continued bottle feeding, try to encourage the kittens to lap the milk replacer from a shallow bowl again.

Once the kittens are comfortable with lapping the milk replacer from the shallow bowl, add small amounts of kitten food (canned wet food or moistened dry food) to the formula. This will help to transition the kittens to solid food.

Please make sure to never feed chilled or listless kittens. Chilled kittens should be warmed gradually, and upon returning to their normal body temperature, they can be offered a small amount of warm water before resuming a regular feeding schedule. If the kittens remain chilled or listless, please see a veterinarian immediately.

Addendum 4: Rabies

Rabies is a viral infection of the central nervous system that is transmitted in the saliva of infected animals. Most infections occur when people are bitten by an infected animal. The rabies virus cannot cross intact skin, but infection can occur if the saliva gets into a person's eyes, nose, or mouth. One cannot get rabies from the blood, urine, or feces of a rabid animal, or from just touching or petting an animal.

Of all the zoonotic diseases, rabies is one of the most feared and misunderstood even though its threat to humans in the United States is very small. Since 2003, rabies has caused a total of 31 human fatalities in the U.S. Ten of those people died after contracting rabies in a foreign country (from a bat, dog, or fox); five others included an undiagnosed organ donor and the four transplant recipients who received his infected organs.

Rabies and Wildlife

For the past 40 years, rabies has been reported more frequently in wildlife than in domestic animals. The Centers for Disease Control (CDC) reported 5,865 cases of animal rabies in the U.S. in 2013, a 4.8 percent decrease from the previous year — 92 percent of the total were wildlife, 85 percent of which were raccoons, bats, and skunks (Dyer et al., 2014). The decline in rabies cases is due to both the improved control and vaccination of domestic animals and to the development of effective post-exposure treatment and vaccines.

In 2013, Canada reported 116 cases of rabies in animals, a 17.7 percent decrease from 2012 and a 58 percent decrease since 2007. Rabies in skunks decreased 15.6 percent from the previous year, though rabies in bats increased by 24.4 percent. Canada reported no cases in humans, cattle, or wolves. Mexico reported 232 cases of rabies in animals, a decrease of 19.4 percent from 2007. Dogs accounted for 13 percent of rabies cases. Mexico confirmed 3 cases of rabies in humans, the source: vampire bats. The primary carriers in 2013 in the U.S. were raccoons (1,898), bats (1,598), skunks (1,447), and foxes (344). Infection is nearly non-existent in rodent populations (Dyer et al., 2014).

Rabies and Bats

Rabies acquired from bats has been the main cause of rabies deaths in humans in the U.S for some time. Even then, this incidence is very low — only 18 times over the last ten years (Dyer et al., 2014). It has not always been clear how humans acquire rabies from bats. In many cases, the fact that those people who died from rabies had contact with a bat was established only after the death of the person. It may be that the bite wounds are so small that they have not been noticed.

The number of rabid bats is indeed very small — only 1,598 in 2013, which is less than six percent of all bats submitted for testing (Dyer et al., 2014). As a precaution, if you ever encounter a sick bat, call a wildlife rehabilitation center for advice and do not handle the bat. If a bat dies or bites a human, rabies tests should be done immediately on the bat. If rabies is confirmed, post-exposure treatment should be started right away.

Rabies and Feral Cats

First, no person in the U.S. has died of rabies acquired from a cat since 1975. This last incident occurred in Minnesota, when a 60-year-old man was bitten on the finger and died approximately seven weeks later (Texas DSHS, 2013). Cats are less susceptible to rabies than many other animals, and in fact there is no cat-specific rabies — cats are infected with whichever species-specific strain is present in the infecting animal, such as raccoons, skunks, or bats. (The same is true for humans.) When cats do get rabies, they usually get the "furious" type; they stop eating, become very aggressive, and make unprovoked attacks on other animals and humans. Rabid cats usually die within four to six days. Generally, the CDC recommends a 10-day rabies quarantine for cats who have come in contact with a wild animal. Some health departments, such as the one in Maryland, insist on a six-month quarantine period.

Lethal Solutions Vs. Nonlethal Solutions

The main response to rabies control in the U.S. in the past has been to try to reduce the vector species by killing groups of those animals. This effort has proven totally ineffective, hastening the spread of the disease by removing healthy animals, and thus creating territorial "vacuums" for other animals of those species to enter. The mid-Atlantic epidemic was actually caused by hunters bringing infected raccoons into the region from Florida.

In Western Europe, the very successful oral vaccine VRG (vaccinia-rabies glycoprotein), developed in the U.S., has proven to be an effective, economical, and humane control for rabies. Wildlife vaccination via food bait has blocked the spread of the disease and prevented small outbreaks from becoming major epidemics by maintaining healthy populations of key vector species as immune barriers (Browne, 1994). A new oral vaccine, ONRAB (AdRG1.3 or human adenovirus-rabies virus glycoprotein), has shown promise in Canadian studies and is being investigated in the U.S. in Ohio, Vermont, New York, New Hampshire, and West Virginia. ONRAB is different in that it cannot induce rabies in humans or domestic animals who come into contact with it (Canadian Centre, 2012). Early trials have shown ONRAB to be significantly more effective than VRG in vaccinating raccoon populations (Fehliner-Gardiner et al., 2012). This is particularly important, as raccoons are the primary carriers of rabies in the U.S. and a threat to pass the virus to community cats.

Alley Cat Rescue Advocates a Comprehensive Nonlethal Rabies Control Program Based on Three Primary Initiatives:

1. Implement widespread oral-vaccine immunization barriers for key wildlife vector species, primarily raccoons and skunks.

2. Educate the public on steps to minimize human risk from wildlife rabies, including vaccinating outdoor cats and dogs and reporting sick bats to wildlife groups or the local health department. (Do not kill bats indiscriminately. They are a vital asset to our environment.)

3. Recognize and support the vaccination and nonlethal management of feral cat colonies as an effective and important part of a comprehensive control program.

The most effective means of stabilizing and reducing populations, controlling rabies, and protecting human health is to sterilize and return healthy vaccinated cats back to their supervised colonies. This helps to reduce roaming for mates, searching for food, and fighting; reducing these behaviors also reduces the transmission of other diseases. As mentioned previously, vaccinated colonies also create a buffer zone between humans and wildlife.

Addendum 5: International Animal Organizations

Below is a list of international animal organizations from around the world you might find helpful during your travels.

Animal Equality
www.animalequality.net
Headquarters in the U.S. and U.K.,
with projects in Germany, Italy, Spain,
Mexico, Venezuela, and India.

Harmony Fund
www.harmonyfund.org
Supports animal rescue in hard to
reach places, such as war zones.
Projects worldwide.

Humane Society International
www.hsi.org
Headquarters in the U.S.,
with offices in Australia, Brussels,
Canada, Costa Rica, India, and the U.K.

International Animal Rescue
www.internationalanimalrescue.org
Offices in the U.K. and U.S.; Cat rescue
project in the U.K., other projects in India,
Indonesia, and Malta.

International Animal Rescue Foundation
www.international-animalrescue-
foundation.org.uk
Headquarters in the U.K., with projects in
Greece, Georgia, South Africa, and others.

International Fund for Animal Welfare
www.ifaw.org
Offices in the U.S. and 14 other countries.

International Cat Care
www.icatcare.org
Headquarters in the U.K.

SPANA (Society for the Protection
of Animals Abroad)
www.spana.org
Headquarters in the U.K., with clinics
throughout Africa and the Middle East.

World Animal Protection
www.worldanimalprotection.org
Headquarters in the U.K., with offices
in 13 other countries, including the U.S.

Glossary

adoption — process used by rescue groups or shelters to place rescued or abandoned cats and kittens in homes. The process can involve interviews, home visits, and questionnaires, and a fee is usually charged. (This partly offsets costs to the shelter, plus it makes for a safer adoption for the cat, as unscrupulous people will likely not pay a fee for a cat they would harm.)

alter — to neuter or spay (applies to both male and female cats.)

animal control agency — most are local government agencies that respond to calls regarding stray and dangerous animals. These animals are then impounded; hence the term "pound." These are usually not animal welfare agencies, as they exist mostly to protect the public more than saving animals. Many, however, now work with local rescue groups to save more animals' lives.

alley cats — feral cats living in alleys, backyards, or under porches.

backyard breeder — a person who chooses not to spay or neuter the cats living in their backyard, or one who allows a family pet to constantly have endless litters.

caregiver — someone who provides food, water, shelter, and veterinary care for their own cat or a feral colony; the term "owner" is rarely used.

carnivore — an animal who derives his/her nutritional requirements from consuming animal tissue or flesh.

castrate — to neuter a male cat to prevent reproduction.

cat collector or hoarder — a person who takes in a greater number of cats than he/she can adequately care for. In these situations cats may not receive enough food and water to stay healthy, may not receive veterinary care, and living conditions tend to be cramped or unsanitary. Collectors are often unaware that living conditions for the cats (and themselves) are poor, that they are causing the cats more harm than good, and are unable to accept that they are overwhelmed. Hoarding is a defined mental disorder similar to obsessive compulsive disorder.

cat fancy — people who breed and show cats.

cat guardian — a new term that is preferred by many to describe a "cat owner." This term refers to the caring of and possibly sharing living space with a cat. This term can refer to someone caring for a pet cat or a feral cat colony.

catch-and-kill — an outdated method of feral cat population management where cats are trapped and killed in an effort to reduce their numbers.

colostrum — milk from a mother cat after a kitten is born. Helps protect the kitten. Colostrum is crucial for newborns. They receive no immunity via the placenta before birth, so beneficial antibodies need to be ingested.

community cat — a cat who lives outdoors, either in a colony with other cats, or by themselves as part of the local community. Can refer to both feral and stray cats. See *free-roaming cat, outdoor cat.*

companion animal — any domesticated animal (i.e. cat, dog, bird) whose physical, emotional, behavioral, and social needs can be met as companions in the home, or in close daily relationship with humans.

desex — to neuter either male or female cats to prevent reproduction. Term usually used in Australia.

domesticate — to tame an animal, especially by generations of breeding, to live in close association with humans as a companion or work animal, and usually creating a dependency so that the animal loses his/her ability to live in the wild.

domestic cat — an animal who has adapted to humans, usually over many generations. One who has a genetic predisposition to being socialized. *See also companion animal.*

eradication — the complete removal of a species from a given area, typically done by culling. Common methods involve poisoning, shooting, or catch-and-kill.

euthanasia — purposefully ending the life of a pet. Often employed when an animal is in poor health, is suffering, and cannot be treated. The decision to euthanize is typically at the discretion of the animal's caretaker.

ex-feral cat — a feral cat now tamed and living with a human. These cats are sometimes only "tame" with the original rescuer.

feline immunodeficiency virus (FIV) — a lentivirus (i.e. slow-acting virus) specific to cats that is usually transmitted through deep bite wounds. FIV is less common than FeLV, and FIV positive cats often live long lives symptom-free. FIV can eventually lead to a weakened immune system, making

cats susceptible to other viruses. Positive cats can live with other cats in a home, as once neutered they usually will not fight to the extent that they will cause the deep bite wounds needed to transmit the disease.

feline leukemia virus (FeLV) — a retrovirus specific to cats, FeLV is the most common cause of cancer in cats. It can lead to blood disorders as well as a weakened immune system , making the cat susceptible to diseases that she might otherwise be able to fight. FeLV is present in a cat's bodily fluids, is contagious, and can spread through bite wounds, mutual grooming, and occasionally through food dish and litter box sharing.

feral cat — a cat who was previously domesticated but became lost or abandoned and reverted to a wild state, or a cat born to a feral mother who has had little or no human interaction. Sometimes called community cat or wild cat. *See community cat.*

feral cat colony — a group of feral cats living together in an area. Usually started by an unneutered female or male cat who became lost while looking for a mate, or a cat who was abandoned, and found a reliable food source behind a shopping mall, cafeteria, or fast-food restaurant.

free-roaming cat — an outdoor cat who wanders freely and chooses her own living space. Can refer to feral and stray cats, as well as domestic cats allowed outdoors. See *outdoor cat, community cat.*

house cat — a cat who lives indoors, often specifically inside a residential area rather than a barn or other living space. Most often a domestic cat, except for re-socialized feral cats. See *indoor cat.*

indoor cat — a cat who lives strictly indoors.

Most often a domestic cat, unless she is a socialized feral cat. See *house cat*.

invasive species — a species that colonizes an area beyond or separate from its traditional environment. Also known as exotic, alien, or non-native species, they are typically thought to negatively impact their new habitat.

kill shelter — usually an animal control agency that euthanizes animals on a regular basis, and that will euthanize for reasons other than poor health and suffering (i.e. cage space).

neonatal kittens — newborn kittens. If they are orphans they will need to be bottle fed and cleaned in a similar manner to the way a mother cat would clean them.

neuter — the surgical removal of a male cat's testicles to prevent reproduction. Some call this to "fix" or "sterilize" a cat, or to "castrate" a male cat. Many refer to "neuter" for both male and female cats, especially in Britain.

no-kill policy — a policy adopted by many humane shelters and organizations that does not allow healthy and treatable animals to be killed, but instead will give each animal the opportunity and resources to live until a home can be found. Euthanasia can be performed, but only in extreme cases where the animal is in poor health and suffering.

outdoor cat — any cat who is not confined to an indoor home. This includes feral and stray cats, as well as domestic cats who live outside some or all of the time. See *free-roaming cat*.

overpopulation — the point at which the size of an animal population grows too large for a particular environment to support. For example, there are still too many dogs and cats born in the U.S., and there are not enough homes to take them. This is why it is so important to always spay or neuter companion animals.

porch cat — usually a stray or feral cat who has found a safe haven under or on a porch.

rabies — an acute and deadly zoonotic disease caused by a viral infection of the central nervous system. The rabies virus is most often spread by a bite, when saliva is transferred from an infected mammal. Although there is an extremely low incidence of contracting rabies in the U.S., the virus still causes great panic.

rescue — an organization that rescues homeless, stray, surrendered, and neglected cats and provides them with veterinary care and finds them new homes.

semi-feral — a cat who is used to living close to humans, but who is not entirely domesticated, such as a barn cat.

semi-owned cat — an outdoor, free-roaming cat fed by a community neighbor who does not consider him/herself an owner, but still provides food for the cat. These are the people we need to teach TNR to.

shelter — a facility that houses stray and/or surrendered pets for adoption.

spay — the surgical removal of a female cat's uterus and ovaries to prevent reproduction.

special-needs — an animal with a disability or with a permanent medical condition that requires ongoing special care.

sterilize — to spay a female cat or to neuter

a male cat is often said to "sterilize" a cat or prevent reproduction.

stray cat — a cat who lives outdoors, but is socialized to humans. Usually, these are cats who have run away from their homes or have been abandoned. They can become pet cats once again, but if they are independent from humans for too long, they may become feral.

surrender — there are many reasons people give up their cat for adoption to a rescue or shelter. This is called "owner-surrender."

tom cat — an un-neutered male cat.

trap-neuter-return (TNR) — a comprehensive program in which feral cats are caught in a humane trap, vaccinated, sterilized, ear-tipped, and returned to their original home. Young kittens and any tame cats are removed and placed for adoption. A caretaker ensures long-term maintenance by providing regular food, water, shelter, and veterinary care when needed.

vasectomise — cutting or otherwise inter-rupting the tubes that carry sperm from the testes, but leaving the testes intact. The cat behaves like a full tom cat, but cannot impregnate a female. Some recommend this for feral colonies, but ACR recommends a full neuter instead; neutering decreases the "annoying" behaviors often associated with feral cats, such as spraying, yowling, and wandering, whereas a vasectomy only halts reproduction.

vector species — an animal that is a carrier of a particular virus or disease; i.e. the raccoon is a vector species for the rabies virus.

wild — often used to describe a feral cat. A true wild cat actually is a non-domestic species, such as the European wildcat, Jungle Cat, or the African wildcat (*Felis lybica),* who is the ancestor of the domestic or feral cat.

zoonotic disease — a disease that can be passed between humans and animals. Actually quite common; scientists have estimated more than half of infectious diseases in humans are spread from animals.

Timeline References

Alliance for Animals. "Our History." *Afaboston.org*. N.p., n.d. Web. 23 Jan. 2015.

"Animal People." *Wikipedia, The Free Encyclopedia* 6 Dec. 2013. *Wikipedia*. Web. 18 Mar. 2015.

Best Friends Animal Society. "No-Kill Timeline." *Bestfriends.org*. N.p., 2015. Web. 30 April 2015.

Bloomberg, Mark S. et al. "Animal Welfare Forum: The Welfare of Cats." *JAVMA*. Vol. 208. No. 4. 497-527." *JAVMA* 208.4 (1996): 497–527. Print.

Cat Fanciers' Association. *A Critical Evaluation of Free-Roaming, Unowned, Feral Cats; Proceedings*. Englewood, CO: N.p., 1997. Print.

Elliott, Jeff. "The Accused." *The Sonoma County Independent* 3 Mar. 1994: 1 & 10. Print.

Grayvik Center. "The ORCAT Program." *Grayvikcenter.com*. N.p., n.d. Web. 26 Jan. 2015.

"List of Governments Supporting Trap-Neuter-Return." *Wikipedia, The Free Encyclopedia* 23 Dec. 2014. *Wikipedia*. Web. 23 Jan. 2015.

Maddie's Fund. "Feral Cat Advocacy: Deep Roots Continue to Blossom in the Bay Area." *Maddiesfund.org*. N.p., 2006. Web. 27 Jan. 2015.

Maddie's Fund. "History of No-Kill." *Mattiesfund.org*. N.p., 2000. Print.

Marx, Kerri. "Madrid Becomes a No-Kill City Saving Homeless Dogs." *HuffingtonPost.com*. Web. 26 March 2015.

Merrimack River Feline Rescue Society. "About." *Mrfrs.org*. Web. 12 March 2015.

Neighborhood Cats. "Our History: From One Colony to a National Movement!" *Neighborhoodcats.org*. N.p., 2014. Web. 2 Feb. 2015.

No Kill Advocacy Center. "About." *Nokilladvocacycenter.org*. N.p., n.d. Web. 27 Jan. 2015.

Operation Catnip. "Operation Catnip Inc - Raleigh, NC - Overview of Volunteer & Donation Opportunities, Services, Mission, Contact Information on Great Nonprofits." *Greatnonprofits.org*. N.p., n.d. Web. 27 Jan. 2015.

Petsmart Charities. "Preventing Litters Tackles Pet Overpopulation at the Source." *Petsmart Charities*. N.p., n.d. Web. 28 Jan. 2015.

Rowan, Andrew R. *Feral Cat Workshop: Friday, June 26, 1992, 10:00 A.m. to 5:00 P.m*. Medford, MA: Tufts University School of Veterinary Medicine., 1992. Print.

Slater, Margaret and Stephanie Shain. "Feral Cats: An Overview." *The State of the Animals 2005* (2005): n. pag. Web. 23 Jan. 2015.

The Humane Society of the United States. "Results of the Outdoor Cat Conference." *Humanesociety.org*. N.p., 1 Mar. 2013. Web. 6 Feb. 2015.

Torre Argentina Roman Cat Sanctuary. "Torre Argentina's Cat News." *Romancats.com*. Web. 31 March 2015.

Winograd, Nathan J. *Redemption: The Myth of Pet Overpopulation and the No Kill Revolution in America*. 2 edition. Los Angeles, Calif.: Almaden Books, 2009. Print.

References

Alley Cat Rescue. *Feral Cat Survey*. N.p., 2012. Web. 4 Oct. 2014.

Alliance for Animals. "Our History." *Afaboston.org*. N.p., n.d. Web. 23 Jan. 2015.

Alliance for Contraception in Cats and Dogs. "Megestrol Acetate." *ACC-D.org*. N.p., 9 Feb. 2009. Web. 6 Oct. 2014.

Alliance for Contraception in Cats and Dogs. "Why Non-Surgical Fertility Control." *ACC-D.org*. N.p., n.d. Web. 24 Oct. 2014.

Alliance for Contraception in Cats and Dogs. *Zeuterin™/EsterilSol™: Non-Surgical Sterilant for Male Dogs*. *ACC-D.org*. N.p., 2014. Web. 24 Oct. 2014.

American Society for the Prevention of Cruelty to Animals. "Pet Statistics." *ASPCA.org*. N.p., n.d. Web. 23 Oct. 2014.

American Veterinary Medical Association. *Vaccine-Associated Feline Sarcoma Task Force*. N.p., 2001. Web. 18 Aug. 2014.

Anderson, W. P., C. M. Reid, and G. L. Jennings. "Pet Ownership and Risk Factors for Cardiovascular Disease." *The Medical Journal of Australia* 157.5 (1992): 298–301. Print.

Arhant-Sudhir, Kanish, Rish Arhant-Sudhir, and Krishnankutty Sudhir. "Pet Ownership and Cardiovascular Risk Reduction: Supporting Evidence, Conflicting Data and Underlying Mechanisms." *Clinical and Experimental Pharmacology and Physiology* 38.11 (2011): 734–38. *Wiley Online Library*. Web. 25 July 2014.

Arup, Tom, and Nicky Phillips. "Curiosity: The Cat-Killing Bait to Protect Native Species." *The Sydney Morning Herald*. N.p., 1 July 2014. Web. 7 July 2014.

Australian Department of the Environment. "Lessons Learned from Devastating Effects of Cat Eradication on Macquarie Island — Australian Antarctic Division." N.p., 13 Jan. 2009. Web. 12 Jan. 2015.

Banfield Pet Hospital. *State of Pet Health 2013 Report*. Portland, Oregon: N.p., 2013. Web. 13 Aug. 2014.

Barratt, D. G. "Predation by House Cats, *Felis Catus* (L.), in Canberra, Australia. II. Factors Affecting the Amount of Prey Caught and Estimates of the Impact on Wildlife." *Wildlife Research* 25.5 (1998): n. pag. Print.

Berkeley, Ellen Perry. "Feral Cats." *Cat Fancy* July 1990: 20–27. Print.

Berkeley, Ellen Perry. *Maverick Cats: Encounters with Feral Cats*. Expanded and Updated Edition. Vermont: The New England Press, 2001. Print.

Berkeley, Ellen Perry. *TNR Past, Present and Future: A History of the Trap-Neuter-Return Movement*. Alley Cat Allies, 2004. Print.

Bester, M. N. et al. "A Review of the Successful Eradication of Feral Cats from Sub-Antarctic Marion Island, Southern Indian Ocean." *South African Journal of Wildlife Research* 32.1 (2002): p–65. Print.

Bester, M.N. et al. "Final Eradication of Feral Cats from Sub-Antarctic Marion Island, Southern Indian Ocean." *South African Journal of Wildlife Research* 30.1 (2000): 53–57. Print.

Best Friends Animal Society. "New Research Exposes High Taxpayer Cost for Eradicating Free-Roaming Cats." *Best Friends Animal Society*. N.p., 18 Mar. 2010. Web. 12 Aug. 2014.

Best Friends Animal Society. "Pussycats or Predators?: The Feral Catfight." *Best Friends*, 2003. Print.

Blua, Antoine. "World: Human Damage To Earth Reportedly Increasing." *RadioFreeEurope/RadioLiberty*. N.p., 30 Mar. 2005. *Radio Free Europe/Radio Liberty*. Web. 16 Mar. 2015.

Bonner, John. "Culling All Cats." *New Scientist*, N.p., 3 July 1999. Web. 18 Nov. 2014.

Brestrup, Craig. *Disposable Animals: Ending the Tragedy of Throwaway Pets*. Leander, Tex.: Camino Bay Books, 1997. Print.

Browne, Malcolm W. "Rabies, Rampant in U.S., Yields to Vaccine in Europe." *The New York Times*, 5 July 1994, sec. Science. Web. 18 March 2015.

Bruno, Debra. "Beijing's Feral Cat Problem Comes Back." *CityLab.com*. N.p., 27 Feb. 2012. Web. 16 Mar. 2015.

Bryner, Jeanna. "Growing Bird Populations Show Conservation Successes." *Livescience.com*. N.p., 16 Jan. 2009. Web. 2 Mar. 2015.

Calhoon, Robert E., and Carol Haspel. "Urban Cat Populations Compared by Season, Subhabitat and Supplemental Feeding." *The Journal of Animal Ecology* 58.1 (1989): 321. *CrossRef*. Web. 15 July 2014.

Campbell, K. J. et al. "Review of Feral Cat Eradications on Islands." *Veitch, CR; Clout, MN and Towns, DR (eds.)* (2011): 37–46. Print.

Canadian Centre for Veterinary Biologics. "Rabies Vaccine, Live Adenovirus Vector (AdRG1.3 Baits), Trade Name: ONRAB – Environmental Assessment." *Inspection.gc.ca*, 2 Nov. 2012. Web. 23 Mar. 2015.

Carey, Bjorn. "Stanford Biologist Warns of Early Stages of Earth's 6th Mass Extinction Event." *Stanford University*. N.p., 24 July 2014. Web. 2 Mar. 2015.

Carey, Sarah. *UF Researchers: Single Dose of Contraceptive Vaccine Controls Fertility in Cats for Years*. University of Florida News, 2011. Web. 26 Oct. 2014.

Catalyst for Cats, Inc. "Home." *Catalystforcats.org*. N.p., n.d. Web. 27 Jan. 2015.

"Cat Haters: Famous People In History Who Disliked Cats." *HubPages.com*. N.p., n.d. Web. 26 June 2014.

Caumes, Eric. "Treatment of Cutaneous Larva Migrans." *Clinical Infectious Diseases* 30.5 (2000): 811–814. *Cid.oxfordjournals.org*. Web. 28 July 2014.

Center for Biological Diversity. *New Data: 2.7 Million Animals Killed by Rogue Federal Wildlife Program in 2014*. Center for Biological Diversity, 13 April 2015. Web. 17 April 2015.

Centers for Disease Control and Prevention. "Parasites - Cryptosporidium (also Known as 'Crypto')." *CDC.gov*. N.p., n.d. Web. 17 July 2014.

Centers for Disease Control and Prevention. "Prevention - Plague." *CDC.gov*. N.p., n.d. Web. 29 July 2014.

Centers for Disease Control and Prevention. "Rabies in the U.S." *CDC.gov*. N.p., n.d. Web. 16 July 2014.

Centers for Disease Control and Prevention. "Salmonella." *CDC.gov*. N.p., n.d. Web. 28 July 2014.

Centers for Disease Control and Prevention. "Toxoplasmosis." *CDC.gov*. N.p., n.d. Web. 17 July 2014.

Centers for Disease Control and Prevention. "Tuberculosis (TB)." *CDC.gov*. N.p., n.d. Web. 28 July 2014.

Centers for Disease Control and Prevention's National Center for Emerging and Zoonotic Infectious Diseases. "Emerging and Zoonotic Diseases — At a Glance." *CDC.gov*. N.p., 29 May 2014. Web. 11 June 2014.

Christiansen, Bob. *Save Our Strays: How We Can End Pet Overpopulation and Stop Killing Healthy Cats & Dogs*. Napa, CA: Canine Learning Center, 1998. Print.

City of Atlantic City. "Business Administrator Ron Cash." *Cityofatlanticcity.org*. N.p., n.d. Web. 8 Apr. 2013.

Clifton, Merritt. "Where Cats Belong — and Where They Don't." *Animal People News* June 2003. Web. 29 Sept. 2014.

Coe, R. J. et al. "Comparison of Flank and Midline Approaches to the Ovariohysterectomy of Cats." *Veterinary Record* 159.10 (2006): 309–13. *Veterinaryrecord.bmj.com*. Web. 17 Nov. 2014.

Coleman, John, S., Stanley A. Temple, and Scott R. Craven. "Cats & Wildlife: A Conservation Dilemma." *Wildlife Control Technologies* 1999: 18–20. Print.

Columbia University's Mailman School of Public Health. "Early Life Exposure To Cats May Reduce Risk Of Childhood Allergies And Asthma Symptoms." *ScienceDaily.com*. N.p., 22 May 2008. Web. 11 Aug. 2014.

Cornell Feline Health Center. "Feline Immunodeficiency Virus." Ithaca, New York: Cornell University College of Veterinary Medicine, 2014. Web. 29 Sept. 2014.

Cornell Feline Health Center. "Feline Infectious Peritonitis." Ithaca, New York: Cornell University College of Veterinary Medicine, 2014. Web. 29 Sept. 2014.

Cornell Feline Health Center. "Feline Leukemia Virus." Ithaca, New York: Cornell University College of Veterinary Medicine, 2014. Web. 29 Sept. 2014.

Cornell Feline Health Center. "Zoonotic Disease: What Can I Catch from My Cat?" Ithaca, New York: Cornell University College of Veterinary Medicine, 2014. Web. 29 Sept. 2014.

Couffer, Jack. *The Cats of Lamu*. New York: Lyons Press, 1998. Print.

Council on Hemispheric Affairs. "Shooting Itself in the Foot, Brazil Spreads Concrete Through the Rainforest." N.p., 12 Nov. 2009. Web. 2 Mar. 2015.

Courchamp, Franck, Michel Langlais, and George Sugihara. "Control of Rabbits to Protect Island Birds from Cat Predation." *Biological Conservation* 89.2 (1999): 219–25. *ScienceDirect.com*. Web. 8 Jan. 2015.

Courchamp, Franck, Jean-Louis Chapuis, and Michel Pascal. "Mammal Invaders on Islands: Impact, Control and Control Impact." *Biological Reviews* 78.03 (2003): 347–83. *Cambridge Journals Online*. Web. 8 Jan. 2015.

Cox, Paul. "Skunks Lurk in Cape May after Feral Cats Are Removed." *The Star-Ledger* 18 Sept. 2008. Web. 7 Oct. 2014.

Cratty, Carol. "Ex-National Zoo Employee Sentenced in Attempted Feral Cat Poisoning - CNN.com." *CNN.com*. N.p., 15 Dec. 2011. Web. 24 Feb. 2015.

Crooks, Kevin R., and Michael E. Soulé. "Mesopredator Release and Avifaunal Extinctions in a Fragmented System."

Nature 400.6744 (1999): 563–66. *www. Nature.com*. Web. 1 July 2014.

Curtis, Patricia. *The Indoor Cat*. Rev Upd Su edition. New York: Perigee Trade, 1997. Print.

Darnton, Robert. "The Symbolic Element in History." *The Journal of Modern History* 58.1 (1986): 218–34. Print.

DeForest, J.W. "Modern Cats." *The Atlantic*. Vol. 33. Atlantic Monthly Company, 1874. 737–44. Print.

DK Publishing. *The Cat Encyclopedia*. Penguin, July 2014. Print.

Doty, K., and R. Hiltunen. "'I Will Tell, I Will Tell': Confessional Patterns in the Salem Witchcraft Trials, 1692." *Journal of Historical Pragmatics* 3.2 (2002): 299–335. *IngentaConnect*. Web. 10 Jan. 2014.

Driscoll, Carlos A., Marilyn Menotti-Raymond, et al. "The Near Eastern Origin of Cat Domestication." *Science* 317.5837 (2007): 519–23. *Sciencemag.org*. Web. 30 May 2014.

Driscoll, Carlos A., Juliet Clutton-Brock, et al. "The Taming of the Cat." *Scientific American* 300.6 (2009): 68–75. *Nature. com*. Web. 29 July 2014.

Duvin, Ed. "Unfinished Business." *Animal Advocates Society*, 2013. Web. 30 May 2014.

Dyer, Jessie, Pamela Yager, Lillian Orciari, et al. "Rabies Surveillance in the United States during 2013." *Journal of the American Veterinary Medical Association (JAVMA)*. 245.10 (2014): 1111-23. Web. 18 March 2015.

Elliott, Jeff. "The Accused." *The Sonoma County Independent* 3 Mar. 1994: 1 & 10. Print.

Engels, Donald W. *Classical Cats: The Rise and Fall of the Sacred Cat*. Psychology Press, 1999. Print.

EPA, Climate Change Division. "Methane Emissions." Overviews & Factsheets. *EPA. gov*, N.p., 2, July 2014. Web. 2 March 2015.

European Commission. *Commission Refers Greece to Court over Animal Welfare Infringements*. Brussels: European Commission, 2007. Web. 16 March 2015.

Fan, Meng, Yang Kuang, and Zhilan Feng. "Cats Protecting Birds Revisited." *Bulletin of Mathematical Biology* 67.5 (2005): 1081–1106. *Link.springer.com*. Web. 8 Jan. 2015.

Fehlner-Gardiner, Christine et al. "Comparing ONRAB® and Raboral V-RG® Oral Rabies Vaccine Field Performance in Raccoons and Striped Skunks, New Brunswick, Canada, and Maine, USA." *Journal of Wildlife Diseases* 48, no. 1 (January 2012): 157–67. Web. 23 March 2015.

Fenwick, George. "House Cats: The Destructive Invasive Species Purring on Your Lap." *Baltimore Sun* 25 Feb. 2013. Web. 1 Mar. 2015.

Feral Cat Coalition. "Welcome to the Feral Cat Coalition Website!" *Feral Cat Coalition San Diego, California*. N.p., n.d. Web. 27 Jan. 2015.

Feral Cat Coalition of Oregon. "History." *Feralcats.com*. N.p., n.d. Web. 27 Jan. 2015.

Feral Cat Spay/Neuter Project. "About the Cats: Feline Myths and Controversies." *FeralCatProject.Org*. N.p., 2006. Web. 12 Aug. 2014.

Fitzgerald, B. Mike and Dennis C. Turner "Hunting Behaviour of Domestic Cats and Their Impact on Prey Populations." In *The Domestic Cat: The Biology of Its Behaviour*, edited by Dennis C. Turner and Patrick Bateson, 152-75. Cambridge University Press, 2000.

Food and Agriculture Organization of the United Nations. "Agriculture's Greenhouse Gas Emissions on the Rise." *FAO.org*, 11 April 2014. Web. 6 August 2015.

Food and Drug Administration. "Suprelorin® F (Deslorelin Acetate) 4.7 Mg Implant." June 2012. Web. 26 Oct. 2014.

Foro, Lynda. "The History of the No-Kill Movement." *Maddiesfund.org*. N.p., 2001. Web. 2 Feb. 2015.

Friedman, Robin. "Israeli City Kills 55 Cats Suspected of Harboring Rabies." *Jweekly. com*. N.p., 26 Feb. 1999. Web. 16 March, 2015.

Friedman, Robin. "Killing of Israeli Cats Galvanizes U.S. Animal Lovers." *Jweekly. com*. N.p., 11 Sept. 1998. Web. 16 March 2015.

Friedmann, Erika, Heesok Son, and Chia-Chun Tsai. "The Animal/human Bond: Health and Wellness." *Handbook on Animal-Assisted Therapy: Theoretical Foundations and Guidelines for Practice*. Academic Press, 2010. 85–107. Print.

Gibson, Inga. "Hawaii Case Study: Developing Productive Partnerships to Protect Cats and Wildlife." The Outdoor Cat Conference. 2012. Web. 6 March 2015.

Goodland, Robert, and Jeff Anhang. *Livestock and Climate Change: What If the Key Actors in Climate Change Were Pigs, Chickens and Cows?*. Washington, D.C.: WorldWatch Institute, 2009. Web. 2 Mar. 2015.

Gray, Richard. "How Easy Is It to Catch Tuberculosis from a Cat?" 28 Mar. 2014. *Telegraph.co.uk*. Web. 29 July 2014.

Grayvik Center. "The ORCAT Program." *Grayvikcenter.com*. N.p., n.d. Web. 26 Jan. 2015.

Grube, Arthur et al. *Pesticides Industry Sales and Usage: 2006 and 2007 Market Estimates*. Washington, D.C.: U.S. Environmental Protection Agency, 2011. Web. 2 Mar. 2015.

Hamilton, Donald. *Homeopathic Care for Cats & Dogs: Small Doses for Small Animals*. Berkeley, California: North Atlantic Books, 2010. Print.

Hammond, Celia. "Long-Term Management of Feral Cat Colonies." *The Ecology and Control of Feral Cats: Proceedings of a Symposium at Royal Holloway College, University of London*. Hertfordshire, United Kingdom: Universities Federation for Animal Welfare, 1980. 90–91. Print.

Handwerk, Brian. "House Cat Origin Traced to Middle Eastern Wildcat Ancestor." *National Geographic News* 28 June 2007. Web. 29 Sept. 2014.

Harlan, Kohr. "Out-of-Control Rats Crossing Albany Power Lines." *KOIN 6 News* 25 July 2013. Web. 18 Aug. 2014.

Headey, Bruce. "Health Benefits and Health Cost Savings Due to Pets: Preliminary Estimates from an Australian National Survey." *Social Indicators Research* 47.2 (1999): 233–43. *Link.springer.com*. Web. 25 July 2014.

Hedge, Zarah. "Surgery Not Required: Updates from the 5th International Symposium on Non-Surgical Methods of Pet Population Control." *Humane Society Veterinary Medical Association*. N.p., 26 Aug. 2013. Web. 6 Oct. 2014.

Herodotus. "The Histories." *Landmark Herodotus.* Ed. Robert B. Strassler. London: Quercus Publishing Plc, 2008. 11: 66–67. Print.

Hoskins, Johnny D., DVM, PhD, DACVIM. "New Strategies, Technologies Are Helping the Overpopulation War." *DVM360 Magazine,* 1 June 2005. Web. 30 July 2014.

Horrigan, Leo, Robert S. Lawrence, and Polly Walker. "How Sustainable Agriculture Can Address the Environmental and Human Health Harms of Industrial Agriculture." *Environmental Health Perspectives* 110, no. 5 (May 2002): 448–49. Web. 5 Jan. 2014.

Howe, Lisa M., Margaret R. Slater, et al. "Long-Term Outcome of Gonadectomy Performed at an Early Age or Traditional Age in Cats." *Journal of the American Veterinary Medical Association* 217, no. 11 (December 1, 2000):1661–65. doi:10.2460/javma.2000.217.1661. Web. 30 July 2014.

Hughes, Kathy L., and Margaret R. Slater. "Implementation of a Feral Cat Management Program on a University Campus." *Journal of Applied Animal Welfare Science* 5.1 (2002): 15–28. *Taylor and Francis+NEJM.* Web. 13 Jan. 2015.

Hughes, Kathy L., Margaret R. Slater, and Linda Haller. "The Effects of Implementing a Feral Cat Spay/neuter Program in a Florida County Animal Control Service." *Journal of Applied Animal Welfare Science: JAAWS* 5.4 (2002): 285–98. *NCBI PubMed.* Web. 29 Sept. 2014.

Human Rabies in the U.S. 1950-Present. Austin, Texas: Zoonosis Control Branch: Texas Department of State Health Services, June 14, 2013. Web. 5 Mar. 2015.

Humane Research Council. "2011-2012 APPA National Pet Owners Survey." N.p., 13 Apr. 2011. Web. 26 June 2014.

Hurley, Kate, and Julie Levy. "Feline Shelter Intake Reduction Program FAQs." N.p., Jan. 2013. Web. 30 May 2014.

Huyser, Onno, Peter G. Ryan, and John Cooper. "Changes in Population Size, Habitat Use and Breeding Biology of Lesser Sheathbills (Chionis Minor) at Marion Island: Impacts of Cats, Mice and Climate Change?" *Biological Conservation* 92.3 (2000): 299–310. *ScienceDirect.com.* Web. 26 June 2014.

Jablonski, Helen. "Where Kitten Personality Comes From." *Cat Channel.* N.p., n.d. Web. 3 July 2014.

Jennings, Lea B. "Potential Benefits of Pet Ownership in Health Promotion." *Journal of Holistic Nursing* 15.4 (1997): 358–72. *Jhn.sagepub.com.* Web. 25 July 2014.

Kirkpatrick, Jay F., and John W. Turner. "Chemical Fertility Control and Wildlife Management." *BioScience* 35.8 (1985): 485–91. *Bioscience.oxfordjournals.org.* Web. 6 Oct. 2014.

Kristensen, Tom. "Feral Cat Control in Denmark." *The Ecology and Control of Feral Cats,* The Universities Federation for Animal Welfare (1980): 68–72. Print.

Kurushima, Jennifer D. et al. "Cats of the Pharaohs: Genetic Comparison of Egyptian Cat Mummies to Their Feline Contemporaries." *Journal of Archaeological Science* 39.10 (2012): 3217–23. *PubMed Central.* Web. 6 Jan. 2015.

Kustritz, Margaret V. Root. "Early Spay-Neuter: Clinical Considerations." *Clinical Techniques in Small Animal Practice* 17, no. 3 (August 2002): 124–28. doi:10.1053 /svms.2002.34328. Web. 29 Sept. 2014.

Lamont, Gil. *Is There a War Against Cats?*. Animal Protection Institute, 1994. Print.

Lawrence, Elizabeth Atwood. "Feline Fortunes: Contrasting Views of Cats in Popular Culture." *Journal of Popular Culture* 36.3 (2003): 623. Print.

Lazenby, Billie T., Nicholas J. Mooney, and Christopher R. Dickman. "Effects of Low-Level Culling of Feral Cats in Open Populations: A Case Study from the Forests of Southern Tasmania." *Wildlife Research* 41.5 (2015): 407–20. Print.

Lee, Irene T. et al. "Prevalence of Feline Leukemia Virus Infection and Serum Antibodies against Feline Immunodeficiency Virus in Unowned Free-Roaming Cats." *Journal of the American Veterinary Medical Association* 220.5 (2002): 620–22. Print.

Levine, Glenn N. et al. "Pet Ownership and Cardiovascular Risk: A Scientific Statement From the American Heart Association." *Circulation* (2013): CIR.0b013e3182920201e1. *Circ. ahajournals.org*. Web. 1 July 2014.

Levy, J. K., N. M. Isaza, and K. C. Scott. "Effect of High-Impact Targeted Trap-Neuter-Return and Adoption of Community Cats on Cat Intake to a Shelter." *The Veterinary Journal* 201.3 (2014): 269–74. *ScienceDirect.com*. Web. 16 Nov. 2014.

Levy, Julie K., David W. Gale, and Leslie A. Gale. "Evaluation of the Effect of a Long-Term Trap-Neuter-Return and Adoption Program on a Free-Roaming Cat Population." *Journal of the American Veterinary Medical Association* 222.1 (2003): 42–46. Print.

Levy, Julie K., and P. Cynda Crawford. "Humane Strategies for Controlling Feral Cat Populations." *Journal of the American Veterinary Medical Association* 225.9 (2004): 1354–60. *Avmajournals. avma.org (Atypon)*. Web. 18 Aug. 2014.

Levy, Julie K. et al. "Long-Term Fertility Control in Female Cats with GonaCon™, a GnRH Immunocontraceptive." *Theriogenology* 76.8 (2011): 1517–25. *ScienceDirect*. Web. 27 Oct. 2014.

Leyhausen, Paul. *Cat Behavior: The Predatory and Social Behavior of Domestic and Wild Cats*. New York: Garland STPM Press, 1979. Print.

Linzey, Andrew. "Against Biodiversity." *The Animals' Agenda* Apr. 2001: n. pag. Print.

Longcore, Travis et al. "An Estimate of Avian Mortality at Communication Towers in the United States and Canada." *PLOS ONE* 7.4 (2012): n. pag. *PLoS Journals*. Web. 2 Mar. 2015.

Lord, Linda K. "Attitudes toward and Perceptions of Free-Roaming Cats among Individuals Living in Ohio." *Journal of the American Veterinary Medical Association* 232.8 (2008): 1159–67. *Avmajournals. avma.org (Atypon)*. Web. 16 Jan. 2015.

Lorenzi, Rossella. "Animals Mummified by the Millions in Ancient Egypt." *DNews*. N.p., 6 Jan. 2012. Web. 6 Jan. 2015.

Loss, Scott R. et al. "Bird–building Collisions in the United States: Estimates of Annual Mortality and Species Vulnerability." *The Condor* 116.1 (2014): 8–23. *Aoucospubs.org (Atypon)*. Web. 2 Mar. 2015.

Low, Tim. *Feral Future: The Untold Story of Australia's Exotic Invaders*. 1st Edition. Victoria, Australia: Penguin Books Australia Ltd., 1999. Print.

Luria, Brian J et al. "Prevalence of Infectious Diseases in Feral Cats in Northern Florida." *Journal of Feline Medicine and Surgery* 6.5 (2004): 287–96. *NCBI PubMed*. Web. 29 Sept. 2014.

Maddie's Fund. "Feral Cat Advocacy: Deep Roots Continue to Blossom in the Bay Area." *Maddiesfund.org*. N.p., 2006. Web. 27 Jan. 2015.

Maddie's Fund. "San Francisco: The Nation's First Adoption Guarantee City." *Mattiesfund.org*. N.p., 2000. Web. 24 Feb. 2015.

Manville II, Albert M. "Bird Strike and Electrocutions at Power Lines, Communication Towers, and Wind Turbines: State of the Art and State of the Science - next Steps toward Mitigation." *Bird Conservation Implementation and Integration in the Americas: Proceedings of the Third International Partners in Flight Conference*. Ed. C. John Ralph and Terrell D. Rich. Vol. 2. Albany, California: U.S. Dept. of Agriculture, Forest Service, Pacific Southwest Research Station, 2005. 20–24, 1051–64. *Treesearch*. Web. 2 Mar. 2015.

Mark, Joshua J. "Cats in the Ancient World." *Ancient History Encyclopedia*. N.p., 17 Nov. 2012. Web. 6 Jan. 2015.

Marrion, Ruth. "New Views on Neutering." *Pet Resource*. N.p., n.d. Web. 29 Sept. 2014.

Marx, Kerri. "Madrid Becomes a No-Kill City Saving Homeless Dogs." *HuffingtonPost. com*. Web. 26 March 2015.

McGrath, Holly, Robert J. Hardie, and Eric Davis. *Lateral Flank Approach for Ovariohysterectomy in Small Animals*. N.p., 2004. Print.

McNeil Jr, Donald G. "First Cases Documented of TB Caught From Cats." *The New York Times* 28 Mar. 2014. *NYTimes.com*. Web. 29 July 2014.

Mercer, Samuel Alfred Browne. *Growth of Religious and Moral Ideas in Egypt*. Morehouse Publishing Company, 1919. Print.

Merrimack River Feline Rescue Society. "About." *Mrfrs.org*. Web. 12 March 2015.

Mineau, Pierre, and Melanie Whiteside. "Pesticide Acute Toxicity Is a Better Correlate of U.S. Grassland Bird Declines than Agricultural Intensification." *PLOS One* 8.2 (2013): n. pag. Web. 2 Mar. 2015.

Møller, A. P., and J. Erritzøe. "Predation against Birds with Low Immunocompetence." *Oecologia* 122.4 (2000): 500–04. *Link.springer.com*. Web. 18 Feb. 2015.

Molsher, Robyn, Alan Newsome, and Chris Dickman. "Feeding Ecology and Population Dynamics of the Feral Cat (Felis Catus) in Relation to the Availability of Prey in Central-Eastern New South Wales." *Wildlife Research* 26.5 (1999): 593–607. Print.

Montoya, J. G., and O. Liesenfeld. "Toxoplasmosis." *Lancet* 363.9425 (2004): 1965–76. *NCBI PubMed*. Web. 29 Sept. 2014.

Moriki, Darin. "Task Force Goal: Zero Feral Cats." *Thegardenisland.com* 18 June 2014. Web. 3 Mar. 2015.

Munro, Estelle. "Living in the Gray Zone." *Bestfriends.org*. N.p., Oct. 2003. Web. 5 Nov. 2003.

Murphy, E. C. et al. *Control and Eradication of Feral Cats: Field Trials of a New Toxin*. IUCN, Gland, Switzerland and Centre for Biodiversity and Biosecurity (CBB), Auckland, New Zealand, 2011. *Researcharchive.lincoln. ac.nz*. Web. 9 Oct. 2014.

National Institutes of Health. "Campylobacter Infection." *Medline Plus*. Web. 17 July 2014.

National Institutes of Health. "Ringworm." *Medline Plus*. Web. 17 July 2014.

National Institutes of Health. "Typhus." *Medline Plus*. Web. 17 July 2014.

National Institutes of Health. "Visceral Larva Migrans." *Medline Plus*. Web. 17 July 2014.

National Research Council (U.S.) Subcommittee on Rabies. *Control of Rabies*. National Academies, 1973. Print.

National Wildlife Research Center. *Development of Injectable and Oral Contraceptive Technologies and Their Assessment for Wildlife Population and Disease Management*. U.S. Department of Agriculture Animal and Plant Health Inspection Service, 2011. Web. 24 Oct. 2014. Wildlife Damage Management.

Natoli, Eugenia et al. "Management of Feral Domestic Cats in the Urban Environment of Rome (Italy)." *Preventive Veterinary Medicine* 77.3-4 (2006): 180–185. *NCBI PubMed*. Web. 29 Sept. 2014.

Neighborhood Cats. "Our History: From One Colony to a National Movement!" *Neighborhoodcats.org*. N.p., 2014. Web. 2 Feb. 2015.

Neville, Peter. *Claws and Purrs*. London: Sidgwick & Jackson, 1992. Print.

Neville, P. F., and J. Remfry. "Effect of Neutering on Two Groups of Feral Cats." *The Veterinary Record* 114.18 (1984): 447–50. Print.

No Kill Advocacy Center. "About." *Nokilladvocacycenter.org*. N.p., n.d. Web. 27 Jan. 2015.

Nolen, R. Scott. "Study Shines Spotlight on Neutering." *Journal of the American Veterinary Medical Association News*, October 16, 2013. Web. 30 July 2014.

North American Bird Conservation Initiative. *The State of the Birds 2009 Report*. Washington, D.C.: U.S. Department of Interior, 2009. Print.

North American Bird Conservation Initiative. *The State of the Birds 2013 Report on Private Lands*. Washington, D.C.: U.S. Department of Interior, 2013. Print.

North American Bird Conservation Initiative. *The State of the Birds 2014 Report*. Washington, D.C.: U.S. Department of Interior, 2014. Print.

Norton, Mary Beth. *In the Devil's Snare: The Salem Witchcraft Crisis of 1692*. Knopf Doubleday Publishing Group, 2007. Print.

Nutter, Felicia B, Jay F. Levine, and Michael K. Stoskopf. "Reproductive Capacity of Free-Roaming Domestic Cats and Kitten Survival Rate." *Journal of the American Veterinary Medical Association* 225.9 (2004): 1399–1402. Print.

Operation Catnip. "Operation Catnip Inc - Raleigh, NC - Overview of Volunteer & Donation Opportunities, Services, Mission, Contact Information on Great Nonprofits." *Greatnonprofits.org*. N.p., n.d. Web. 27 Jan. 2015.

Owens, Jared. "Greg Hunt Calls for Eradication of Feral Cats That Kill 75m Animals a Night." *The Australian* 2 June 2014. Web.

Pacelle, Wayne. "Setting Aside Semantics: Not Killing Pets Must Be Our Goal." *Humane Nation*. HSUS, 8 Nov. 2007. Blog. 5 January 2014.

Patronek, Gary J. "Letter to the Editor." *Journal of the American Veterinary Medical Association* 209.10 (1996): 1686-87. Print.

Pet Cancer Center. "Vaccine-Associated Fibrosarcoma in Cats." *Petcancercenter.org*. N.p., 10 Apr. 2013. Web. 18 Aug. 2014.

Peterson, Nancy. "Caring for Feral Cats in the Clinic." *Veterinary Technician* (2006): 503. Print.

Peterson, Roger Tory. "The Joy of Birds." *The Birds Around Us*. Alice E. Mace. San Francisco, CA. Ortho Books, 1986. 10-11. Print.

PetMD. "Bacterial Infection (Campylobacteriosis) in Cats." *PetMD*. N.p., n.d. Web. 17 July 2014.

Petsmart Charities. "Preventing Litters Tackles Pet Overpopulation at the Source." *Petsmart Charities*. N.p., n.d. Web. 28 Jan. 2015.

"Population Growth." *Wikipedia, The Free Encyclopedia* N.d. *Wikipedia*. Web. 2 Mar. 2015.

Quammen, David. *The Boilerplate Rhino: Nature in the Eye of the Beholder*. Simon and Schuster, 2012. Print.

Qureshi, Adnan I. et al. "Cat Ownership and the Risk of Fatal Cardiovascular Diseases. Results from the Second National Health and Nutrition Examination Study Mortality Follow-up Study." *Journal of Vascular and Interventional Neurology* 2.1 (2009): 132–35. Print.

Randi, E. et al. "Genetic Identification of Wild and Domestic Cats (Felis Silvestris) and Their Hybrids Using Bayesian Clustering Methods." *Molecular Biology and Evolution* 18.9 (2001): 1679–93. Print.

Ratcliffe, Norman et al. "The Eradication of Feral Cats from Ascension Island and Its Subsequent Recolonization by Seabirds." *Oryx* 44.01 (2010): 20–29. *Cambridge Journals Online*. Web. 29 Sept. 2014.

Rauzon, Mark J. et al. *Eradication of Feral Cats at Wake Atoll*. 15th ed. Vol. 1–2. Atoll Research Bulletin: National Museum of Natural History, Smithsonian Institution, 2008. Print. 560.

Rayner, Matt J. et al. "Spatial Heterogeneity of Mesopredator Release within an Oceanic Island System." *Proceedings of the National Academy of Sciences* 104.52 (2007): 20862–65. *Pnas.org*. Web. 15 Jan. 2015.

Remfry, Jenny. *Cat Neutering Programmes*. British Veterinary Association. Web. 18 Nov. 2014.

Remfry, Jenny. "Control of Feral Cat Populations by Long-Term Administration of Megestrol Acetate." *Veterinary Record* 103.18 (1978): 403–04. Print.

Remfry, Jenny. "Feral Cats in the United Kingdom." *Journal of the American Veterinary Medical Association* 208.4 (1996): 520–23. Print.

Remfry, Jenny. *Feral Cats: Suggestions for Control*. Second Edition. Potters Bar, Herts.: Universities Federation for Animal Welfare, 1989. Print.

Remfry, Jenny. *Ruth Plant: A Pioneer in Animal Welfare*. Hertfordshire, England: Jenny Remfry, 2001. Print.

Ridgley, Heidi. "Backyard Habitat: Why Curtailing Your Cat Is for the Birds." *National Wildlife Federation*. N.p., 1 Apr. 2003. Web. 3 Mar. 2015.

Rodríguez, Cristina, Roxana Torres, and Hugh Drummond. "Eradicating Introduced Mammals from a Forested Tropical Island." *Biological Conservation* 130.1 (2006): 98–105. *ScienceDirect.com.* Web. 8 Jan. 2015.

Romagnoli, Stefano (in press). "Progestins to Control Feline Reproduction: Historical Abuse of High Doses and Potentially Safe Use of Low Doses." *Journal of Feline Medicine and Surgery* 17.9 (September 2015). Print.

Rosen, Zac. *Tel Aviv's Feral Cat Population Out of Control.* The World, PRI, 2012. Print.

Rosenow, Daniela. "The Naos of 'Bastet, Lady of the Shrine' from Bubastis." *The Journal of Egyptian Archaeology* 94 (2008): 247–66. Print.

Rout, T.M. et al. "When to Declare Successful Eradication of an Invasive Predator?" *Animal Conservation* (2013): 125–32. Web. 14 Nov. 2014.

Rowan, Andrew N. "Cat Demographics." The Outdoor Cat: Science and Policy from a Global Perspective. 2012. Web. 9 Feb. 2015.

Royal Society for the Protection of Birds. "Are Cats Causing Bird Declines?" *RSPB. org.* N.p., 3 Dec. 2014. Web. 18 Feb. 2015.

RSPCA. "Stray Cats - Feral Cats | RSPCA." *RSPCA.org.uk.* N.p., n.d. Web. 29 Jan. 2015.

Sakagami, Taketo, and Mitsuaki Ohta. "The Effect of Visiting Zoos on Human Health and Quality of Life." *Animal Science Journal.* 81.1 (2010): 129–34. *NCBI PubMed.* Web. 29 Sept. 2014.

Salman, M.D., John G. New, Jr., Janet M. Scarlett, Philip H. Kris, Rebecca Ruch-Gallie, and Susanne Hetts. " Human and Animal Factors Related to the Relinquishment of Dogs and Cats in 12 Selected Animal Shelters in the United States." *Journal of Applied Animal Welfare Science,* J(3), 1998. 207-26. Web. 5 Feb. 2014.

Scarlett, Janet, and Naomi Johnston. "Impact of a Subsidized Spay Neuter Clinic on Impoundments and Euthanasia in a Community Shelter and on Service and Complaint Calls to Animal Control." *Journal of Applied Animal Welfare Science* 15.1 (2012): 53–69. *Taylor and Francis+NEJM.* Web. 19 Jan. 2015.

Scheer, Roddy, and Doug Moss. "Pet Overpopulation | EMagazine.com." *Emagazine.* N.p., 11 Sept. 2011. Web. 30 May 2014.

Schmidt, Paige M., Roel R. Lopez, and Bret A. Collier. "Survival, Fecundity, and Movements of Free-Roaming Cats." *Journal of Wildlife Management* 71.3 (2007): 915–19. *Bioone.org (Atypon).* Web. 30 May 2014.

Scott, Karen C., Julie K. Levy, Shawn P. Gorman, and Susan M. Newell Neidhart. "Body Condition of Feral Cats and the Effect of Neutering." *Journal of Applied Animal Welfare Science* 5.3 (2002): 203–13. *Taylor and Francis+NEJM.* Web. 18 Aug. 2014.

Scott, Karen C, Julie K Levy, and P Cynda Crawford. "Characteristics of Free-Roaming Cats Evaluated in a Trap-Neuter-Return Program." *Journal of the American Veterinary Medical Association* 221.8 (2002): 1136–38. Print.

Serpell, J. "Beneficial Effects of Pet Ownership on Some Aspects of Human Health and Behaviour." *Journal of the Royal Society of Medicine* 84.12 (1991): 717–20. Print.

Serpell, James A. "Domestication and History of the Cat." *The Domestic Cat: The Biology of Its Behaviour*. Ed. Dennis C. Turner and Patrick Bateson. Cambridge University Press, 2000. 179–92. Print.

Seymour, Frankie. "The Great Feral Cat Con Job: The Ungentle Art of Scapegoating and Scaremongering." N.p., n.d. Web. 29 Sept. 2014.

Simmon, Mike, and Trish Simmon. "The Maine Coon, America's Native Longhair." Organization. *Maine Coon Breeders & Fanciers Association*. N.p., n.d. Web. 29 Sept. 2014.

Slater, Margaret R. *Community Approaches to Feral Cats*. First. Washington, D.C.: Humane Society Press, 2002. Print. Public Policy Series.

Slater, Margaret, and Stephanie Shain. "Feral Cats: An Overview." *The State of the Animals 2005* (2005): n. pag. Web. 23 Jan. 2015.

Smallwood, K. Shawn. "Comparing Bird and Bat Fatality-Rate Estimates among North American Wind-Energy Projects." *Wildlife Society Bulletin* 37.1 (2013): 19–33. *Wiley Online Library*. Web. 2 Mar. 2015.

Stanley, Alessandra. "Venice Journal; With Claws Drawn, Italians Duel Over 250 Cats." *The New York Times*, April 7, 1999, sec. World. Web. 16 March 2015.

Strickland, Eliza. "Attempt to Control Invasive Species Backfires Spectacularly on an Antarctic Island." *80beats, Discover Magazine*. N.p., 12 Jan. 2009. Web. 31 July 2014.

Syufy, Franny. "Sterilization Drugs for Cats." *About.com*. N.p., n.d. Web. 25 Oct. 2014.

Tabor, Roger. *Cat Behaviour: The Complete Feline Problem Solver*. David & Charles, 1997. Print.

Tabor, Roger. *Cats: The Rise of the Cat*. London, England: BBC Books, 1991. Print.

Tabor, Roger. "General Biology of Feral Cats." *The Ecology and Control of Feral Cats: Proceedings of a Symposium Held at Royal Holloway College, University of London, 23rd and 24th September, 1980*. Potters Bar, Hertfordshire: Universities Federation for Animal Welfare, 1981. Print.

Tabor, Roger K. *The Wild Life of the Domestic Cat*. London: Arrow Books, 1983. Print.

Tabor, Roger. *Understanding Cats*. Newton Abbot: David & Charles, 1995. Print.

Terborgh, John, and Dr. James A. Estes, eds. *Trophic Cascades: Predators, Prey, and the Changing Dynamics of Nature*. 1 edition. Washington DC: Island Press, 2010. Print.

The Humane Society of the United States. "Common Questions about Animal Shelters." *The Humane Society of the United States*. N.p., 3 May 2013. Web. 30 May 2014.

The Humane Society of the United States. "Pets by the Numbers." N.p., 30 Jan. 2014. Web. 26 June 2014.

The Humane Society of the United States. "Results of the Outdoor Cat Conference." *Humanesociety.org*, March 1, 2013. Web. 6 February 2015.

The National Council on Pet Population Study and Policy (NCPPSP). *The Shelter Statistics Survey, 1994-97*. N.p., 1997. Web. 31 Oct. 2014.

Thomet, Laurent. "First Domestic Cat Purred in Middle East." *Australian Broadcasting Corporation* 29 June 2007. Web. 29 Sept. 2014.

Torre Argentina Roman Cat Sanctuary. "Torre Argentina's Cat News." *Romancats.com*. Web. 31 March 2015.

Tufts University School of Veterinary Medicine. *Catnip*. N.p., October 1995. Print.

Tufts University School of Veterinary Medicine. "What the Cat Dragged In." *Catnip* 1995: 4–6. Print.

Twain, Mark. *Mark Twain's Letters from Hawaii*. Univ. of Hawaii Press, 1975. Print.

U.S. Department of Agriculture: Animal and Plant Health Inspection Service. "2014 Program Data Reports." *Aphis.usda.gov*, 10 April 2015. Web. 17 April 2015.

U.S. Department of Health and Human Services. "H5N1 Avian Flu (H5N1 Bird Flu)." *Flu.gov*. N.p., n.d. Web. 25 Oct. 2014.

VCA Animal Hospitals. *A Few Benefits and Risks for Indoor/outdoor Cats*. VCA Inc., 2012. Web. 16 Mar. 2015.

Veitch, C.R., M.N. Clout, and D.R. Towns, eds. "Island Invasives: Eradication and Management." *International Conference on Island Invasives*. University of Auckland, New Zealand: International Union for Conservation of Nature and Natural Resources, 2011. 37–46. Print.

"Veterinarian Orientation | Program Administration | TNR Clinic Model." *Operation Catnip of Gainesville*. N.p., n.d. Web. 15 Mar. 2015.

Vigne, J.D. et al. "Early Taming of the Cat in Cyprus." *Science* 304.5668 (2004): 259. *Sciencemag.org*. Web. 30 May 2014.

Vittecoq, Marion et al. "Cat Ownership Is Neither a Strong Predictor of Toxoplamsa Gondii Infection nor a Risk Factor for Brain Cancer." *Biology Letters* (2012): rsbl20120625. *Rsbl. royalsocietypublishing.org*. Web. 17 July 2014.

Wade, Nicholas. "Study Traces Cat's Ancestry to Middle East." *The New York Times* 29 June 2007. *NYTimes.com*. Web. 30 May 2014.

Wallace, Jennifer L., and Julie K. Levy. "Population Characteristics of Feral Cats Admitted to Seven Trap-Neuter-Return Programs in the United States." *Journal of Feline Medicine and Surgery* 8.4 (2006): 279–84. *NCBI PubMed*. Web. 29 Sept. 2014.

WebMD. "Feline Toxoplasmosis." *Pets. WebMD.com*. N.p., n.d. Web. 25 July 2014.

Wenstrup, J., and A. Dowidchuk. "Pet Overpopulation: Data and Measurement Issues in Shelters." *Journal of Applied Animal Welfare Science: JAAWS* 2.4 (1999): 303–19. *NCBI PubMed*. Web. 29 Sept. 2014.

Wildlife Services. *Oral Rabies Vaccination Program in the East*. U.S. Department of Agriculture Animal and Plant Health Inspection Service, 2011. Web. 29 Sept. 2014.

Wilkinson, Charles Kyrle, and Marsha Hill. *Egyptian Wall Paintings: The Metropolitan Museum of Art's Collection of Facsimiles*. New York: Metropolitan Museum of Art (New York, N.Y.), 1983. Print.

Winograd, Nathan J. "Breaking Ranks: The Evolution of Dr. Kate Hurley." *NathanWinograd.com*. N.p., 24 May 2013. Blog. 1 Sept. 2013.

Winograd, Nathan J. *Redemption: The Myth of Pet Overpopulation and the No Kill Revolution in America*. 2 edition. Los Angeles, Calif.: Almaden Books, 2009. Print.

Wolf, Peter J. "Repeat After Me." *Vox Felina*. N.p., 3 Aug. 2010. Blog. 1 Mar. 2015.

World Health Organization. *Expert Consultation on Rabies: Second Report.* Geneva, Switzerland: N.p., 2013. Web. 16 Mar. 2015.

World Health Organization. "Lyme Borreliosis (Lyme Disease)." *WHO.* N.p., n.d. Web. 28 July 2014.

World Health Organization. "Plague." *WHO.* N.p., n.d. Web. 28 July 2014.

World Health Organization. "Severe Acute Respiratory Syndrome (SARS)." *WHO.* N.p., n.d. Web. 25 Oct. 2014.

World Health Organization. "Zoonoses and the Human-Animal-Ecosystems Interface." *WHO.* N.p., n.d. Web. 11 June 2014.

Worldwatch Institute. *2010 State of the World.* New York, New York: W. W. Norton & Company, 2010. Print.

Youth, Howard. *Winged Messengers: The Decline of Birds.* Worldwatch Institute, 2003. Print.

Zaunbrecher, Karl I., and Richard E. Smith. "Neutering of Feral Cats as an Alternative to Eradication Programs." *Journal of the American Veterinary Medical Association* 203.3 (1993): n. pag. Print.

Zawistowski, S., *Simulating Different Approaches for Managing Free-Roaming Cat Populations, in 2013 National Council on Pet Population Research Symposium Presentations: CATS: The Ins and Outs: Improving their Future Through Research* 2013, Society of Animal Welfare Administrators Tempe, AZ.

Zax, David. "A Brief History of House Cats." *Smithsonian.* N.p., 30 June 2007. Web. 6 Jan. 2015.

Zeugner, Emily. "Feline Geneticist Traces Origin of the Cat." *Associated Press* 9 June 2008. Web. 29 July 2014.

Photography Credits

Adrigu: page 105. *IMG_4437*. 2006. Flickr. Accessed 8/12/15. https://www.flickr.com/photos/97793800@N00/339258273/in/set-72157594238864563. CC BY 2.0 - https://creativecommons.org/licenses/by/2.0/

Alley Cat Rescue: pages xiii, 21, 27, 48, 52, 58, 62, 78, 79, 93, 96, 100, 103, 112, 114, 122, 134, 164, 165, 166, 172, 235.

Cara Frye: pages 18, 53, 149.

City Critters, Inc.: page 23.

Desireé Stapley: pages 29, 33, 47, 119.

George Smith: page 61.

Jenny Remfry: page ix.

Judy M. Zukoski: pages 14, 51, 64, 82, 140.

Linda Tanner: page 36, *The Wharf Cat Family*. 2011.

Louise Holton: pages 3, 5, 10, 13, 19, 26, 56, 75, 86, 90, 111, 133, 152, 177.

Luc Viatour (www.lucnix.be): page 4. *A European Wildcat*. 2013. Wikimedia Commons. Accessed 8/12/15. http://commons.wikimedia.org/wiki/File:Felis_silvestris_silvestris_Luc_Viatour.jpg#/media/File:Felis_silvestris_silvestris_Luc_Viatour.jpg CC BY-SA 3.0 - http://creativecommons.org/licenses/by-sa/3.0/

Maggie Funkhouser: pages 102, 128, 132.

Magnus Johansson: page 156. *Cat in a Tree*. 2014. Flickr. Accessed 8/12/15. https://www.flickr.com/photos/120374925@N06/15022426058 CC BY-SA 2.0 - https://creativecommons.org/licenses/by-sa/2.0/

Nancy North: pages 67, 83, 107, 117.

Operation Catnip of Gainesville: page 106.

Roger Tabor: pages viii, 8, 43, 135.

Roy Pederson: page 138. *Young Alley Cat Searching through Some Rubbish*. Shutterstock. http://www.shutterstock.com/cat.mhtml?searchterm=young+alley+cat+searching+through+some+rubbish&autocomplete_id=1430696823211237700008&language=en&lang=en&search_source=&safesearch=1&version=llv1&media_type=

Serena: page 158. *Spellbound*. 2008. Flickr. Accessed 8/12/15. https://www.flickr.com/photos/zenera/3141853919 CC BY-SA 2.0 - https://creativecommons.org/licenses/by-sa/2.0/

ShaidaTala Sabin: pages 54, 109.

Troy Snow: pages 148, 169.

Waterloo Alley Cat Project: pages 77, 80.

Alley Cat Rescue, Inc.

www.saveacat.org (301) 277-5595

Feral Cat Survey 2012

Question	Answer & Percentage	
1. Do you have a physical shelter?	Yes	38.66%
	No	50.42%
2. What is your organization's capacity? (How many animals can it hold?)	10-20	9.24%
	21-40	13.45%
	41-60	6.72%
	61-80+	37.82%
3. How many paid employees do you have?	0-3	60.50%
	4-6	4.20%
	7-10	4.20%
	11-15+	18.49%
4. Do you have a foster program/network?	Yes	74.79%
	No	17.65%
5. How many volunteers, including fosters, do you have?	1-10	21.85%
	11-20	19.33%
	21-30	15.97%
	31-40+	31.93%
6. Have many years have you been in operation?	1-5	19.33%
	6-15	42.86%
	16-25	15.13%
	26-36+	12.61%
7. Besides providing TNR for feral cats, do you offer spay/neuter services to "owned" cats?	Yes	78.99%
	No	12.61%
8. If yes, how many "owned" cats do you sterilize per year?	1-20	15.97%
	21-50	14.29%
	51-80	6.72%
	81-110+	42.86%

Question	Answer & Percentage	
9. Do you sterilize cats before you adopt them out?	Yes	80.67%
	No	0.84%
10. If yes, how many cats in your adoption program do you sterilize per year?	40-60	20.17%
	61-80	5.04%
	81-110	7.56%
	111-130+	44.54%
11. How many "community" cats are there in your state?	100,000-500,000	8.40%
	500,000-1,000,000	6.72%
	1 million-5 million	22.69%
	5 million-10 million	15.13%
	10 million-15 million	1.68%
12. How many "community" cats are there in your county?	0-1,000	2.52%
	1,000-10,000	9.24%
	10,000-100,000	28.57%
	100,000-500,000	20.17%
	500,000-1 million	0.84%
	1 million-3 million	0.84%
13. How many cats has your group TNR'd TOTAL?	200-500	12.61%
	501-1,000	16.81%
	1,001-5,000	31.09%
	5,001-10,000	12.61%
	10,001-15000	8.40%
	15,001-20,000	0.84%
	20,001-25,000	2.52%
	25,001-30,000+	5.04%
14. How many do you TNR per year?	1-100	17.65%
	101-300	20.17%
	301-500	11.76%
	501-700	12.61%
	701-900	1.68%
	901-1,500	7.56%
	1,501-2,000+	11.76%

Question

Answer & Percentage

Question	Answer	Percentage
15. What is the average size of colonies in your area? (How many cats per colony?)	5-10	35.29%
	11-20	34.45%
	21-30	7.56%
	31-40+	2.52%
16. How many colonies do you take care of?	1-5	42.02%
	6-10	11.76%
	11-15+	5.88%
	16-20	3.36%
	21-25	1.68%
	26-30+	6.72%
17. How many colonies do others in your area take care of?	1-5	15.13%
	6-10	12.61%
	11-15	6.72%
	16-20+	39.50%
18. What is the average age of the cats in these colonies?	1 month-1 year	4.20%
	2-6 yrs	63.87%
	6-10 yrs	10.92%
	10+	3.36%
19. What are the oldest ages of some of the cats?	3-5 yrs	4.20%
	6-8 yrs	24.37%
	9-12 yrs	35.29%
	13+	14.29%
20. How long do you hold a cat for recovery after surgery?	a few hours	15.13%
	1 day	48.74%
	2 days	21.01%
	3 days	7.56%
21. Do you ear-tip all cats you TNR?	Yes	80.67%
	No	6.72%
	sometimes	0.84%

Question	Answer & Percentage	
22. Do you test for FIV and FeLV?	Yes	10.08%
	No	31.09%
	sometimes	47.06%
23. If you do test, how many cats have tested positive for FeLV?	1-5	31.09%
	6-10	7.56%
	11-15	4.20%
	16-20+	9.24%
24. If you do test, how many cats have tested positive for FIV?	1-5	23.53%
	6-10	13.45%
	11-15	6.72%
	16-20+	8.40%
25. Do you provide rabies vaccines?	Yes	80.67%
	No	10.08%
26. Do you provide other vaccinations and/or treatments? (Circle all that apply.)	distemper	64.71%
	leukemia	11.76%
	dewormer	62.18%
	deflea	63.87%
27. How many kittens were reported prior to TNR?	5-10	8.40%
	11-15	10.92%
	16-20	8.40%
	21-25	2.52%
	26-30+	33.61%
28. How many kittens were reported after TNR?	0-5	42.86%
	6-10	9.24%
	11-15	3.36%
	16-20	0.84%
	21-25+	7.56%
29. How many kittens have been removed for adoption?	5-10	10.92%
	11-15	10.08%
	16-20	7.56%
	21-25	5.04%
	26-30+	37.82%

Question

Answer & Percentage

Question		
30. How many adult cats have been removed for adoption?	0-5	31.09%
	0-5	14.29%
	6-10	5.88%
	11-15	3.36%
	21-25+	16.81%
31. How many cats have been relocated?	0-5	36.97%
	6-10	13.45%
	11-15	7.56%
	16-20	4.20%
	21-25+	9.24%
32. After performing TNR, on average, how many new cats moved into the colonies?	0-5	46.22%
	6-10	8.40%
	11-15	3.36%
	16-20	2.52%
	21-25+	0.84%
33. How many cats have died from natural causes?	0-5	34.45%
	6-10	16.81%
	11-15	3.36%
	16-20	0.84%
	21-25+	3.36%
34. How many died due to suspicious circumstances?	0-5	49.58%
	6-10	5.04%
	11-15	2.52%
	16-20	0.00%
	21-25+	1.68%
35. How many were killed by cars?	0-5	45.38%
	6-10	7.56%
	11-15	2.52%
	16-20	0.00%
	21-25+	1.68%

Question

Answer & Percentage

Question	Answer	Percentage
36. How many were euthanized?	0-5	51.26%
	6-10	6.72%
	11-15	2.52%
	16-20	2.52%
	21-25+	2.52%
37. What is your average cost to neuter a male feral cat?	$25-50	68.91%
	$51-75	14.29%
	$76-100	4.20%
	$101-125+	0.84%
38. What is your average cost to spay a female feral cat?	$25-50	53.78%
	$51-75	22.69%
	$76-100	10.08%
	$101-125+	1.68%
39. What do you charge the client to neuter a male feral cat?	$0-25	51.26%
	$26-50	22.69%
	$51-75	5.88%
	$76-100+	1.68%
40. What do you charge the client to spay a female feral cat?	$0-25	48.74%
	$26-50	26.05%
	$51-75	3.36%
	$76-100+	3.36%
41. Does your local animal control agency approve of TNR?	Yes	54.62%
	No	23.53%
42. Does your local animal control offer TNR to local people?	Yes	21.85%
	No	61.34%
43. Has your animal control ever trapped-and-killed whole colonies?	Yes	36.13%
	No	36.13%
44. If yes, have other cats moved in to the area?	Yes	27.73%
	No	2.52%

Question

Answer & Percentage

45. If yes, new cats moved in, how long after the eradication did they move in?	less than 1 month	8.40%
	2-3 months	11.76%
	4-5 months	4.20%
	6+ months	0.84%
46. Is the public aware of feral cats in your area?	Yes	79.83%
	No	7.56%
47. Is the public sympathetic to feral cat colonies?	Yes	18.49%
	No	5.04%
	somewhat	65.55%
48. Does your group promote educational/outreach programs regarding TNR and feral cats?	Yes	82.35%
	No	8.40%
49. How affective have such outreach programs been?	not at all	1.68%
	somewhat	65.55%
	extremely	17.65%
50. How would your organization classify working with county-run animal shelters?	easy	21.01%
	intermediate	31.09%
	difficult	26.89%
51. How would you classify working with local govt/city officials regarding animal issues?	easy	15.13%
	intermediate	31.93%
	difficult	37.82%
52. How would you classify working with local wildlife groups (i.e. Fish & Wildlife Service, Game Commission, Audubon)?	easy	2.52%
	intermediate	25.21%
	difficult	31.93%

Thank you

to the Edith Goode Foundation for providing funding to conduct this survey.

Become An Activist for Cats

Now that you've read through the handbook and learned the issues surrounding cats, here are a few steps you can take to get active on their behalf.

- Implement a Trap-Neuter-Return (TNR) program for free-roaming cats in your community.

- Advocate for TNR programs in your community by sending polite and educational letters to city council members, accompanied by a supporting petition with collected signatures. You might even want to include a copy of this handbook to offer additional information.

- Address neighborhood concerns and complaints by educating them on the importance and effectiveness of TNR; offer to setup sprinklers and other harmless deterrents to keep cats out of gardens; and build outdoor litter boxes and scoop daily.

- Encourage your veterinarian to treat feral cats and offer TNR services.

- Respond to negative press by submitting editorial letters that present the facts on TNR and cat predation.

- Contact wildlife and bird conservation groups and encourage them to adopt nonlethal forms of animal management, including TNR for community cats.

- Request ACR's TNR brochure to distribute.

- Volunteer, foster, and donate to your local cat organizations.

- Support colony caretakers by building shelters and/or feeding stations and donating food.

- Adopt an alley cat.

Helpful Resources

Humane box traps are available from the following companies:

ACES (Animal Care Equipment & Services, Inc.)
(800) 338-ACES(2237)
www.animal-care.com

Safeguard Traps
800-433-1819
www.safeguardproducts.com

Tomahawk Live Trap
(800) 272-8727
www.livetrap.com

Tru-Catch Traps
1-800-247-6132
www.trucatchtraps.com

Information on drop traps can be found at:

Droptrapdesign.blogspot.com

Tomahawk Live Trap
(800) 272-8727
www.livetrap.com

Transfer cages and cat dens:

Tomahawk Live Trap
(800) 272-8727
www.livetrap.com

Holding pens, playpens, and carriers can be purchased from:

Chewy.com
1-800-67-CHEWY (672-4399)

Drs. Foster & Smith:
(800) 826-7206
www.drsfostersmith.com

Petsmart, Petco

Nets for safely catching cats can be purchased at:

ACES (Animal Care Equipment & Services, Inc.)
(800) 338-ACES(2237)
www.animal-care.com

Specialized fencing and catios:

Affordable Cat Fence
1-888-840-CATS(2287)
www.catfence.com

Cat Fence In
1-888-738-9099
www.catfencein.com

Purrfect Fence
1-888-280-4066
www.purrfectfence.com

Feeding stations:

Carter Pets
602-245-4247
www.outdoorpetfeeder.com
With every purchase, a donation is made to ACR; simply mention our name while placing your order.

FeralVilla.com

Outdoor shelters:

FeralVilla.com

Petsmart, Petco

Heating pads and warming beds:

Chewy.com

CozyWinters.com
800.340.1528

Petsmart, Petco

Cat scat mats and cat repellent products are available from:

Beaphar (company in Holland)
Reppers Outdoor Sticks
www.beaphar.com

Chewy.com

Gardener's Supply Company
1-800-876-5520
www.gardeners.com

Petsmart, Petco

Calming products can be purchased at most pet supply stores and online:

- Feliway - sprays, diffusers
- Whisker City - sprays, water additive
- Rescue Remedy by Bach - water additive

Parasite prevention can be purchased at most pet supply stores, online, or through a veterinarian:

- Advantage Multi (Bayer) - fleas, ticks, ear mites, heartworms, roundworms, hookworms
- Capstar - fleas
- De Flea (Natural Chemistry) - sprays, shampoos
- Frontline Plus - fleas, lice, tick
- Heartgard - heartworms, hookworms
- Profender - tapeworms, roundworms, hookworms
- Revolution - fleas, ticks, ear   mites, heartworms, roundworms, hookworms

Other helpful resources:

Alley Cat Rescue
www.saveacat.org

City Critters, Inc.
www.citycritters.org

Little Buddies
www.littlebuddies.org

Nikki Hospice Foundation for Pets
www.csum.edu\pethospice

Spay USA
www.spayusa.org

Vox Felina
www.voxfelina.com
Providing critical analysis of claims made in the name of science by those opposed to feral/free-roaming cats and trap-neuter-return (TNR).

*Managing Community Cats:
A Guide for Municipal Leaders*
Written by the Humane Society of the United States. Concisely focused on what local leaders want and need to know, this guide offers an in-depth look at community cat management programs, addresses proactive approaches, and the importance of collaborative efforts in local communities. Download your copy at: http://www.animalsheltering.org/resources/all-topics/cats/managing-community-cats.pdf

Forms

Sample City Council Letter

Name of City Council Member
Address

Date

Dear Council Member _____(insert last name)_____ ,

I am writing this letter to address our town's current homeless cat population and to offer some helpful suggestions to the council in humanely managing the situation. As you are probably aware, there are several methods of controlling cat populations; however, only one method provides not only a humane solution, but also an effective and less costly solution. The method I am referring to is Trap-Neuter-Return or TNR.

The preferred nonlethal method of controlling feral or stray cats is by implementing a Trap-Neuter-Return program. In practicing TNR, cats are caught in humane traps, spayed/neutered, vaccinated, and returned to the site. Kittens/cats who are friendly or can be socialized are placed into an adoption program to find permanent homes. Cat rescue organizations, such as Alley Cat Rescue, have over 40 years of experience working with feral cats, which has taught us that TNR immediately reduces colony sizes, because all kittens and tame cats are removed. Feral cats, who cannot be adopted, are returned to the site, where supervised, long-term care is ensured by dedicated volunteers.

The benefits of TNR are numerous. TNR stabilizes populations at manageable levels, by stopping the reproductive cycle. Over time, the natural cycle of attrition will maintain the stable numbers and any new cats to the colony will be sterilized. Sterilization eliminates common complaints associated with mating behaviors, such as fighting, yowling, and spraying.

TNR is also more effective and less costly than repeated eradication attempts. Complete eradication attempts fail and in some cases are counterproductive because they cause a "vacuum effect." Biologist Roger Tabor explains that removing cats all together will allow for more cats to quickly fill in the vacant space. However, "if a colony is neutered and returned to its area it will continue to hold the location and keep other cats out by its presence." In addition, in numerous cases when feral cats are removed from an area, the rodent populations explode, causing further problems. Lastly, TNR is humane to the animals and fosters compassion within the community.

Also, <u>cats who have been trapped and evaluated by a veterinarian are healthier and are less likely to transmit diseases</u> (to other cats and to humans). Females who have been spayed are less susceptible to uterine, ovarian, or mammary cancer, and males who are neutered are less likely to get testicular tumors or have prostate problems. In addition, cats who are "fixed" tend to be less aggressive (fight less, which decreases disease transmission) and wander less (they will keep other cats from joining the colony and it makes managing them easier). Lastly, a rabies vaccine is administered; which provides a buffer zone between wildlife and humans, and decreases the risk of the public coming in contact with an unvaccinated cat.

The traditional catch-and-kill method has been proven not to work, as I explained above, and another outdated approach to the problem is to pass ordinances prohibiting people from feeding community cats. Such regulations will only heighten the problem rather than help. The logic behind such bans is that if there is no food available, the cats will go away. This is not true. "Starving out" cats will only make the situation worse for the community and for the cats. Plus, it will put those individuals willing to take care of and give homes to community cats under fire, when all they are trying to do is help the animals. Instead of blaming the feeders and criminalizing their actions, we should encourage their acts of compassion by assisting them with the resources and information available to care for and sterilize the animals. After all, it is not their fault the cats are homeless; they are just trying to be upstanding citizens, by taking it upon themselves to help the animals.

Simply prohibiting individuals from feeding community cats will not solve the problem. Where there is a large number of people living (food source), there will be cats. And if individuals continue to not spay/neuter their pets, allowing them to reproduce, there will be more stray/feral animals. Ultimately, we all need to work together, if we are to control the pet overpopulation. The current trend of scapegoating cats is very dangerous, for it fosters cruelty to animals, and the time spent placing blame is only time wasted. Plus, nonlethal methods for controlling their populations exist and should be advocated by all who are trying to instill a more compassionate ethic towards the earth and all its inhabitants.

Should you need further information on TNR and feral cats, please visit Alley Cat Rescue's website at www.SaveACat.org. ACR has published a feral cat handbook to shed some light on the facts and myths surrounding feral cats; if you should need assistance in your decision-making process and to help you in organizing and managing TNR programs, please let ACR know and they will send you a copy. ACR can be reached at acr@saveacat. org or by calling 301-277-5595. Thank you for your time and compassion for our feline friends!

Sincerely,

(Your signature)

Your Name Printed
Your Contact Information

Sample Petition

Support Trap-Neuter-Return (TNR) Programs for ___(insert town name)___ 's Stray and Feral Cats

Target: ___(insert town council or local government)___

Background information:

The preferred nonlethal method of controlling feral or stray cats is to implement a Trap-Neuter-Return (TNR) program. In practicing TNR, cats are caught in humane traps, spayed/neutered, vaccinated, and returned to the site to live out their lives. Kittens/cats who are friendly or can be socialized are placed into an adoption program (coordinated by a rescue organization) to find permanent homes. TNR immediately reduces the size of colonies, because all kittens and tame cats are removed. Cats who are truly feral should be returned to the site, where supervised, long-term care is ensured by dedicated volunteers.

The benefits of TNR are numerous. TNR stabilizes populations at manageable levels, by stopping the reproductive cycle. Over time, the natural cycle of attrition will maintain the stable numbers and any new cats to the colony will be sterilized. At the same time, TNR reduces euthanasia rates at local county shelters, by reducing the number of unwanted kittens being born and freeing up space at the shelters for cats who are relinquished by their owners.

TNR is also more effective and less costly than repeated eradication (catch-and-kill) attempts. Catch-and-kill attempts fail and in some cases are counterproductive because they cause a "vacuum effect." Biologist Roger Tabor explains that removing cats all together will allow for more cats to quickly fill in the vacant space. However, "if a colony is neutered and returned to its area it will continue to hold the location and keep other cats out by its presence." In addition, in numerous cases when feral cats are removed from an area, the rodent populations explode, causing further problems.

Sterilization also eliminates common complaints associated with mating behaviors, such as fighting, yowling, and spraying. TNR is humane to the animals and fosters compassion within the community. Lastly, cats who have been trapped and evaluated by a veterinarian are healthier and are less likely to transmit diseases (to other cats and to humans). A rabies vaccine is administered, which creates a buffer zone between wildlife and humans, and also reduces the risk of the public coming in contact with an unvaccinated cat.

Petition:

We, the undersigned, call on ___(insert town council)___ to support the implementation of Trap-Neuter-Return (TNR) programs for all stray and feral cats living in ___(insert town name)___.

We support TNR programs whereas friendly cats and kittens and those who can be socialized are removed and placed into foster and adoption programs to find permanent homes.

We support TNR programs that sterilize, vaccinate, ear-tip, and return unsocialized or feral cats to their sites to live out the rest of their natural lives, where they will be supervised and cared for by a dedicated volunteer.

Thusly, we support TNR programs as the preferred nonlethal management plan for all stray and feral cats, and petition ___(insert town council)___ to pass an ordinance making it legal for TNR programs to be implemented and made the standard method of managing cat populations in ___(insert town name)___.

Name (print)	Signature

Sample Guidelines for Adopting A Cat or Kitten

 Alley Cat Rescue, Inc.

www.saveacat.org (301) 277-5595

Alley Cat Rescue wants our rescued cats placed in homes where they will be treated as a member of the family for the rest of their lives which, with care, can be for 12 years or longer. If you do not agree with our guidelines, we suggest that you reconsider whether or not adopting a cat is right for you. When you adopt a cat from us, you must sign a legal contract stating that you will comply with our requirements, which are to give the cat a long healthy life in a loving home. If you have any questions or concerns in fulfilling these requirements, please discuss them with us prior to signing.

1. **Member of the family**. A cat is not a possession, but a member of your family to be treated with love and respect. She should share the house and not be left outdoors, isolated in a cage, or left in a room separating her from the people in the family.

   Reason: A cat who is not an accepted member of the family will not be happy and may become withdrawn or exhibit other behavioral problems.

2. **Neutering and spaying**. Your cat must be neutered (male) or spayed (female) by five months of age. (The cat you adopt from ACR will already be spayed/neutered).

   Reason: There are already too many unwanted cats killed in shelters each year. ACR campaigns to put an end to this killing. A female cat can become pregnant as early as five months of age. Spaying and neutering will prevent homeless kittens and will help your cat live a longer, healthier life. Neutered and spayed animals are less prone to cancers. Unneutered males often spray on furniture.

3. **Declawing**. Our cats must not be declawed. If you want a declawed cat, let us know. We sometimes have cats who have already been declawed by their previous guardians before relinquishing them to ACR.

   Reason: Cats have a psychological need to claw as part of grooming and stretching. They remove the sheath that grows over their claws. Just as a cat cleans her fur, she also takes care of her claws. Clawing also helps keep her muscle tone. It is cruel and inhumane to remove a cat's claws, which function as part of her fingers and toes. Declawing is like removing the entire first joint of your finger. Many cats do not walk properly after being declawed and some exhibit aversions to litter boxes, because it hurts their feet to dig. Declawed cats often bite more, since they no longer have claws for defense. If you do adopt a declawed cat, she should not go outside without supervision.

   Frequent nail clipping can help alleviate scratching problems. Your vet can show you how to do this. You can also help by giving your cat plenty of things to scratch on and by gently correcting her when she scratches something inappropriate; a spray bottle filled with water works as a good deterrent. A product called Soft Claws is a more humane alternative to declawing. These are vinyl nail covers which are glued on to your cat's natural nails. Soft Claws will cover the nail tips, so that no damage is caused when your cat scratches. They are available at most pet supply stores.

4. **Indoor/Outdoor cats**. You should keep the cat indoors or allow her outside only under supervision. ACR recommends a cat-proof, fenced-in yard if the cat goes outside. (Visit www.CatFence.com for more information.) Cats must be kept inside at night. We also have information available on a variety of outdoor structures so that she can enjoy the outdoors safely. And a harness and leash can be used for outdoor exercise.

   Reason: Domestic cats left outdoors without supervision could face dangers and risk being injured, lost, or stolen. It is much safer to only allow your cat outside under supervision.

5. **Medical care**. Your cat will need to visit the veterinarian at least once a year for her annual check-up. Many veterinarians now recommend a three-year vaccination cycle, instead of annual boosters. When ill, a cat needs to be promptly treated by a veterinarian. You are responsible for medical bills, except for the initial set of vaccinations we supply.

   Reason: The FVRCP booster prevents your cat from contracting distemper and other ailments. Rabies vaccinations prevent your cat from contracting rabies and may be required by law in your state. Expect your cat to catch an occasional cold, ear infection, respiratory infection, etc., and to develop some ailments as she gets older, so plan your budget accordingly to include these medical conditions.

6. **Children.** If you have a child under six years of age, it is recommended that you adopt a cat or kitten six months of age or older.

   Reason: Young kittens have not yet learned to retract their claws and could scratch if handled improperly. The younger a kitten is, the more fragile, and the easier she could be accidentally injured by a small child. No matter how good your young child is with animals, children are often unable to properly carry and handle little kittens. Also, children frequently have high-pitched voices, which can frighten a young cat.

7. **Preferably no single cats**. It is highly recommended that cat, especially a kitten, be placed in a home with another cat or a dog.

   Reason: Cats are social creatures and having a single kitten in a house could get very lonely and may exhibit behavior problems. She can also drive you crazy begging for affection when you come home. A young cat needs companionship and someone to play with.

8. **Cats must be permitted where you live.** If you rent your home or apartment, or live in a condominium, you need to be sure that cats are permitted. Your lease or bylaws should specifically state that you are allowed to have cats. Cats are a life-long commitment, so you must always live in situations where cats are permitted.

Reason: Many people get a companion cat and are then told by their landlord or condo association to give up the animal or move out. Rental housing permitting animals can be difficult to find. ACR can assist your efforts to get permission.

9. **Post-adoption**. We reserve the right to investigate the living conditions of your new cat through follow-up telephone calls and/or visits.

   Reason: ACR wants our cats placed into loving, caring homes as members of the family. The vast majority of people provide excellent homes for their cats. Occasionally, there will be a personality conflict between a cat and a person. If this occurs and is not resolved in a couple of weeks, it is best to return the cat to us. Follow-up calls and visits help us to ensure that our cats are being treated with the love and respect laid out in our guidelines. ACR wants to help you through your adjustment period with your new companion(s) and we will be happy to answer any questions and address any concerns that you may have.

10. **Relinquishment of your cat**. If you must give up your cat, she *must be returned to Alley Cat Rescue*. You must not turn the cat over to a shelter or another person. If you do relinquish a cat, no questions will be asked. We do not want you to feel guilty.

    Reason: ACR will accept your cat at any time if you must give her up. We want to know that our cats are cared for all their lives, so we will take them back and find a new home. Do not, for any reason, leave one of our cats at an animal shelter. They may be killed before we can rescue them.

11. **Literature**. There are several excellent books on cat care and cat behavior. Books and magazines are an excellent resource for answering your questions. ACR suggests these books and magazines. The list also includes books on outdoor, stray, and feral cats.

    - *Adopting Cats & Kittens,* by Connie Jankowski
    - *The Purina Encyclopedia of Cat Care,* by Amy Shojai
    - *Kitten Care & Training*, by Amy Shojai
    - *Cats for Dummies,* by Gina Spadafori
    - *Understanding Cats*; *Understanding Cat Behavior*, by Roger Tabor
    - *The Cat Behavior Answer Book*, by Arden Moore
    - *Cat vs. Cat: Keeping Peace When You have More than One Cat*, by Pam Johnson-Bennett
    - *ComPETability: Solving Behavior Problems in Your Multi-Cat Household*, by Amy Shojai
    - *The New Natural Cat: The Complete Guide for Finicky Owners*, by Anitra Frazier
    - *The Stray Cat Handbook*, by Tamara Kreuz
    - *The Wild Life of the Domestic Cat*, by Roger Tabor
    - *Maverick Cats: Encounters with Feral Cats,* by Ellen Perry Berkeley
    - *The Cat Who Cried for Help*, by Nicholas Dodman
    - Magazines: *The Whole Cat Journal, Catnip, and Cat Watch*

Sample Adoption Contract

Alley Cat Rescue, Inc.

www.saveacat.org (301) 277-5595

Name(s) of Cat(s) being adopted: _____

I, _____ , agree to the following:

1. The cat will live in a private residence as a companion animal and will be provided with fresh food and water daily, as well as a clean litter box.
2. I will never strike or harm the cat in any way.
3. **I will NOT have the cat declawed. I will NOT allow anyone else to declaw the cat. I understand that doing so may result in legal action being taken against me.**
4. I agree to provide future vaccinations and veterinary care if the cat becomes ill or injured. I will take the cat to the vet for checkups as recommended by my veterinarian (usually once a year). I will do whatever it takes to keep the cat living a good quality life.
5. **I will NOT euthanize the cat unless he or she is suffering and no alternative options are available.**
6. I will never use, sell, give, or transfer the cat for purposes of research/ experimentations, fighting, for consumption, or use in products.
7. I certify that I am permitted to have a cat in my home or apartment, and everyone living there has agreed to live with the cat. Upon request, I will provide proof to Alley Cat Rescue that I am permitted to have a cat in my house or apartment.
8. I consent to home inspections by Alley Cat Rescue.
9. If I cannot keep the cat for any reason, I agree to:
   a. Return the cat to Alley Cat Rescue (301-277-5595; ACR@saveacat.org),
   b. Never take the cat to a shelter or animal control facility for any reason,
   c. Never transfer the cat to another home without consulting Alley Cat Rescue.
   Alley Cat Rescue will <u>ALWAYS</u> take back a cat who was adopted from us.
10. I certify that I am 18 years or older and of sound mind and understand the ramifications of entering into a binding contract.

_____   _____   _____
Signature   Printed Name   Date

_____   _____
Date of Birth   License or Social Security No.

Address: _____

Home Phone Number: _____   Cell: _____

Email Address: _____

Index

About The Author

LOUISE HOLTON has founded two international cat advocacy organizations in the U.S., including Alley Cat Allies and Alley Cat Rescue, of which she is currently the president. Louise helped pioneer Trap-Neuter-Return (TNR) in the U.S., bringing her experience of working with feral cats from her home country of South Africa.

Louise and Tequila, who was rescued in Mexico.

Over the past four decades, she has assisted over 40,000 cats, presented at numerous conferences and symposiums, and won several awards, including a Muse Medallion from the Cat Writers' Association for her informational booklet, "Feral Cat Colony Management and Control: Facts and Myths about Feral Cats" and her series of articles published in *The Animals' Voice*. Louise has been presented with the National Humane Achievement Award from the Humane Coalition of Massachusetts and the Animal Kingdom Kindred Spirit Award and Animal Champion Pin from the Doris Day Animal Foundation.

She lives in Maryland with some of the unadoptable cats ACR has rescued over the years, including some who are feral and could not be returned to their colonies, plus an alley cat who was diagnosed with FIV. Also sharing her home are two dogs, Lily and Bandit, rescued from Mexico when ACR ran their mash-style clinic there.